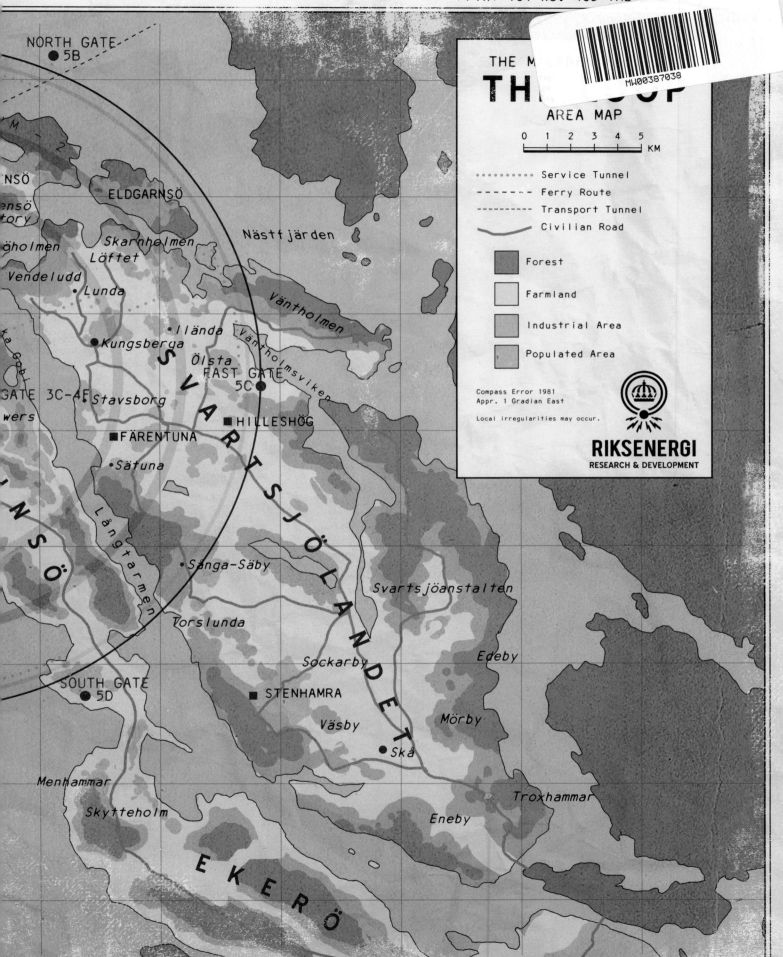

THE MÄLARÖ

# THE LOOP

AREA MAP

0 1 2 3 4 5 KM

········· Service Tunnel
- - - - - - Ferry Route
-------- Transport Tunnel
⌒⌒⌒ Civilian Road

▨ Forest
☐ Farmland
▨ Industrial Area
▨ Populated Area

Compass Error 1981
Appr. 1 Gradian East

Local irregularities may occur.

## RIKSENERGI
RESEARCH & DEVELOPMENT

NORTH GATE
● 5B

ELDGARNSÖ

Nästfjärden

...NSÖ

ensö
tory

...öholmen

Skarnholmen
Löftet

Vendeludd

● Lunda

Väntholmen

● Ilända

Väntholmsviken

● Kungsberga

Ölsta
EAST GATE
5C

...ka Gabi

GATE 3C-4F
...wers

Stavsborg

■ HILLESHÖG

■ FÄRENTUNA

● Sätuna

SVARTSJÖLANDET

Långtarmen

...NSÖ

● Sånga-Säby

Svartsjöanstalten

Torslunda

Sockarby

Edeby

SOUTH GATE
● 5D

■ STENHAMRA

Väsby

Mörby

● Skå

Menhammar

Troxhammar

Skytteholm

Eneby

EKERÖ

Not approved for general distribution,
Statens lantmäteriverk April 27, 1981

# 01.

## WELCOME TO THE LOOP

# 02.

## THE AGE OF THE LOOP

# 03.

## THE US LOOP

RIKSENERGI

# 04.

## THE KIDS

# 05.

## TROUBLE

# 06.

## THE MYSTERY

RIKSENERGI

# 07.

## THE MYSTERY LANDSCAPE

# 08.

## THE FOUR SEASONS OF MAD SCIENCE

# 09.

## SUMMER BREAK AND KILLER BIRDS

RIKSENERGI

# 10.

## GROWN-UP ATTRACTION

# 11.

## CREATURES FROM THE CRETACEOUS

# 12.

## I, WAGNER

RIKSENERGI

**RIKSENERGI**

# WELCOME TO THE LOOP

*The landscape was full of machines and scrap metal connected to the facility in one way or another. Always present on the horizon were the colossal cooling towers of the Bona Reactor, with their green obstruction lights. If you put your ear to the ground, you could hear the heartbeat of the Loop – the purring of the Gravitron, the central piece of engineering magic that was the focus of the Loop's experiments.*

It was the middle of summer, and my little sister, Klara, had tried to follow me and my friend around for weeks. Her best friend was out of town and my mother tried, without much success, to arouse my sympathy. I had always taken care of Klara, not only because of her hearing impairment, but because there has always been something fragile about her, as if she can be easily damaged or broken. However, this summer had awakened the desire in me to ride as far away as possible on my bike, and to do things on my own. When Klara suddenly disappeared, guilt hit me like a blow to the stomach, and I remembered she had talked about meeting a new friend called Bettan.

We found them on the other side of the strait; I still don't know how they managed to cross. We crept toward them through the tall grass as the wind tore at the pines. A woodpecker could be heard in the distance. Klara sat on a stone and leaned forward to place a daisy chain on the head of a runaway robot, her new friend "Bettan." I signaled to my friends to keep quiet and snuck around to the other side. When I looked back, Bettan was staring at me, its eyes narrowing to tiny black dots as it took my sister in its arms.

RIKSENERGI

7

*EXAMPLE*

**The Gamemaster:** *Bettan has clearly seen you. What do you do?*

**Player 1 (Klara's brother Olle):** *I crouch down in the tall grass and try to calm myself, but feel my heart beating even faster.*

**Player 2 (Olle's friend Anita):** *I guess it hasn't seen me? I try to sneak around it.*

**The Gamemaster:** *Roll Sneak.*

**Player 2:** *Five dice. (Rolls dice to get at least one six.) Yes, one success!*

**The Gamemaster:** *Tell us what you do.*

**Player 2:** *I sneak from tree to tree until I'm on the other side, and kneel behind an overgrown jasmine bush. I am prepared to rush the cyborg if it tries to leave with Klara.*

**Player 1:** *Do I know anything about how cyborgs work, how to stop them?*

**The Gamemaster:** *Roll Calculate.*

**Player 1:** *Two dice. (Rolls dice.) Success!*

**The Gamemaster:** *You have read a lot about robots because your father previously worked at a job producing spare parts for robots. You know there is sometimes a big red button on the chest for an emergency stop; if pressed hard, the robot collapses lifeless.*

**Player 1:** *Are there any rocks close by?*

**The Gamemaster:** *Absolutely.*

**Player 1:** *I grab a large piece of granite and slowly stand up. I try to spot the button and see if I can throw the stone at it.*

**The Gamemaster:** *The cyborg stands turned towards you with Klara in its arms, her face against its chest. It strokes her hair. The button on its body is concealed by Klara. What do you do?*

**Player1:** *I slowly place the stone on the ground and talk to it with a soft voice: "I'm her brother. I will not hurt you."*

This story is an example of what can happen when you play the *Tales from the Loop* roleplaying game, which takes place in the fantastic world created by Simon Stålenhag.

A roleplaying game is a conversation where you and your friends build a story with a beginning, a mid-

dle, and an end. A typical story takes between three to six hours of play. Most often you sit at a table and you need paper, pens, and at least ten six-sided dice.

## THE TALES FROM THE LOOP

In this game, a story is called a Mystery. It deals with a group of friends who try to solve Mysteries together. The friends are Kids, aged 10-15 years old, living in the late 1980s. Everyday Life is full of nagging parents, never-ending homework, and classmates bullying and being bullied.

The Mysteries allow the Kids to encounter strange machines and creatures that exist as a result of the nearby Loop, a huge underground particle accelerator built in the late 1960s. The Kids get to escape their everyday lives and problems and be part of something meaningful and magical, yet also dangerous. They risk getting injured and also changed by the Troubles they have to overcome to solve the Mysteries.

## ROLEPLAYING - HOW DOES IT WORK?

All players, except one, create a character; a Kid whom they will play in the story. In-game, you choose what your Kid does and says, and you tell the others what she looks like and what she thinks and feels. You should pretend to be the Kid, like an actor in a movie or a play. It is usually easier to play the Kid if you refer to the character as "me" or "I," instead of "she" or "her."

One of the players will be the Gamemaster. She plays all people except the Kids, and controls all creatures and machines. These are called Non-Player Characters, or NPCs. The Gamemaster also describes what everything looks like in the game, the smells and the sounds. She is responsible for making the story move forward and cuts from scene to scene, just like a director in a movie.

The Gamemaster shouldn't decide what will happen in the story. She presents situations and puts the Kids in Trouble. The players decide how the Kids try to overcome that Trouble, and that creates the story.

To support the story, the Gamemaster has a Mystery, a script that describes locations and NPCs that the Kids can encounter, and what Trouble they may need to overcome. The Mystery is only a guide, as the Gamemaster can choose to improvise and make up her own events, but she can always fall back on the Mystery when she is unsure of what to say or do.

The Gamemaster's task is clearly a bit more difficult than that of the others, but is also even more rewarding. The Gamemaster can invent intriguing mysteries, play robots and mad scientists, and she may, with the help of the players, describe the fantastical world of the Loop. The Gamemaster should cheer on the Kids just like you do with the heroes of a movie, but at the same time, put them in Trouble so that she can enjoy how they overcome it and solve the Mystery.

The players and the Gamemaster take turns telling what the characters do, what the scenery looks like, and what happens. It is important that everyone gets space and time to participate. The group should listen to, and take in, each other's ideas. The story should be created together, and it's important to help one another, not compete for attention.

---

### TWO LOOPS, SWEDISH AND US

There are two settings included in this book. The primary setting is an alternate version of the Swedish Mälaren Islands, west of the capital Stockholm. This setting is described in Chapter 2. The second, alternative setting is based on the US town of Boulder City, Nevada, which has a Loop of its own and is a sister facility to the Swedish Loop. The US setting is described in Chapter 3. The Mystery Stories (scenarios) later in this book are primarily based on the Swedish setting, but they contain hints on how to adapt them to Boulder City. All comments in orange brackets [like this] in the scenario texts refer to the American setting.

---

Sometimes situations arise where the Kids try to do something difficult. In those situations, you roll dice and let chance determine if you succeed or fail.

### A LOOP IN YOUR OWN HOME TOWN?

It's entirely possible to set your game in your own home town, where you live or where you grew up. In your game universe, maybe that's where the Loop was built? Creating your own game setting requires some more work, but can be a lot of fun!

THE MYSTERY LANDSCAPE

An alternative way to play the game is for the Gamemaster to use the Mystery Landscape. The Mystery Landscape consists of weird or problematic Locations spread out over the game setting. The Kids are expected to seek out the Locations and solve whatever problems they encounter. These two methods can be combined by using the pre-written Mysteries as a part of the Mystery Landscape. Read more about the Mystery Landscape in Chapter 7.

RIKSENERGI

## ROLLING DICE

The Kids have numeric ratings for what they are good at: understanding machines, fast talking, climbing trees, and running fast. The rating indicates how many six-sided dice you get to roll when trying to overcome Trouble. A six means a success. You rarely need more than one success. If you fail, you may try again, but then you risk getting hurt, upset or scared. This is explained further in Chapter 5.

## PRINCIPLES OF THE LOOP

The *Tales from the Loop* roleplaying game is permeated by six principles that the players and the Gamemaster will use to create stories with the right kind of feeling and plot. They are also tools to finding a way to get along, if players have different opinions about what should happen in the story and how it should be described. The principles are first presented as a numbered list, and then explained in more detail, written as instructions and inspiration to you who are reading this text.

1. Your home town is full of strange and fantastic things.
2. Everyday life is dull and unforgiving.
3. Adults are out of reach and out of touch.
4. The land of the Loop is dangerous but Kids will not die.
5. The game is played scene by scene.
6. The world is described collaboratively.

### 1. YOUR HOME TOWN IS FULL OF STRANGE AND FANTASTIC THINGS

When fusion, particle accelerators and the magnetrine effect were discovered in the 1950s, it broke the boundaries between the possible and the impossible. Huge transport vessels fly, cyborgs and robots can think, scientists create time portals and objects that replace people's identities. Strange beasts roam the landscape, and humanity can contact people and creatures from other times and places.

Not infrequently, things are created because of experiments that go wrong or random events that spawn something new and unexpected. Only the imagination limits what can happen in the land of the Loop in the late 1980s. The Kids should discover all these strange things.

See the world through the eyes of Kids, as they are about to leave childhood with all of their lives ahead of them. They can do anything, and will do it to solve the Mysteries.

Use your own experiences from being a kid – whether you are one now or it was many years ago – to create magic and wonder. Think of how it feels to sneak out in the middle of the night to secretly meet your friends, to dive deep underwater to gather stones or ride your bike as fast as you can on hilly trails through the woods. Think of how it feels to sit sweating in a secret tree hut with friends and how those first days of summer break feel. Think of what it is like to spy on the creepy guy with the dogs, or listen to the older kids' stories about burglars or the strange old lady. Let yourself be enchanted.

### 2. EVERYDAY LIFE IS DULL AND UNFORGIVING

The alarm clock rings every morning, and homework must be done every night. It does not matter that the magnetrine ships sail by outside the window, that mom

RIKSENERGI

and dad still quarrel, and your brother seems to hate you. Your house smells fishy and you don't get enough pocket money to buy that tape you want. The garbage has to be thrown out every day, bullies give you nicknames, and your bike is broken. It's raining, and you have no raincoat.

Life is full of setbacks and obstacles. The adults decide and do as they please, and Kids are forced to do as they say. Sure, sometimes a problem is solved and you enjoy a nice moment, but it only lasts a short while, then it's the same as before. Everyday life.

### 3. ADULTS ARE OUT OF REACH AND OUT OF TOUCH

It does not matter what you say; the adults neither listen nor understand. They live in their own world, distinct from the Kids. There's no point in asking them for help with problems, Mysteries to be solved or Troubles that must be overcome. The Kids are at the mercy of each other. The adults won't even believe in all the strange things that the Kids encounter.

The adults nag and whine and argue with each other. They are busy with themselves and their work.

**RIKSENERGI**

Moreover, they are ignorant. It is usually their mistakes that the Kids need to fix – machines that run amok, experiments gone bad, aircraft that crash or explode.

The worst are the adults who actually see the Kids and want to exploit or harm them.

Sometimes adults help, like when your dad comforts you, or you call the police and they catch the burglars, but it never lasts and it often comes with a price. The police take all the glory, your stepmom wants you to mow the lawn all summer as payment for her help, or your teacher sees you as an ally and expects you to help her keep an eye on the bad guys in class.

## 4. THE LAND OF THE LOOP IS DANGEROUS BUT KIDS WILL NOT DIE

The Kids can be hurt, locked up, mocked, displaced, robbed, or broken-hearted, but they cannot die in this game.

## 5. THE GAME IS PLAYED SCENE BY SCENE

Just like in the movies, the Mystery is played in scenes. First, the characters talk to each other in the house, then we skip to when they meet their teacher at school. Don't play out every little step they take on the way between home and school. Skip the boring or less important parts.

In *Tales from the Loop*, the Gamemaster is the one who "sets" the scenes, often with the help of the players. Setting a scene means to initiate the scene and end it when it seems done. The Gamemaster should consult the players when unsure.

The Gamemaster can set scenes on her own initiative, like this:

*"When you come home at night, you hear someone crying in the kitchen. Your father is sitting at the table. When he sees you, he puts on a fake smile. What do you do?"*

The Gamemaster should also ask the players to suggest which scene should be set. A good rule of thumb is to allow players to set at least every other scene.

*EXAMPLE*

**The Gamemaster:** *Does anyone have a scene?*
**Player 1 (Olle):** *I would like to try to break into the school to see what they are hiding there.*
**The Gamemaster:** *Do you go there alone?*
**Player 1:** *Yes.*
**The Gamemaster:** *The sun is going down above the oaks when you lean your bike against the fence behind the gymnasium. It is quiet and empty, and all the windows are dark.*

### 6. THE WORLD IS DESCRIBED COLLABORATIVELY

The Gamemaster is responsible for setting scenes and describing things in the story, but that doesn't mean she should do all the work herself. The Gamemaster should ask the players for help all the time. Ask them what the school looks like, what the weather is, why the neighbors are arguing, and so forth.

The Gamemaster should ask the Kids questions: What does your mother look like? What's fishy about the lady of the house next door? What is the mood like in the house when you get home? How do you feel? What are you thinking? What have you done that makes her hate you? What are you wearing? How come you love her? The Gamemaster should use the players' imaginations by asking questions all the time, and making sure the group creates the world together.

If the players make up flying schools and parents who work as Alien Hunters, the Gamemaster should remind them of the principle "Everyday life is dull and unforgiving." The strange and the mysterious should be in the Mysteries. The Gamemaster has the final say.

RIKSENERGI

# THE AGE OF THE LOOP

*The Loop's presence was felt everywhere on the Mälaren Islands. Our parents worked there. Riksenergi's service vehicles patrolled the roads and the skies. Strange machines roamed in the woods, the glades, and the meadows. Whatever forces reigned deep below sent vibrations up through the bedrock, the flint lime bricks, and the Eternit facades – and into our living rooms.*

One of the core elements of the game setting is that the *Tales from the Loop* RPG takes place in a distinct and iconic period of time: the 1980s. It's a time you probably know well – you might even have grown up during this era, and if not, you have probably experienced it through a score of iconic movies like *E.T., The Goonies,* and *Wargames.*

It is the decade that gave us global pop stars like Michael Jackson and Madonna, when hard rock and synth pop dominated the radio, and the Commodore 64 was the world's best-selling computer. In a way, it was the first really modern decade. The VCR made its way into homes, and a generation of kids watched movies that previously were out of sight and reach for them.

After the pessimistic '70s, the '80s looked ahead and upwards. Everything seemed possible. Yet it was also a decade of fear and conflict. Looming over every-thing was the spectre of the Cold War, and the global threat of nuclear war. To be scared of The Bomb was as natural as being afraid of climate change today. This, and everything else that happened during this era, is part of this game. But there is more to it as well – this game is about an '80s that never was.

## THE '80S THAT NEVER WAS

Things are not quite as you remember them. The '80s of this game are filled with strange technology and top secret, government-run projects. The twin large parti-cle accelerators in Sweden and the US are still active. "Balanced autonomous systems" (commonly known as robots) are commonplace and 10,000 ton gauss freighters traffic the Tundra route to Siberia. This is the era of the *Tales from the Loop.*

RIKSENERGI

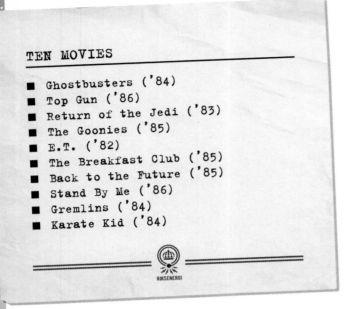

TEN MOVIES

- Ghostbusters ('84)
- Top Gun ('86)
- Return of the Jedi ('83)
- The Goonies ('85)
- E.T. ('82)
- The Breakfast Club ('85)
- Back to the Future ('85)
- Stand By Me ('86)
- Gremlins ('84)
- Karate Kid ('84)

RIKSENERGI

In the years after the second World War, the major powers invested huge amounts of time and money in experimental research programs. Most of these yielded almost no results, but a few of them paid off handsomely. The so-called magnetrine effect was discovered by scientists in the Soviet Union, and gave birth to the majestic gauss freighters that, in the decades that followed, became a common sight, especially in the northern hemisphere. The magnetrine effect is distinctly weaker in the southern hemisphere, limiting its use to smaller gauss ships there.

In the US, the world's first particle accelerator was constructed in Boulder City, Nevada, in the 1950s. Part of a military program, its scientific findings were unclear, and rumors calling it a failure spread. That did not stop scientists in Sweden from following suit. In the 1960s, the Swedish government formed Riksenergi, an agency tasked with building the world's largest particle accelerator on the Mälaren Islands outside of Stockholm. The Facility for Research in High Energy Physics was inaugurated in 1969, and top scientists from all over Sweden relocated to the area so as to partake in one of the most ambitious scientific endeavors of its time. It did not take long for the inhabitants of the islands to come up with a new name for the facility: The Loop.

Meanwhile, the Japanese company Iwasaka perfected the self-balancing machine in laboratories in Osaka. In the '70s and '80s, these machines, most often simply called robots, became a more common sight in industries and defense forces.

## MAKING THE FANTASTIC MUNDANE

The world of the *Tales from the Loop* is our world, but it's also quite different. The discovery of the magnetrine effect and the perfecting of robot technology in the late '60s have made things we consider fantastic commonplace in this world. Keep in mind that while seeing a huge gauss ship cruise above the ground is an awe-inspiring sight for the Kids in this game, it is not something magical or fantastical. They grew up in this reality; for them, hovering magnetrine ships and robots are as normal as jets or computers are to us. *Tales from the Loop* is science fiction, but it is not about technology. At its heart, this game is about growing up in the shadows of strange things and solving mysteries. It is about the Kids.

### SCIENCE – A TIMELINE

#### 1950-59

- Scientists in the Soviet Union discover the Magnetrine Effect.
- The world's first particle accelerator is built in Boulder City, Nevada.

#### 1960-69

- Iwasaka, a Japanese company, develops the self-balancing machine, laying the foundation for the development of what are today known as robots.
- Riksenergi, the government agency tasked with operating the Swedish accelerator, is founded.
- Department of Advanced Research into Teleportation is started by the US government agency ARPA.
- The construction of the Swedish accelerator. The Facility for Research in High Energy Physics, more commonly called the Loop, is completed.

RIKSENERGI

## THE SWEDISH LOOP

From its inception in 1969, the Facility for Research in High Energy Physics, or simply "The Loop," is the largest particle accelerator of its kind in the world.

### SWEDEN IN THE '80S

Sweden in the 1980s is a very different country from what it is today. Some call it a socialist utopia, others a failed experiment of finding a middle way between capitalism and communism. It is a country governed by the monolithic Social Democratic party, who have ruled more or less single-handedly since World War II. It's a far cry from the communist countries of Eastern Europe, but the belief that the government should care for its citizens from the cradle to grave is still strong. Education is free for everyone, as is health care. Alcohol is only sold in state owned Systembolaget stores, there are only two TV channels - both state owned and showing a mix of American soap operas, Swedish social realist dramas, and cartoons from behind the Iron Curtain.

Sweden is officially neutral, and is not aligned with NATO or the Warsaw Pact. Indeed, it was one of the few countries in Europe that was not occupied and did not fight in World War II, a subject that has been much debated among its less lucky neighbors. But regardless of what Finns or Norwegians think about Sweden's way of not taking sides, it is firmly entrenched in the Swedish psyche. The Social Democratic government has good diplomatic relations with both the Soviet Union and the US. But even if the official stance always is to never pick a side, it is an open secret that the

Swedish military, many politicians, and a large part of the population only really see one obvious enemy: the Soviet Union.

There are rumors that cooperation with NATO countries is more widespread than commonly believed, and some talk about secret research and intelligence projects in cooperation with US representatives. When the Soviet submarine U-137 runs aground outside Blekinge in southern Sweden in 1981, the threat suddenly becomes very real.

---

### EIGHT TECH COMPANIES

- Vectra — Vehicles
- Rogosin Locke Industries — Service machinery
- Lieber-Alta — Makers of ABM100 and AMAT 2
- Paarhufer — Service machines and robots
- Maltemann — Utility machines and robots
- Wiman Shipyards — Small gauss freighters
- Bendlin-Akulov — Large gauss freighters
- Iwasaka — Creators of the self-balancing machine

RIKSENERGI

---

### 1970-79

- Scientific work commences at the Loop. Scientists from all over Sweden, and indeed Europe are recruited to the project.
- The first civilian autonomous robots enter service.
- Robot-wave tactics used by Chinese in the Baikal Wars fail, bringing military use of robots to an end.

### 1980-89

- Hans Albrechtsson takes over as Director of the Loop.
- The Swedish Armed Forces introduces the AMAT-1, crewed self-balancing machines.
- Strange sightings are reported around the Loop. Wildlife patrols are increased.

RIKSENERGI

After the incident, the Swedish navy steps up its efforts, and submarine hunting becomes a regular thing throughout the rest of the decade, although with no tangible results.

Sweden is also a changing society. Influence from the West, and especially the US and the UK, is growing stronger both in popular culture and in economic policies. So-called "yuppies" are celebrating the capitalist way in Stockholm, with one hand on an absurdly large mobile phone and the other on the steering wheel of a Porsche. Kids are playing with *Garbage Pail Kids, He-Man* and *Transformers*. The personal computer can be found in many homes, most often in the form of the Commodore 64.

Pen and paper roleplaying games, like *Drakar och Demoner* and *Mutant*, sell 100,000 copies. Going on charter vacations becomes a national pastime. The shift from the idealistic and political '70s to a more individual and pleasure-seeking way of life in the '80s is gradual, but clear. In February 1986, Swedes awake to momentous news: the iconic Prime Minister Olof Palme has been murdered in cold blood in downtown Stockholm. The murder will never be solved, and some claim that this marks the end of the age of innocence in Sweden.

Throughout the decade, the Swedes carry on with their lives the way they have always done. Enduring the long cold winters, spending the short but beautiful summers in country houses, and the rest of the year longing for next summer.

## GROWING UP IN SWEDEN

Being a kid in 1980s Sweden feels like being stuck between the past and a bright, shining future. There are still only two channels on the TV, the computers in school are hopelessly outdated ABC 80s, and a vocal minority of the adult world sees parts of popular culture, such as horror films, computer games, and heavy metal, as soul-corrupting garbage.

Still, things are exponentially better than the drab, grey '70s when your older siblings grew up. VHS tapes of American movies are copied and distributed among friends, pirated cassettes full of Commodore 64 games are tiny slices of heaven for enthusiasts, and the music scene is alight with decadent and deliciously dangerous metal groups as well as stylish and glitzy synth pop duos.

Teen magazines such as *Okej* (glam rockers), *Dator-magazinet* (computer games), and *Frida* (love and heartache) are required reading for the young, as well as comics such as the popular *Fantomen* (The Phantom), *Spindelmannen* (Spider-Man), and *Min Häst* (for horseriding youth).

Parents have a less controlling parenting style in the '80s, and often let Kids keep to themselves without any major interference. Kids are allowed to roam the countryside as they please, as long as they return before dark. It is also a decade where divorce becomes commonplace, and many kids grow up in separate homes. Turbulence at home and the existential uncertainty that comes with this casts a shadow over many kids who seek to understand what is happening to their once so-called safe families.

School is mandatory and free. All kids go to the *grundskola* (basic school) at the age of seven, and continue for nine years before they go on to two to four years in *gymnasiet* (college). English is taught from an early age, and because all television shows and movies only have subtitles in Swedish, kids learn to speak English very well, although often with Hollywood-like accents rather than the British English that is most often taught in school.

The school system is relatively fair and progressive, but echoes of archaic methods from the '60s still remain. Teachers are often kind and well-meaning, but hopelessly out of touch with the realities of the kids. Bullying is a real and commonplace problem, and teachers and parents alike struggle to handle it properly. For some, the school years are torture at the hands of their so-called comrades, and the only respite they find is in like-minded friends or an escape into dreams of something else.

## THE MÄLAREN ISLANDS: A SLICE OF SUBURBIA

In many ways, the group of small islands called the Mälaren Islands (Mälaröarna in Swedish) is the archetypical suburban landscape of middle-class Sweden. Located just a short car ride from the capital of Stockholm, the Mälaren Islands are not quite in the city nor in the countryside. It's a bit of both. The landscape is dotted with red cottages and farms. Vast fields stretch towards the water of Lake Mälaren that surrounds the islands. Swaths of forest full of birch, oak, and pine trees break up the landscape. There are a handful of schools, several supermarkets, and even a 17th century palace on the islands. But mostly they are home to regular Swedes: families, workers, loners, and now, also scientists.

### GETTING AROUND

The main roads on the Mälaren Islands are paved and in good condition; these are made for car and bus traffic and quite narrow, making cycling on them an exciting and dangerous prospect. For Kids, the three main ways of getting around the islands are walking, cycling, and taking the communal bus. The 18-year-old age minimum for getting a driver's license makes cars a distant fantasy, but as you only need to be 15 to use a moped, this is often the vehicle of choice for cool, older Kids.

For the most part though, the bike reigns supreme, and is used all the time to visit friends, go to school or go exploring the countryside. BMX bikes are very popular, as are, to a lesser degree, road handlebar bikes, although they are less useful in rough terrain. Popular brands are Crescent (its model "Världsmästarcykeln" is iconic), Monark (made of paper and bark as the saying goes) and DBS.

Buses from Stockholms Lokaltrafik (SL) traverse the islands and connect them with greater Stockholm. Most kids that have a long trip to school have SL cards that allow them to use the buses as often as they want. Less fortunate kids have to pay the fare, which often makes the difference between having the money to buy a soda or not.

Still, as the islands are quite heavily forested and full of difficult terrain, walking is often the method of choice for exploring the surrounding lands. Even though Kids are often free to come and go as they please, most keep close to their homes and school. Going farther than a couple of kilometers from home feels like going on an expedition into strange lands.

RIKSENERGI

# THINGS TO DO IN THE '80S

Being a Kid in '80s Sweden is living with the constant stress from homework, the social games in school, and demands from parents and siblings at home. It's hard to be a Kid; what with school tests, local bullies, and other, much cooler kids, it sometimes feels like life is out to get you. When this happens (and it does, a lot) your only allies are your real friends and the dreams about something else. Whatever forms they take. Boredom is ever-present, days feel like they never end, visits to grandparents are mind-numbingly slow, and chores at home seem to always turn up when you least want them. It's no wonder that Kids have perfected a number of ways to pass the time together.

## HANG OUT AT THE LOCAL KIOSK

Wherever you go in Sweden, there is always a kiosk somewhere to gather near. These small newspaper stands stock magazines, candy, and tobacco. They are often staffed by grumpy old men who are very skeptical of the youngsters constantly hanging about but almost never buying anything. In some towns, these are replaced by grill kiosks, with the same basic concept, but selling hot dogs and hamburgers instead of magazines. Regardless, whenever a Kid happens to get a cash windfall, his next stop is invariably the kiosk.

## GO TO A SCHOOL DISCO

There are no proms in Swedish schools, but there are school discos. These always awkward affairs are equally filled with angst and short-lived bliss. Most often arranged in some local building decorated with balloons and confetti, these discos consist of kids standing in groups hugging the walls, while more daring youths take to the floor to dance to the latest pop hits. Alcohol being off limits, popcorn and lemonade are consumed in great quantities before the obligatory slow dance begins.

The slow dance is the real deal, the thing everybody has been waiting for. To songs such as "Carrie" by Europe or "Winds of Change" by Scorpions, Kids ask for a dance (it's considered bad form to say no) and dance while holding each other by the backs and slowly rocking from one foot to the other, desperately trying not to step on the dance partner's feet. Outside of these events, it's not uncommon to find older Kids listening to boom boxes and drinking folköl (weak beer that can be bought in stores if you are 18).

## PLAY GAMES

Games become extremely popular in the '80s, both in digital and analogue versions. The personal computer is finally affordable for an average family, and the Commodore 64 dominates the major part of the decade, to be followed by the Atari ST and the Amiga. C64 tapes are hard currency in school yards around the country, especially the so-called "turbo tapes," where up to 40 games are compressed on a single tape (although most of them won't work). A common practice is to gather at a friend's place after school and play games until dinner time.

Pen and paper roleplaying games are sold in great numbers throughout the decade. Thanks to the Swedish company Äventyrsspel, Sweden has one of the highest number of RPG players per capita in the world. The Swedish games *Drakar och Demoner* and *Mutant* are the best sellers, while older Kids prefer to play games in English, such as *Advanced Dungeons & Dragons*, *Call of Cthulhu* and *Rolemaster*. For some Kids, playing RPGs offers a way to channel creativity and imagination previously unheard of. It's popular to create homebrew games, drawing complicated maps, and writing adventures. Roleplaying is even done during school breaks, without dice or rules, just telling stories and acting in them.

## TEN SONGS

- Take On Me – A-ha ('85)
- Billie Jean – Michael Jackson ('82)
- Karma Chameleon – Culture Club ('83)
- The Final Countdown – Europe ('86)
- Jump – Van Halen ('84)
- Girls Just Want To Have Fun – Cyndi Lauper ('83)
- We Built This City – Jefferson Starship ('85)
- Take My Breath Away – Berlin ('86)
- Rock You Like A Hurricane – Scorpions ('84)
- We're Not Gonna Take It – Twisted Sister ('84)

### WATCH VIDEOS

Video stores are popular, but as most families won't own a VHS player until the mid '80s, the rentable moviebox is the solution of choice. This is a VHS player in a sturdy plastic carrying case that is rented for a day. As you need to be 18 years old to rent video films, this is the domain of parents and older siblings. A kid who happens to have a moviebox at home is envied by all, and often keeps court in which friends re-watch the rented movies in the middle of the day.

Getting the moviebox and films back to the video store before 6 pm is often an adventure in itself, as the Kids struggle to view all of the movies before time's up. The debate about the so-called video violence is a major topic in the media of the time. Talk shows on TV discuss the negative impact of American horror movies, and the older generation of Swedes struggles with how to deal with these gory movies suddenly being so easy to get hold of. This is not something that most Kids notice. For most of them, every VHS tape is a box filled with mysteries.

## SVARTSJÖLANDET: BLACK WATER AND DEEP FORESTS

Svartsjölandet (Black Lake Lands in English), also known as Färingsö to some, is the main island of the setting. It covers an area of 82 square kilometers and is surrounded on all sides by Lake Mälaren. Below are some of the important places on Svartsjölandet listed with short descriptions.

### FÄRENTUNA

A small village housing 60-70 inhabitants. Mostly known for its old, stone church constructed in the 12th century, and which still stands today. Enclosed in the 900-year-old walls are the so-called Uppland rune writings, artifacts of the pagans that lived here before Christianity conquered the lands. The runes read "… his wife… and… Odrik, his father. God help his soul."

### KUNGSBERGA

A minor settlement where a few hundred people live. Kungsberga has nothing to distinguish it from other settlements, only a small food store and a newspaper kiosk.

### STAVSBORG'S FACTORY

An abandoned factory in ruins. No one really knows what was made here, but most agree that it had something to do with explosives. Today, most people stay clear of the old buildings; rumors say it's being used by local criminals for shady business.

### STENHAMRA

The largest settlement on the island, Stenhamra is home to a few thousand people, and has all the basic facilities needed. Here, you can find two schools, a library, a supermarket, a small boat harbor, and a pizzeria. The town is mostly known for its abandoned stone quarry that has given the village its name (Stenhamra is roughly translated to Stonehammer).

The quarry, one of the largest of its kind in Sweden, employed workers that toiled around the clock. It was worked from 1884 until 1919 – providing the lion's share of Stockholm's stone work. Scores of workers died during those years, many of them in grisly accidents, others of tuberculosis. Today, the quarry has been left for nature to reclaim, and is mostly filled with dark water. Occasionally, film crews come here for the spectacular scenery, but otherwise wild animals, loners, and nosy kids are the only ones visiting the Stenhamra quarry today.

### SVARTSJÖ PALACE

A stone palace built in the rococo style by the Swedish king Fredrik I in the 18th century, as a gift to his queen Ulrika Eleonora. Partly built by the British royal architect William Chambers, it stands on the ruins of another royal castle that burned to the ground in the 17th century. After a century of decay, it was converted to a facility for forced labor so as to mine the granite deposits nearby. It served as a prison up until 1965. Today, it stands mostly unused, a shadow of its former glorious self. The prison walls have been demolished, and the cells abandoned. But the beautiful facade still hides many dark secrets from the past.

T 23 26

INFLUX KOLBÄCK →

ACCELERATOR PRIM – 1

Accelerator Tunnel P – 1

ACCELERATOR P

ALHOLMEN

M Ä L A R E N

Björkfjärden

ACCELERATOR AUX

LAGNÖ

D.

D.

Löten

BASTLAGNÖ

GATE 2D–3B

OUTFLUX MÄLSÅKER ←

Sätra •

• Bona

THE BONA REACTOR

A D E L S Ö

Svinsundet

• Wäsby

Cooling

• Dalby

WEST GATE
5D ●

Tofta

• Stenby

Lundkulla

Hovgårdsfjärde

Prästfjärden

OUTFLUX BOTKYRKA

Adjustments to map by
Rikskartor, Stockholm 1981

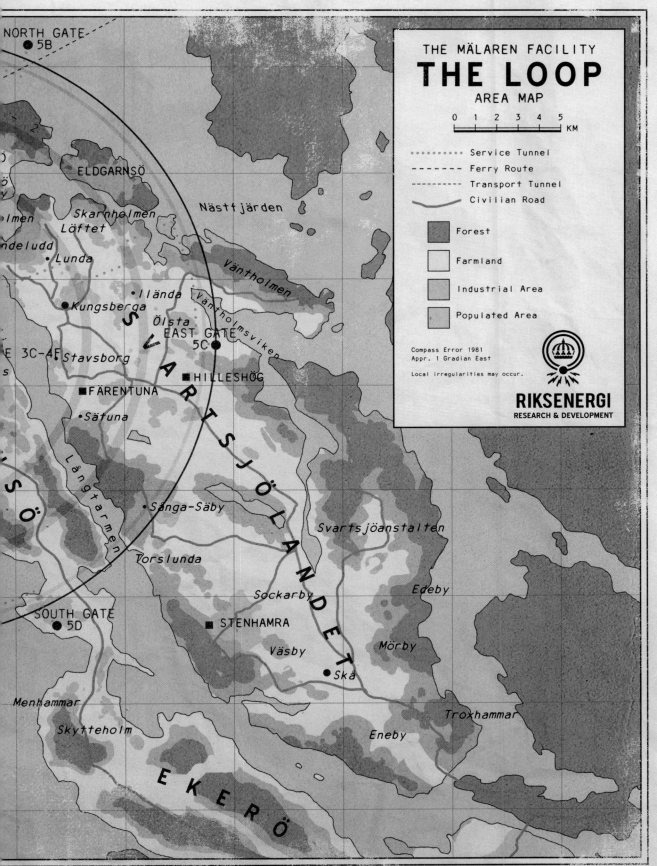

THE AGE OF THE LOOP

## THE MÄLAREN FACILITY
# THE LOOP
### AREA MAP

0 1 2 3 4 5 KM

·········· Service Tunnel
-------- Ferry Route
--------- Transport Tunnel
〜〜 Civilian Road

�(forest) Forest
▢ Farmland
▢ Industrial Area
▢ Populated Area

Compass Error 1981
Appr. 1 Gradian East

Local irregularities may occur.

**RIKSENERGI**
RESEARCH & DEVELOPMENT

NORTH GATE
● 5B

ELDGARNSÖ
Skarnholmen
Löftet
ndeludd
● Lunda
● Ilända
● Kungsberga
Ölsta
EAST GATE
5C ●
■ HILLESHÖG
■ FÄRENTUNA
● Sätuna
E 3C-4F Stavsborg

Nästfjärden
Väntholmen
Väntholmsviken

S V A R T S J Ö L A N D E T

Långtarmen

● Sänga-Säby

Torslunda

Svartsjöanstalten

Sockarby
Edeby

SOUTH GATE
● 5D

■ STENHAMRA

Väsby
Mörby
● Skå

Menhammar

Skytteholm

E K E R Ö

Troxhammar

Eneby

130930

**23**

### SVARTSJÖ PRISON

When the prison in the palace was dismantled, Svartsjö Prison was constructed to replace it. Divided into a men's wing and a women's wing, the prison is made up of a score of low, flat buildings inside the perimeter of security fencing. Used for low-risk criminals, the prisoners live a reasonably comfortable life here, mostly caring for themselves and cooking their own food. Being a prison, there are, of course, rumors about the inmates and their crimes. Some say there is a known hole in the fence, and that some prisoners use this to move freely on the island.

## MUNSÖ: HOME OF THE LOOP

The island of Munsö is home to the heart of the scientific installations of the Mälaren Islands, the Loop itself. Still open to the public, the northern part is where the main buildings and installations are found. Around these, the immediate surroundings are sealed off for everyone other than cleared personnel.

### THE BONA TOWERS

The three massive cooling towers of Bona are a landmark visible from far away. The tallest of them reaches 253 meters into the air. The purpose of the towers is to release the heat created by the huge amount of energy released by the Gravitron, the heart of the Loop that powers the entire particle accelerator deep underground. Around the towers are scores of red wooden houses. These are home to the scientists working at the Loop and their families.

### DEFENSE RESEARCH FACILITY 14

The FOA (Försvarets forskningsanstalt or the Swedish Defense Research Agency) facility at Sätra is classified as Top Secret and off limits to the public. Obviously, this fuels rumors as to what is really going on behind its wired fences. Some say the FOA researchers work on a military application of the Loop, others that they perform weird experiments on local animals, and even people. What is known is that military robot prototypes have been spotted on the premises, and that the facility is guarded around the clock.

RIKSENERGI

## ADELSÖ: REMNANTS OF THE PAST

Of the three islands detailed here, Adelsö is the wildest and least built up. Covered by deep forests, the island's only real inhabitants are a few farmers in small settlements. Once an important island during the Viking Age, the island is dotted with graves from the Bronze Age and forward. Two old stone fortresses can be found here, mostly overrun by nature, but their once proud selves can still be glimpsed.

### LILLA STENBY

A small village with roughly 140 inhabitants, Lilla Stenby houses a small food store and a harbor with a ferry that connects it to the island of Munsö.

### HOVGÅRDEN

Once a royal estate, Hovgården consists of ancient grave fields, rune stones, a castle ruin, and an old "tingsplats" (meeting place from the Viking Age). Among the old stones and grassy hills are a few houses and a church. North of the church are the three Kungshögarna ("Royal Mounds"), burial chambers within mounds, the largest being almost six meters tall. According to the historical chronicle The Life of Ansgard by Rimbart, these are the graves of the kings Olof, Björn, and Erik. These kings were the ones that first received the Christian missionaries to Sweden, and probably resided here in Hovgården.

### SÄTRA YOUTH CORRECTIONAL FACILITY

On the northern tip of the island, there is a remote building that houses a youth correctional center. Home to a dozen kids of various backgrounds, and a number of staff that live and work here, the building only sees regular visitors when food and other supplies arrive every other week. Sometimes kids manage to escape from the facility, prompting the police to come looking for them, and most often finding them quickly. However, people are still talking about the two kids from Norrland that disappeared a few years back, never to be seen again. Some say they drowned in Lake Mälaren trying to swim to the mainland, others claim they were seen sneaking around the tombs of Hovgården before they got lost.

## RIKSENERGI

In the 1960s, the Swedish government decided that it would construct a large-scale particle accelerator on the Mälaren Islands close to Stockholm. The location was chosen because of the proximity to the capital, but also because the bedrock here was considered suitable for constructing an underground facility of this magnitude.

To oversee this huge project, the state agency Riksenergi was created, and immediately granted plentiful funds. Considered by some a sister organization to Televerket, the state-owned telephone and communications operator, in reality Riksenergi has next to nothing to do with its more mundane sibling. Under the first director, Sten Ankarsjö, the agency started recruiting top scientists from around the country. Attracted by the proposition of working on the world's largest

RIKSENERGI

accelerator and by the rewarding relocation package, hundreds of scientists took the offer and committed to working on the project for years to come.

Riksenergi is by far the largest employer on the Mälaren Islands, and as such, is generally viewed favorably by the population. Some consider the agency as "theirs" and are very protective about its activities, even when bad rumors sometimes circulate. Even though security around the vital installations (especially the installations below ground) is tight, movement on the islands is relatively unrestricted. This "open door" policy has been questioned by some as naive, and there are persistent rumors of foreign-sounding strangers camping around the island, claiming to be birdwatchers but with their binoculars firmly trained on the scientific installations.

## THE LOOP

From its inception in 1969, the Facility for Research in High Energy Physics, or simply "The Loop," is the largest particle accelerator of its kind in the world. The Mälaröarna Facility was built by the newly formed government agency Riksenergi, together with the state-owned corporation Atomenergi, on the island of Munsö, some 26 kilometers northwest of downtown Stockholm. Construction began in 1961, using the best of Swedish engineering and know-how. Tunnels were blasted deep into the bedrock, creating the enormous loops for the world's largest particle accelerators, centered around a huge chamber housing the Gravitron. The facility was powered by the Bona reactor, a subterranean nuclear power plant whose most prominent feature are the three huge cooling towers, the tallest rising 253 meters above the rural surroundings.

RIKSENERGI

The scale of the Loop – or rather Loops – is daunting. The main particle accelerator, Prim-1, has a diameter of 26 kilometers, unsurpassed anywhere in the world. It is capable of performing experiments that were previously only dreamt of. There is also the secondary accelerator, Prim-2, at 20 kilometers in diameter, and lastly, the auxiliary accelerator, Aux-1, with a diameter of a "mere" 16 kilometers. Add to this the access tunnels and other underground installations, and one has one of the most impressive engineering feats ever seen. It isn't known how a small nation like Sweden could afford such a massive undertaking, as large parts of the project's budget were classified, but there's speculation that private investors, international corporations, universities, and the US government provided funds in exchange for access to the facility and the results of the research conducted there.

To enter the main entrance of the Loop, a visitor needs to pass through two security checks, have valid credentials, and be scheduled to work or visit, making it next to impossible for any unwanted intruders to slip in. It is safe to say that no Kids will be allowed in here through any means. However, there are a number of service tunnels stretching below and around the islands, and these have separate entrances. Though guarded by security systems, and requiring special codes and cards to open, there have been rumors that some locals have managed to open one of these entrances, and have snuck around in the tunnels for short periods before being discovered.

Not much is publicly known about what kind of experiments are performed at the facility. Some claim that Riksenergi has failed to get the installation to perform at its full capacity, others that the nature of the experiments have changed drastically since the second director, Hans Albrechtsson, took over the reins at Riksenergi. What is known is that US delegations, some of them uniformed, have visited the facility, fueling speculations that the science worked on at the Loop might somehow have military applications.

Most of the projects and experiments conducted at the Loop are secret, which has resulted in a lot of speculation. The nature of some of the anomalies appearing in the area gives some hints, though. The high energies released in combination with experiments with anomalous materials are believed to cause minor and major resonance cascades, which in turn, opens rifts in the space-time continuum. There are persistent rumors of large, reptilian animals having been seen in the woods on the Mälaren Islands. Most people disregard this as kids' fantasies about dinosaurs, but some have noticed that the Riksenergi game warden team has been unusually active lately and seemingly on constant alert. Using JR-17 hunting robots and MSPB-13 magnetrine armored reconnaissance cars, the warden team patrols the area around the Loop facilities, officially to make sure "wild animals" are not a reason for concern to the scientific installations.

There are rumors of an illness among the workers, scientists, and other staff working in proximity to the Gravitron. This so-called "Loop sickness" has symptoms of psychological disorders, including nightmares, depression, rage, alcoholism, and drug use, sometimes leading to suicide. It appears that the longer someone is exposed to the Gravitron, the higher the risk of developing the disorder. Unconfirmed rumors claim that Riksenergi employees fill a whole wing at the Beckomberga psychiatric hospital in west Stockholm.

One intriguing, and not completely understood, type of machinery is the echo sphere, which appears here and there in the landscape. These metal spheres, up to a few meters in diameter, each accessible through a round hatch, lie seemingly abandoned in the countryside around the Loop. The spheres can feel warm to the touch (or icy cold), give off a tingling sensation, cause nausea, or emit flashing lights emanating from the inside. Some carry a sign marked "Rogosin Locke Industries, Bethesda, Maryland," while others are unmarked.

It's possible that the echo spheres are the remains from a previous experiment by Riksenergi, as no one has claimed ownership of the spheres, and they are often left to rust. What their true purpose was – or is – is not known. Maybe they are still active somehow. Unconfirmed reports from locals claim that animals (and even people) that have entered some spheres have vanished into thin air. Whatever the truth of the matter is, most agree that echo spheres are best left alone.

## CIVILIAN TECHNOLOGY

The discovery of the magnetrine effect in 1943 facilitated the revolution in transport technology that was to last for half a century. The Earth's magnetic fields were strong enough to provide the needed lift north of a line spanning from the Mexican border to the Mediterranean, through the Middle East and along the Himalayas, and curving up towards Japan. This meant that magnetrine ships (also known as Gauss freighters) can only travel along routes in the northern hemisphere, spanning the northern three quarters of the Eurasian continent, North America, and the north Atlantic and Pacific oceans. Traditional shipping by ocean-going ships is still very much in use, both in the rest of the world and in the magnetrine shipping zone. In Sweden, exports like cars, iron ore, paper, and timber are shipped via magnetrine ships to destinations ranging from Japan in the east to California in the west.

The powerful magnetic fields created by the larger magnetrine ships make it inconvenient to have them travel through densely populated areas, as they affect local electronics. They have to follow routes, usually the same as traditional ships, but also specially designated "corridors" across land. Smaller ships are less risky, but they aren't used in cities or other built-up areas, which is why older technology like trucks and trains are still used. Most coastal cities have magnetrine ship ports, where the cargo is usually loaded on trucks for local and regional distribution. Railway transport is faster than magnetrine vessels, and the same goes for road transport. That's why there's a need for traditional wheeled vehicles. Airplanes still have their role, too, as they are faster and not limited by the magnetic fields, but there are magnetrine luxury liners for those who like to travel in style.

The principle of the magnetrine drive is simple: magnetrine discs mounted along the bottom part of a hull are charged, the resulting magnetic field repelling the ship against the magnetic field of the Earth, providing the lift needed. The discs on modern vessels are auto-correcting, adjusting to local variations in the magnetic field. In order to propel the vessel, the discs are engaged in sequences, rapidly changing the polarity of the discs in what is known as "caterpillar drive," creating a pull-and-push effect that provides locomotion. Most magnetrine ships are diesel-powered single or twin turbine vessels with a deadweight tonnage (DWT, the weight of everything the ship carries, excluding the ship itself) of up to 80,000 metric tons. Some of the largest freighters are nuclear-powered. The ships come in four classes:

RIKSENERGI

- **MAGLIGHT** (5,000 to 10,000 DWT), up to 100 meters in length.
- **MAGMID** (10,000 to 25,000 DWT), up to 200 meters in length.
- **MAGMAX** (25,000 to 50,000 DWT), up to 250 meters in length.
- **SUPERMAG** (50,000 to 80,000 DWT), up to 300 meters in length.

There are also the smaller vessels for local transport, service and maintenance, military operations, and so forth. Magnetrine discs are used for other purposes, too, such as unmanned drones, road traffic control, construction of buildings, and suspending billboards in the air.

## MILITARY TECHNOLOGY

The military applications of the magnetrine technology are plentiful – on paper. After many weapons projects,

the strengths and weaknesses of the technology have become evidently manifest. First out of the block were the Soviets, as Mikhail Vorobyev had discovered the effect back in 1943. World War II was over before it could be applied to weapons (it was originally a spin-off find while researching long-distance missile guidance systems), but during the first years of the Cold War, Soviet scientists experimented with magnetrine technology and armored vehicles. After Soviet scientist Vladimir Degtaryev defected to the West in 1951, the US got access to the technology, and soon several other Western countries did, too.

One obvious area of research was armored vehicles. Magnetrine hovertanks proved to be problematic, though. The limitations of armor-to-lift ratios made the tanks too lightly armored, and coupled with the raised silhouette, hover tanks proved to be unsuitable for the modern battlefield. The area where magnetrine technology proved useful was in supply and trans-

port. Magnetrine transports filled the niche between wheeled trucks and helicopters, combining capacity with all-terrain access. Magnetrine cargo and troop transports became part of frontline units, as well as lightly armored reconnaissance vehicles. As the magnetrine tech worked best in the northern hemisphere, it couldn't be utilized in the Vietnam War or in many other conflicts in the Third World, and thus saw limited combat use.

When the self-balancing issue was solved by Iwasaki in the late 1960s, military self-balancing autonomous systems – or robots – soon saw the light of day. Classic, humanoid robots proved to be inferior on the battlefield, as they simply couldn't react and adapt like human soldiers. Instead, they were useful for sentry duty and load carrying. Larger robots were more or less autonomous, most commonly patrolling border areas or remote-controlled by human operators, either with line-of-sight "control glove" systems, or via sat-

ellite uplink from control centers. As artificial intelligence improved, robots became more independent, like the Swedish-built ABM-100.

Problems with military robots have usually been associated with poor or rogue AIs. The Baikal Wars in the 1970s saw Chinese "robot wave" tactics fail due to weak command and control systems. As for Sweden, secret research conducted at the FOA facility at Sätra on Munsö included military robots. Despite safety measures, some of the robots are known to have escaped. It is possible that their AI is a little too good, as there are rumors that not all of them have been rounded up. Swedish Army AMAT-2 quadruped robots, painted in a standard army camouflage pattern, have been deployed from time to time in order to deal with extraordinary incidents on and around the islands. The AMAT-2 and its predecessor, AMAT-1, have been successful exports, serving in the armies of Norway, Austria, Brazil, South Africa, and Malaysia.

# Magnetrine flight -How it works:

### 1. The Earth's magnetic field.

The interaction between the Earth's rotation and the movement of its liquid core creates a magnetic field around our planet.

You could say the whole planet works like a gigantic magnet. The field is strongest around the poles, where the field's bearing angle is vertical, and weakest along the equator, where it is horizontal. The buoyant force is negative towards the South Pole, and the major transport routes are located to the north, and not to the south, because of these properties of the magnetic field. The strength of the magnetic field is measured in a unit called "Gauss".

### 2. The Magnetrine Effect.

In 1943, Mikhail Vorobyev stumbled upon what we today call the "Magnetrine Effect."

Vorobyev was an engineer in Russia during the Second World War, and he worked on developing a new kind of guidance system for long-range missiles. While experimenting with different types of gyroscopes, he discovered that if you enclosed a rapidly-rotating neodymium rod in a plate-shaped iron pod then the resulting device repels against the Earth's magnetic field. Vorobyev quickly realized what this implied and refined his design. Soon he had a disc with considerable lift; the first magnetrine disc was born.

### 3. Safety.

Today, almost all locomotive ships use autocorrecting Sinter discs that adjust lift and angle the discs to match the local characteristics of the magnetic field.

Lieber-Alta's locomotive ships use discs that are powered by the most efficient and environmentally-friendly diesel engines on the market. In the unlikely event of an engine failure, a crash is practically impossible. Since the '60s, Sinter discs have had a so-called "float breaker," which ensures that the charge (and thus the lift) stays in the disc. A locomotive ship without power falls at a rate of three centimeters per week. A fifteen meter fall would take ten years!

### 4. Power.

The effectiveness of magnetrine discs is phenomenal. Over the past thirty years Lieber-Alta has shipped a total of 300 billion tons, with an average of five million tons annually per Gauss freighter.

We are continually investing in new technologies, and the future looks bright. In 1988 our fleet will grow with twenty new Allistair ships, which will offer our customers a new level of effectiveness for mid-size ships. At the same time we will be launching our own logistics solution, TransAlta.
Keep your eyes on the sky so you won't miss the innovations of the future!

## ▰▰LIEBER-ALTA
### We make dreams take flight.

RIKSENERGI

RIKSENERGI

# THE US LOOP

*A project as big as the Loop could never have been realized without international collaboration. Even if Swedes would have liked to see it as a Swedish project through and through, it was clear that a lot of the technology and expertise behind the facility was developed in other countries, primarily in the USA. American experience and technology from similar projects in the Nevada desert turned out to be invaluable in the construction of the Loop. Some even say that the whole project was only possible because of an American desire to have a technological presence in the Baltic Sea area. There was much speculation about what part the Loop played in the Cold War, and some questions may never be answered.*

The Loop might have reached its highest level of notoriety in Sweden, but it got its start as a top-secret military project in the USA. Specifically, it began in Boulder City, Nevada, a sleepy little town just a half-hour's drive southeast of Las Vegas, overlooking Lake Mead. While it started out in the early days of the Cold War in the 1950s, the US Loop peaked in the heady years of the 1980s.

The Loop was originally meant to investigate the possibility of instantaneous teleportation between two points on the planet. It was formed under the auspices of the Defense Advanced Research Projects Agency (DARPA), which was known simply as ARPA at the time. President Dwight D. Eisenhower himself ordered the creation of the Department of Advanced Research into Teleportation (DART), hoping to employ the fruits of its labors as a means of moving troops around the globe at a moment's notice.

But that initial promise – secret as it might have been – was never fulfilled, and the city seems to have suffered for it.

## LIVING IN AMERICA

Although Boulder City can sometimes seem like a deserted island in the middle of an endless sea of sand, it's actually not a terrible place to grow up.

### AMERICA IN THE '80S

America in the age of the Loop isn't quite the same as the one you might remember. Strange airships scud across the sky, floating atop gigantic magnetrine discs. Robots perform a lot of the heavy labor, often guided by human operators – but sometimes not.

RIKSENERGI

**TEN TV SHOWS**

- Magnum P.I. (1980-1988)
- Cheers (1982-1993)
- Knight Rider (1982-1986)
- The A-Team (1983-1987)
- Friday Night Videos (1983-2002)
- V (1983-1985)
- Miami Vice (1984-1989)
- Pee-Wee's Playhouse (1986-1990)
- Max Headroom (1987-1988)
- Star Trek: The Next Generation (1987-1994)

RIKSENERGI

This all seems perfectly normal to the Kids born into this world, of course, but that doesn't mean there isn't plenty there that can still mystify and shock them.

The '80s is the era of Ronald Reagan, the former actor who becomes the nation's oldest-ever President by promising a "morning in America." It's a time when Americans want to have faith in their government restored to them after it's been shattered by Watergate and President Nixon's resignation. The threat of an imminent nuclear holocaust may cast a shadow over everything, but by the end of the decade, the Soviet Union is knocked onto the ropes, and it seems there's nothing America can't do.

At the same time, that faith turns out to be founded on a pack of lies. Reagan doesn't just free the hostages from Iran in 1981. Instead, in 1980, he negotiates for them to be held until his inauguration, to help him win the election.

Not too much later, the CIA refuses to obey Congress' ban on helping prop up the Contra rebels in Nicaragua. Congress also cuts off funding to CIA efforts to overthrow the Sandinistas in that war-torn nation, but CIA agents illegally procure their own funds for the cause by selling weapons to America's enemies in Iran instead.

For the most part, though, no one knows this until later in the decade. And to Kids in America, little of this matters directly to them anyway.

At the start of the decade, underage drinking reaches deep into high schools, because the drinking age in much of the country is 18 – although it had been 21 in Nevada since the end of Prohibition. That starts to change in 1984, when Congress forces the states to raise the national drinking age to 21. At the same time, the Reagan administration heats up the War on Drugs, sending First Lady Nancy Reagan out with the slogan, "Just Say No." While widely mocked, teen use of drugs drops during the decade from its highs in the '70s.

Meanwhile, the era of Free Love comes to an end with the rise of HIV and AIDS. This world-wide epidemic infects millions of people who share dirty needles or have unprotected sex. Now, sexually transmitted diseases (STDs) don't just make you sick: they can literally kill you.

Military service is entirely voluntary. While men have to register for the draft at age 18, no one's been conscripted into the US military since the early '70s. Perhaps because of this, the '80s are comparatively peaceful. The US invades the Caribbean island of Grenada in 1983 and Panama in December of 1989, but both operations are swift, limited, and conclusive.

There are only four major TV stations in most of the country: ABC, CBS, NBC, and PBS (Public Television). In 1986, Fox joins the fray. Cable TV is still rolling out over much of the nation, bringing new channels like HBO, MTV, and ESPN to American households. Cartoons start being broadcast in the afternoons, after school, rather than just on Saturday mornings.

During the decade, the Federal Communication Commission ends the prohibition of toy companies making cartoons based on their products. They flood the airwaves with toy-based shows, including *Transformers, My Little Pony, He-Man and the Masters of the Universe, G.I. Joe,* and *Thundercats.*

### GROWING UP IN AMERICA

Being a kid in 1980s America feels like being stuck between a wild, dangerous past and an even stranger and more complicated future. Your grandparents fought in World War II. Your parents either fought in or protested the Vietnam War. The Cold War seems to be heating up to the ignition point, and if you manage to survive that, you can see a corporate-owned, cyberpunk future

RIKSENERGI

heaving toward the digital horizon. You ride the wave of nostalgia that seems like it's sure to crash on the shoals of nuclear armageddon, and the only thing you can hope for is that you can keep surfing long enough to grab a fresh wave laced with future shock.

The only cell phones anyone has at this point are the size and weight of a brick, and they usually come attached to a car. If you want to get a hold of someone when you're out of the house, you have to hunt for a pay phone and hope you have a quarter to plug into it.

You don't have GPS. You have paper maps that no one can seem to fold back together, and you have your memories. The upside is that no one can reach you unless you want to be found, and the idea of someone tracking you using an array of satellites ringing the planet seems like something out of Star Trek.

The only apps anyone has come before dinner at your favorite restaurant.

In America, you start school with kindergarten at the age of five. Grade school ranges from 1st through 5th or 6th grade, after which you go to middle school or junior high. High school usually starts with 9th grade and ends at 12th. Most kids go to public schools, which are free, although some parents pay tuition to send their kids to private schools instead. After high school, you head off to college or technical school – both of which you must pay for – or enter the job market straight away.

Divorce rates reached a peak in the 1980s, leaving lots of kids living in single-parent homes. Most kids in such situations wind up living with their mothers. Sometimes they spend every other weekend with their fathers, who end up playing a smaller part in their lives.

Almost all kids spend a good chunk of their waking hours in school. In homes where the parents both work – or there's only one parent around – the kids often come home to an empty house, giving rise to a generation of latchkey kids. They tend to themselves, and sometimes younger siblings, until their parents get home from their jobs. If they don't come straight home from school, there's no one around to notice.

In their spare time, many kids listen to tunes – including this new thing called rap music – on the radio or on cassettes. Some play their cassettes on portable players like the Sony Walkman or tote them around on their shoulders inside massive boom boxes that use six

to eight D-cell batteries. They also watch movies and TV shows on VCRs – both in VHS and Betamax formats – and swap copies of tapes recorded off broadcast TV with each other.

Some kids play a lot of tabletop games, including *Dungeons & Dragons, Traveller,* and *Middle-Earth Roleplaying (MERP).* In certain areas, these games are banned – along with heavy metal music recordings – for fear that they might have a demonic influence on the kids who play them. The Satanic Panic causes a lot of hand-wringing, but the added notoriety seems to sell even more games and records than before.

Most homes don't have a computer in them, but in those that do, the Apple II and the Commodore 64 top the list, mostly because they offer video games more intricate than the ones you can find on the Atari, Colecovision, or Intellivision systems of the day, things like Zork and Castle Wolfenstein. This changes in 1985 when the relatively inexpensive Nintendo Entertainment System reaches America, and Super Mario Bros. storms the nation.

## BOULDER CITY: "BEST CITY BY A DAM SITE"

Boulder City is a sleepy little town in the middle of the Mojave Desert in southern Nevada. It started out as a town for the workers who labored on the Hoover Dam – which was originally known as the Boulder Dam. It was intended to be a model city for the area, but once the dam was finished, most of the businesses – and people – in the area moved off to Las Vegas or parts unknown instead. Most of the city went up between 1930 and 1934, so by the start of the 1980s, no building is over fifty years old.

Unlike most cities in Nevada, gambling is prohibited inside Boulder City, which makes it feel a bit more normal than gambling meccas like Las Vegas. There are casinos that sit just outside the city's borders, but Kids don't have much to do with them.

Less than 10,000 people live in the city at the start of the 1980s. By the end of the decade, there are about 12,500 in total. Everything is spread out over an area of 208 square miles, giving everyone in the city plenty of room. By land size, it's the largest city in Nevada.

The wealthiest people live on the top of the slope that leads down toward Lake Mead in the distance. The middle class lives below them, and the poorest people are at the bottom of the slope. The lots for homes at the top of the slope are spacious and friendly, but as you move down the slope, they become smaller and rougher.

The citizens of Boulder City are about 95% white. Hispanics make up 4% of the city, and members of other races are few and far between. In the game, of course, Kids can be any race they like.

The city sits on the eastern edge of the Pacific Time Zone (UTC-8). When you cross into Arizona, which lies on the eastern side of the Hoover Dam, you're in Mountain Time (UTC-7) instead.

### GETTING AROUND

Most Kids walk around Boulder City or ride their bikes, but they can also grab a ride on the local bus system, which even has intercity connections to Las Vegas. Lots of Kids ride standard BMX-style bikes, but as they get older, they often move up to road bikes. Few people have even heard of mountain bikes at the time.

Older kids can get a license once they turn sixteen years old, and many kids go and take their driver's test on their sixteenth birthday. Motorcycles and mopeds are popular because they're cheaper than cars, and unlike in colder climates, they can be used all year round.

## THINGS TO DO IN THE '80S

As a Kid in Boulder City in the 1980s, there's not a lot to do outside of school, homework, and sports, which can seem to consume your entire life. Toss in stress induced by bullies and budding romances, and it sometimes seems like the only people you can truly count on

### TEN TABLETOP RPGS

- Advanced Dungeons & Dragons (1977)
- Rolemaster (1980)
- Top Secret (1980)
- Call of Cthulhu (1981)
- Champions (1981)
- Gangbusters (1982)
- Star Frontiers (1982)
- Chill (1984)
- Pendragon (1985)
- Cyberpunk (1988)

RIKSENERGI

in your life – at least to keep you from being bored out of your mind – are your friends.

Although Boulder City is relatively close to Las Vegas, it's not easy to reach without a car – or the determination to bicycle the 25 miles across the blazing desert. It's less than 8 miles to Hoover Dam in the opposite direction, but once you've seen it, there's not a whole lot of entertainment out that way. Most Kids hang out in town instead.

### HANG OUT AT THE POOL

As hot as Boulder City can be, many kids head straight to the city pool once school lets out. In some ways, it's an extension of the school, since kids tend to gather in the same cliques here as they do during the day. Some kids stick around until sunset, although most head home after 5 PM to join their families for dinner.

There's an indoor pool that's heated, and kept

open year round. Most Kids wouldn't be caught dead in it for about three quarters of the year, as the adults in town claim it mostly for swimming laps rather than playing around. During the winter, though, a die-hard few will venture inside for the daily hours of free play between 3:30 and 5 PM.

### PLAY GAMES

When you're stuck inside with the air conditioning and need to escape the boredom of living in a small town in the middle of nowhere, games are just the ticket. The wealthier kids might have Nintendo Entertainment Systems or even an old Atari machine kicking around. Others turn toward tabletop games which are cheap and endlessly renewable entertainment.

Tabletop roleplaying games – led by *Dungeons & Dragons* – are in their golden age in the 1980s. Without a means of communicating with each other, most gamers have to figure out how to play the games themselves, rather than being taught. Fortunately, it's easy to modify such games via house rules to fit any particular group's style of play.

Miniatures games like *Warhammer Fantasy Battles* (1983) and *Warhammer 40,000* (1987) become incredibly popular during this time, too. Kids spend hours painting their armies of lead figures and then pitting them against each other on dining room tables and disused ping-pong tables across the country.

RIKSENERGI

## TEN MUSIC VIDEOS

- "Safety Dance" by Men Without Hats (1982)
- "Burning Down the House" by the Talking Heads (1983)
- "Thriller" by Michael Jackson (1983)
- "Total Eclipse of the Heart" by Bonnie Tyler (1983)
- "Take on Me" by A-ha (1984)
- "Self Control" by Laura Branigan (1984)
- "We're Not Gonna Take It" by Twisted Sister (1984)
- "Land of Confusion" by Genesis (1986)
- "Sledgehammer" by Peter Gabriel (1986)
- "Never Gonna Give You Up" by Rick Astley (1987)

RIKSENERGI

### WATCH MUSIC VIDEOS

Music videos have their heyday in the 1980s. For kids that have cable, MTV is where they get their fix, but others are restricted to watching Friday Night Videos every week instead. This new art form popularizes music of all kinds, driving them to even greater heights of sales.

Most kids buy their music on cassettes. While the music CD debuts in 1982, CD players cost hundreds of dollars at the time and only wind up attached to high-end audio systems for most of the 1980s.

## INSIDE BOULDER CITY

Kids who live in Boulder City spend most of their time there. If their parents like the big city, the Kids might get hauled off to Las Vegas for shopping trips, concerts, or shows. If they like the great outdoors, they might visit the Red Rock Canyon National Conservation Area on the far side of Las Vegas, or they could even take a day trip to the Grand Canyon. For the most part, though, Boulder City is the landscape of the Kids' lives.

### PIERSON'S SALVAGE

Billy Pierson runs this junkyard on the south side of town. It's filled with rusty wrecks of all kinds, including cars, magnetrine freighters, and even the occasional robot. If you're looking for spare parts for any sort of project, this is the place to be. Billy has an encyclopedic memory for everything he's ever bought for the place, and he's eager to sell.

### THE BOULDER THEATER

The Boulder Theater is the center of the downtown shopping district. Built in 1933, it's a bit rundown

these days. Since it can only show one film at a time, it can't compete with the big cineplexes in nearby Henderson or Las Vegas, but for Kids on their own, it's the only theater in town.

### THE BOULDER DAM HOTEL

This sun-bleached small hotel once housed important people visiting the dam when it was being built. Citizens are mustering an effort to restore it to its former glory, but it's a work in progress. Still, important outsiders often stay here because of its central location.

### BOULDER CITY AIRPORT

The airport once serviced the dam project, but it's since closed down. The Elks Club purchased the place in 1958, and turned the terminal into its clubhouse. Some kids claim the airstrip still gets used by secret government planes traveling in the dead of night, but no one has any actual proof.

### BOULDER BOWL

This 8-lane bowling alley opened in 1947, and still feels like a throwback to that time. Kids often come here to kill some time in the air conditioning.

RIKSENERGI

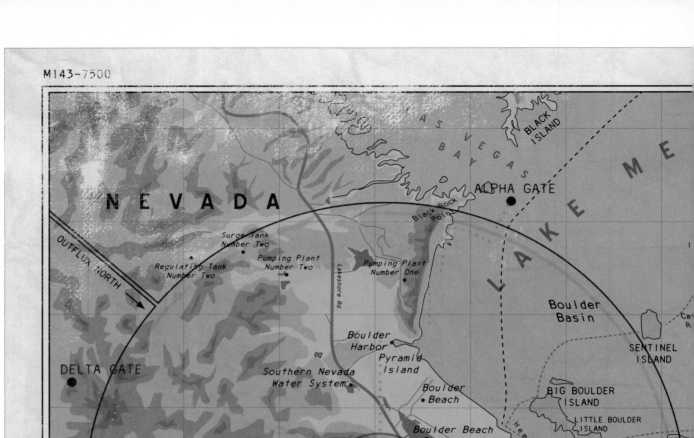

M143-7500

NEVADA

LAS VEGAS BAY

BLACK ISLAND

ALPHA GATE

Black Rock Point

LAKE ME

Surge Tank Number Two

Regulating Tank Number Two

Pumping Plant Number Two

Pumping Plant Number One

Lakeshore Rd

Boulder Basin

SENTINEL ISLAND

OUTFLUX NORTH

Boulder Harbor

Pyramid Island

DELTA GATE

Southern Nevada Water System

Boulder Beach

BIG BOULDER ISLAND

LITTLE BOULDER ISLAND

Boulder Beach Campground

Hemenway Harbor

ROCK ISLAND

River Mountains

Seven Dry Falls

Lake Mead Marina

OUTFLUX WEST

MAIN REACTOR

Cooling Towers

Lakeshore Rd

ECHO GATE

FOXTROT GATE

Hemenway Hall

Red Mountain Rd

93

93

HOOVER D

Red Mountain

Hemenway Pass

Great Basin Hwy

Hoover Dam Lodge

DARPA FACILITY

Hemenway Park

ACCELERATOR

Camino Rd

Great Basin Hwy

Colorado

BOULDER CITY

93

CHARLIE GATE

Canyon Point Rd

OUTFLUX SOUTH

Boulder City Airport

BOULDER CITY

# THE LOOP

AREA MAP

0   1   2   3   4   5
km

Park/Forest

Hills/Mountains

Populated Area

Buildings

·········· Service Tunnel

------- Ferry Route

---------- Transport Tunnel

Civilian Road

DART

DEPARTMENT OF ADVANCED

## BOULDER CITY

CANYON RD

Wilbur Sq

Boulder Theatre

Boulder City Police Department

Boulder Canyon

Bowling Hall

COLORADO ST

Boulder Dam Hotel

St Christopher's Church

93

Fisher Space Pen

Mitchell Elementary School

Boulder City High School

Whalen Baseball Field

NEVADA HIGHWAY

ADAMS BVD

SOUTH GATE 5D

Boulder City Hospital

Boulder City Library

St Andrew's Catholic Church

BUCHANAN BLVD

Oasis Park

Pier's Salvage

Boulder City Golf Course

Helicopter Sightseeing

Boulder City Airport

0   500   1000   1500   2000   2500
m

A R I Z O N A

River

GATE

RIKSENERGI

130930

The Boulder City High School teams practice here, but anyone is welcome to the other alleys at any time.

### FISHER SPACE PEN

The Fisher Space Pen Company moved here in 1976, and quickly became one of the biggest employers in town, making the company's famous Silver Bullet pens, which use pressurized ink chambers so they can function in space. Rumor has it that DART is the company's largest customer.

## LAKE MEAD

Lake Mead is an artificial lake created by the construction of the Hoover Dam to block the Colorado River, which forms the local border between Nevada to the west and Arizona to the east. It's the largest such reservoir in the nation when it reaches its peak capacity in 1983, although drought and water demand later in the decade cause it to shrink.

### HOOVER DAM

The Hoover Dam provides water and hydroelectric power to Las Vegas and all other nearby places. It was built and operated by the US Bureau of Reclamation, a division of the Department of the Interior, which is still one of the biggest employers in Boulder City. The massive concrete structure stretches over 1,200 feet across the Black Canyon, and stands over 725 feet from the top to bottom.

### LAKE MEAD NATIONAL RECREATIONAL AREA

Lake Mead isn't just a water reservoir; it's also a fantastic lake upon which people boat, fish, and play. It runs from the mouth of the Grand Canyon all the way to the Hoover Dam. People from Boulder City head east on Highway 93 until they reach Lakeshore Road, from which they can reach the Las Vegas Boat Harbor, the Boulder Beach Campground, and Boulder Beach.

It stretches four and a half miles south from Las Vegas's actual city limits to just shy of the famous "Welcome to Las Vegas" sign, and it includes such notables as the Dunes, the Sands, the Sahara, the Stardust, and the gigantic, emerald-colored MGM Grand, at which an electrical fire kills 87 people in 1980.

### AREA 51

In the 1950s, aliens supposedly landed in this legendary part of the Nevada Test and Training Range run by the US Air Force, although no evidence of this has ever been produced. It's actually used to test experimental aircraft and weaponry. It sits over 80 miles north-northwest of Las Vegas, out past the Nevada Test Site, where the US military used to test atomic bombs.

### NUCLEAR TESTING

In the 1950s, casinos in downtown Las Vegas actually advertised suites from which visitors could watch the glow from the nuclear explosions light up the night. Fortunately, the prevailing winds didn't carry the fallout to Boulder City, and above-ground tests ended in 1963.

### VALLEY OF FIRE STATE PARK

Just west of the northernmost tip of Lake Mead sits the Valley of Fire, so named for the red sandstone formations that jut out of the desert floor. Native Americans known as the Anasazi once lived here, and the petroglyphs they left behind can still be found on sheltered walls and inside caves.

## LAS VEGAS AND BEYOND

A wider world awaits beyond the borders of Boulder City. Heading west on Highway 93 brings you to Henderson, Nevada, and some 14 miles beyond that lies Las Vegas. This is the largest city in Nevada, and you can see the lights from its casinos blazing through the desert sky all night long.

### THE STRIP

The Strip is a series of world-famous casinos that sit along South Las Vegas Boulevard.

## THE DART

With the Hoover Dam providing a massive surplus of electricity for the region, DARPA decided in the early 1950s to begin construction of the world's largest particle accelerator on the western edge of Lake Mead. President Eisenhower ordered the development of the Department of Advanced Research into Teleportation (DART) to oversee the project.

Since the project's actual goals were top secret, no one was allowed to reveal to the public what the organization's acronym actually stood for. Most outsiders assumed it was the Department of Advanced Research and Technology, and no government official ever dared correct them.

The smartest physicists in the nation were recruited to work there by the project's original director, Malcolm Grayson, who often resorted to siphoning people off other government projects – at least temporarily. Most of DART's employees live in Boulder City with their families, occupying homes formerly owned by the people who built the Hoover Dam.

RIKSENERGI

45

They're all sworn to secrecy about the nature of their work, even to the point that they cannot tell their spouses or kids.

The fact that Lake Mead and the Hoover Dam have become tourist destinations for people visiting nearby Las Vegas causes the DART security team fits at times, but others see that as conveniently providing cover for them to indulge in their most paranoid fantasies about spies and other potential breaches. DART's current director, Dr. Alma Madeira, hasn't shown any impulse to restrain them so far.

## THE US LOOP

The DART Loop is gigantic, although at nearly 15 miles across, it's still smaller than the Loop in Sweden. It runs deep underneath all of Boulder City, encompassing a large chunk of the municipality within its circumference. Most of Boulder City's residents live within the DART Loop, and don't even realize it.

No one is allowed into any DART facilities without the proper credentials being presented at the main offices, which are located in a high-fenced compound that sits next to the golf course on the outskirts of town. Dogs and guards patrol the compound's perimeter, which is lined with motion detectors and concertina wire.

Some people have noticed a number of Swedish scientists are regularly roaming in and out of town, staying at local hotels. This is supposedly part of an exchange program set up with similar particle accelerators around the world – even though it's rare to see any visitors from a nation other than Sweden.

No Kids are allowed inside the DART Loop, not even on Take Your Kid to Work Day. There are a dozen or so maintenance shafts that lead down to the Loop at various points around the city though, and these aren't quite so obviously guarded. With the right tools, someone might be able to sneak down into the tunnels beneath the city, and maybe even get into the main headquarters before they were detected.

If anyone's managed this so far, though, they haven't announced what they've found. Anytime someone disappears from town without warning, however, the rumors that they were caught somewhere they weren't supposed to be – and then swept away to a secret federal prison – start flying.

RIKSENERGI

RIKSENERGI

RIKSENERGI

# THE KIDS

*The echo sphere lay there in the gravel pit. A faint tune hummed from within the sphere when the wind resonated between the steel walls. Kalle and Olof immediately ran inside and started shouting to test the echo. A pair of nervous ospreys wheeled above the sphere. I remained outside, reminded of that first day there with my grandfather. Thinking back on it now I realize that this is probably my first memory of experiencing nostalgia. Odd; a summer's day and three nine-year-olds, one of whom was stopped in the middle of playing by a childhood memory.*

Each player creates a Kid. The process is shown step-by-step and then explained more thoroughly.

1. Choose your Type.
2. Decide your age, from 10 to 15 years.
3. Distribute a number of points equal to your age in the four attributes, 1 to 5 points in each.
4. Determine your number of Luck Points, equal to 15 minus your age.
5. Distribute 10 points in skills. You may take up to level 3 in the three key skills of your Type. For other skills, a starting skill level of 1 is the maximum.
6. Pick an Iconic Item.
7. Pick a Problem.
8. Pick a Drive.
9. Pick a Pride.
10. Define your Relationships to the other Kids and to the NPCs.

11. Select an Anchor.
12. Name your Kid.
13. Write a short description.
14. Choose your favorite song.

**DO THIS TOGETHER:**
15. Define the group's Hideout.
16. Answer the Gamemaster's questions.

## TYPES

Choose which Type your Kid is. There should preferably be only one Kid of each Type in the group.

RIKSENERGI

# BOOKWORM

*When you read, you travel thousands of miles to foreign countries. You speak with mad poets and discuss the meaning of life with philosophers who died hundreds of years ago. You have secret rendezvous at Alpine peaks and shootouts with Russian agents. In real life, you wish that your pimples would not show as much as they do, and you long for the day you will leave this place, so that your real life can truly begin.*

**KEY SKILLS: CALCULATE, INVESTIGATE, COMPREHEND**

### ICONIC ITEM
Choose one or make up one on your own:
- Dog named Plutten [Tiny]
- Encyclopedia
- Magnifying glass

### PROBLEM
Choose one or make up one on your own:
- Nobody tells me how my dad died.
- My sister is really sick.
- That weird man is following me.

### DRIVE
Choose one or make up one on your own:
- I want to find answers to the big questions in life.
- I need something to brag about.

### PRIDE
Choose one or make up one on your own:
- I'm the smartest kid in school.
- Nothing scares me.

### RELATIONSHIPS TO OTHER KIDS
Choose one for each other Kid or make up on your own:
- He/she is my competitor.
- I will make him/her love me.
- We are siblings and friends.

### RELATIONSHIPS TO NPCS
Choose two or make up two on your own:
- Mona [Mary], the school librarian, was my friend until she disappeared. I am sure that the school janitor [Jeffrey] knows more than he's saying.
- Olof [Gary] in my class was attacked by animals while riding his bike home from training. I can't believe that everyone at school thinks he was attacked by werewolves.
- When Lena Thelin [Diane Petersen] was fired from the Loop, I heard her vow to take revenge on all who live here.

### ANCHOR
Choose one or make up one on your own:
- Mom/dad
- Teacher
- Local author

### TYPICAL NAMES
Choose one or make up one on your own:
- **Girls names:** Felicia, Ann-Christin, Magdalena, Gabriella [Elizabeth, Erin, Rachel, Susan]
- **Boys names:** Nils, Kristian, Magnus, Jan [Aaron, Darren, Joshua, Thomas]
- **Nicknames:** Ugglan, Vårtan, Plattfisk, Janne [Frodo, Professor, Wart, Owl]

# COMPUTER GEEK

*You know exactly what is important in life – to break the record in Super Mario Bros, to build revolutionary programs on your computer, to understand how a robot works, or to cast just the right spell to save the party during roleplaying nights. Who cares what all the others think?*

**KEY SKILLS:** **CALCULATE, PROGRAM, COMPREHEND**

### ICONIC ITEM
Choose one or make up one on your own:
- Computer
- Pocket calculator
- Toy lightsaber

### PROBLEM
Choose one or make up one on your own:
- The tough guys hit me.
- My parents are always arguing.
- She/he doesn't even know I exist.

### DRIVE
Choose one or make up one on your own:
- I love puzzles.
- Peer pressure makes me do it.

### PRIDE
Choose one or make up one on your own:
- When the shit hits the fan, I don't back down.
- I'm the smartest kid in school.

### RELATIONSHIPS TO OTHER KIDS
Choose one for each other Kid or make up on your own:
- We are best friends.
- We are different but still friends.
- He/she treats me badly but I won't sink to the same level.

### RELATIONSHIPS TO NPCS
Choose two or make up two on your own:
- My friend Lina [Leeanne] told me that strange creatures have moved into the Cooling Towers. She thinks they are aliens.
- Everyone seems to be having nightmares about that horrible teenager Peter.
- My friend Elisabeth has built a computer program that cracks codes, and we used it to listen to a scrambled radio communication. Some guys, who called each other fish names, talked about her mother as "one of the targets."

### ANCHOR
Choose one or make up one on your own:
- Mother/father
- Science teacher
- The guy who owns the comic shop

### TYPICAL NAMES
Choose one or make up one on your own:
- **Girls names:** Monika, Anette, Isabella, Lea [Shannon, Patricia, Karen, Julie]
- **Boys names:** Kristoffer, Martin, Lukas, Börje [Andrew, Eric, Daniel, Timothy]
- **Nicknames:** Haren, Glasögonorm, Sköldpaddan, Svettis [Turtle, Lazer, Data, Ducky]

# HICK

*Your classmates smile at you because of your tan, your pronunciation and your jokes, but what does it matter when you get to go out in the fields and the woods every day? The smell of corn and the grateful sounds that the cows make at morning milking have been a part of your life since you were born. You know how to build and repair an engine, how to drive a tractor, and how to hunt and slaughter animals.*

**KEY SKILLS: FORCE, MOVE, TINKER**

### ICONIC ITEM

Choose one or make up one on your own:
- German Shepherd
- Crowbar
- Tractor

### PROBLEM

Choose one or make up one on your own:
- Someone is poisoning our animals.
- Mom/dad doesn't want to accept that she/he is sick.
- I seriously hurt someone by mistake.

### DRIVE

Choose one or make up one on your own:
- There is more to this world than what meets the eye.
- They need me.

### PRIDE

Choose one or make up one on your own:
- My machines will one day conquer the world.
- I help other people.

### RELATIONSHIPS TO OTHER KIDS

Choose one for each other Kid or make up on your own:
- He/she wouldn't survive one day in the woods.
- How can I show her/him what I really feel?
- A reliable friend.

### RELATIONSHIPS TO NPCS

Choose two or make up two on your own:
- The school janitor seems so lonely since Mona [Mary], the school librarian, disappeared. I wish I could help him.
- The Police officer Ing-Marie Blankäng [Karen Richards] asked me if we could help her out on her boat this weekend.
- I have seen that stranger, the former rock singer Nille Landgren [Mikey Hayes], sneaking around in the forest near the company NAAB [NAI].

### ANCHOR

Choose one or make up one on your own:
- Dad/mom
- Fellow hunter
- Riding instructor

### TYPICAL NAMES

Choose one or make up one on your own:
- **Girls names:** Lena, Greta, Åsa, Hanna-Sofia [Mary, Lee-Anne, Laura, Dawn]
- **Boys names:** Lars, Anders, Olof, Pär [Benjamin, Jeremy, Ronald, Todd]
- **Nicknames:** Traktor-Bengt, Gris-Leif, Nordman, Nicke [Diesel, Scratch, Banjo, Buzz]

# JOCK

*You feel at home in sweaty locker rooms and at lit training fields in the autumn darkness. Nothing beats the feeling of a perfect shot, the aching muscles after training, and the companionship with teammates. You wish everything in life was as easy.*

**KEY SKILLS: FORCE, MOVE, CONTACT**

### ICONIC ITEM

Choose one or make up one on your own:
- Baseball bat
- Hockey stick
- BMX bike

### PROBLEM

Choose one or make up one on your own:
- My brother refuses to go out of his room since the accident.
- My teacher hates me.
- I cannot read very well, and they want to move me to a special class.

### DRIVE

Choose one or make up one on your own:
- I'm in it for the thrill.
- It's the right thing to do.

### PRIDE

Choose one or make up one on your own:
- My father is a firefighter.
- No one calls me chicken!

### RELATIONSHIPS TO OTHER KIDS

Choose one for each other Kid or make up on your own:
- I wonder if we can count on her/him?
- He/she knows everything!
- Annoying little sister/brother.

### RELATIONSHIPS TO NPCS

Choose two or make up two on your own:
- That new police officer, Ing-Marie Blankäng [Karen Richards], has rented a boat to investigate something in the lake, but she hasn't told anyone what it is.
- Several of my teammates are having strange dreams.
- A scientist named Olivia Martinez came to our training session and asked the coach if we wanted to take part in some kind of medical experiment, but I could tell she was lying about something.

### ANCHOR

Choose one or make up one on your own:
- Father/mother
- Coach for the team
- Brother/sister

### TYPICAL NAMES

Choose one or make up one on your own:
- **Girls names:** Stina, Lisa, Hanna, Camilla [April, Heather, Kimberly, Tammy]
- **Boys names:** Henrik, Kristian, Patrik, Sami [Chad, Brock, Brad, Billy]
- **Nicknames:** Pucken, Pelle, Mackan, Slangen [Iceman, Butch, Scooter, Sneak]

RIKSENERGI

# POPULAR KID

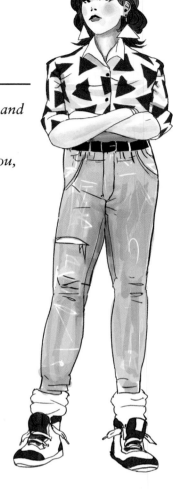

*It is you who decide what is lame and what's cool in school, and you know who's in love with who and who did what at the kiosk on Saturday night. Others listen when you talk, and you're used to being liked. It doesn't matter why they love you, just that they do.*

**KEY SKILLS: CONTACT, CHARM, LEAD**

### ICONIC ITEM

Choose one or make up one on your own:

- Pack of chewing gum
- Diary with juicy secrets
- Hairspray bottle

### PROBLEM

Choose one or make up one on your own:

- My aunt lives in our basement and she is crazy.
- Mom/dad is having a secret love affair.
- Your rival knows what you are trying to hide.

### DRIVE

Choose one or make up one on your own:

- It's a relief to get away from the burden of popularity.
- I hate secrets.

### PRIDE

Choose one or make up one on your own:

- Everybody likes me.
- I know everything about everyone.

### RELATIONSHIPS TO OTHER KIDS

Choose one for each other Kid or make up on your own:

- I know she/he loves me.
- She/he is freaky but I like it.
- He/she is useful.

### RELATIONSHIPS TO NPCS

Choose two or make up two on your own:

- That new teen Lisa and her friends from the Wild-life Club are scary. I wonder what they are up to?
- The school janitor, Per [Jeffrey], seems to hate me, but I know he is hiding something.
- Nobody knows it, but the former rock star Nille Landgren [Mikey Hayes] lives in a cottage at Väntholmen [Hemenway Park]. I talked to him and he said something horrible is happening at Svartsjölandet.

### ANCHOR

Choose one or make up one on your own:

- Older sibling
- Mom/dad
- Famous friend of the family

### TYPICAL NAMES

Choose one or make up one on your own:

- **Girls names:** Johanna, Linnea, Nikolina, Linda-Marie [Shannon, Kelly, Melissa, Tiffany]
- **Boys names:** Andreas, Martin, Peter, Håkan [John, Jason, Ryan, Sean]
- **Nicknames:** Krille, Madde, Gabbe, Milla [Baby, The King/Queen, Blue-eyes, Sunny]

RIKSENERGI

# ROCKER

*It was a worn cassette tape that changed your life. When that song had finished playing, you had found a home. You are an insane hard rocker who is high on life and play music so loud that the windows crack. In any case, you wish it would be like that. But you've just learned to play a C on your electric guitar and soon you will form a band down at the recreation center.*

**KEY SKILLS: MOVE, CHARM, EMPATHIZE**

### ICONIC ITEM
Choose one or make up one on your own:
- Boombox
- Electric guitar
- Leather jacket

### PROBLEM
Choose one or make up one on your own:
- My parents are about to divorce.
- I steal money.
- Unrequited love.

### DRIVE
Choose one or make up one on your own:
- I'm doing it for love.
- Hunger for everything in life.

### PRIDE
Choose one or make up one on your own:
- I play the guitar.
- I stood up for my friend.

### RELATIONSHIPS TO OTHER KIDS
Choose one for each other Kid or make up on your own:
- I love him/her.
- We don't like each other but he/she is part of the band.
- He/she rocks!

### RELATIONSHIPS TO NPCS
Choose two or make up two on your own:
- My mom thinks that she is being followed because she's a scientist, but dad thinks she´s going crazy.
- My older sister has joined the Wildlife Club; now she's stopped talking to me, and she sneaks out in the middle of the night.
- The strange scientist, Lena Thelin [Diane Petersen], is my aunt, but that doesn't mean I like her.

### ANCHOR
Choose one or make up one on your own:
- Music teacher
- Older brother/sister
- The guy at the music store

### TYPICAL NAMES
Choose one or make up one on your own:
- **Girls names:** Frida, Janis, Branka, Tove [Lori, Amanda, Crystal, Jamie]
- **Boys names:** Ingmar, Niklas, Tommy, Alexander [Justin, Gary, Kevin, Mark]
- **Nicknames:** Slash, Axl, Ziggy, Micke [Tommy-Lee, Spike, Ozzy, Fuzz]

# TROUBLEMAKER

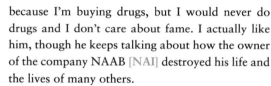

*You're a tough guy or girl who never holds back. Your classmates are afraid of you or look up to you, the teachers hate you, and everybody is nagging you to change. But they don't understand that you don't live in the same world as they do. When life turns on you, humiliates you, and hurts you, there is only one thing to do. Fight back.*

**KEY SKILLS: FORCE, SNEAK, LEAD**

**ICONIC ITEM**

Choose one or make up one on your own:

- Lighter and cigarettes
- Knife
- Skateboard

**PROBLEM**

Choose one or make up one on your own:

- My parents say that I'm good for nothing.
- My mother/father drinks a lot.
- We are short of money.

**DRIVE**

Choose one or make up one on your own:

- I'll do anything to get away from home.
- My friends and what we do is the only thing not broken in my life.

**PRIDE**

Choose one or make up one on your own:

- I helped a bird with a broken wing.
- I stood up to the teacher.

**RELATIONSHIPS TO OTHER KIDS**

Choose one for each other Kid or make up on your own:

- She/he thinks she/he is better than the rest of us!
- I'll do anything for him/ her.
- She/he knows what I'm going through.

**RELATIONSHIPS TO NPCS**

Choose two or make up two on your own:

- I wonder why the Priest in Wäsby [St Christopher's] bought explosives, and why his clothes are so filthy?
- They think I meet with Nille [Mikey] at Väntholmen [Hemenway Park] because he was famous or because I'm buying drugs, but I would never do drugs and I don't care about fame. I actually like him, though he keeps talking about how the owner of the company NAAB [NAI] destroyed his life and the lives of many others.
- My teacher Niklas [Neil] is the only teacher I have ever liked, and now he is in the hospital and he won't wake up from whatever nightmare he is having.

**ANCHOR**

Choose one or make up one on your own:

- Janitor at school
- School psychologist
- Grandma

**TYPICAL NAMES**

Choose one or make up one on your own:

- **Girls names:** Sussy, Monika, Jenny, Emma [Marylee, Jenna, Stacey. Charlene]
- **Boys names:** Lenny, Dennis, Benny, Stellan [Ray, Jerry, Troy, Steve]
- **Nicknames:** Knota, Hajen, Kicki, Nettan, Mange [Knuckles, Ninja, Sharky, Bird-killer]

RIKSENERGI

# WEIRDO

*They make fun of you for your clothes, your interests, your choice of words and call you "weirdo", but you don't care. They know nothing about your thoughts and feelings, or what you've been through. You want the world to see that you are different. One day you will outshine them all.*

**KEY SKILLS: SNEAK, INVESTIGATE, EMPATHIZE**

## ICONIC ITEM
Choose one or make up one on your own:
- Razorblade
- Drawing pad
- Pet rat

## PROBLEM
Choose one or make up one on your own:
- My father is a communist.
- My brother is doing weird things in his room.
- I get bullied at school.

## DRIVE
Choose one or make up one on your own:
- They say I'm the most curious person alive.
- Drawn to anything different or strange.

## PRIDE
Choose one or make up one on your own:
- I'm not heterosexual.
- Mom says that I am beautiful.

## RELATIONSHIPS TO OTHER KIDS
Choose one for each other Kid or make up on your own:
- He/she doesn't know that I love him/her.
- Her/his parents let me live with them.
- He/she doesn't like me, but I will prove him/her wrong.

## RELATIONSHIPS TO NPCS
Choose two or make up two on your own:
- The Priest in Wäsby [St Christopher's], Hans-Erik [Joseph], is the only adult whom I trust. Now he has disappeared.
- That kid Björn [Bryan] told me that his friend, Peter, who works at the Dream Shop, is about to do something bad.

- She wants me to call her Majsan [Stacey], and she's older than me, and lives by herself in a house in Kungsberga [outside Hemenway]. She hates all grownups.

## ANCHOR
Choose one or make up one on your own:
- Grandmother
- Another Kid's mom/dad
- Neighbor

## TYPICAL NAMES
Choose one or make up one on your own:
- **Girls names:** Marianne, Sara, Anna-Lena, Ida [Sandra, Amy, Michele, Christina]
- **Boys names:** Nikodemus, Carl-Ingvar, Simeon, Gustaf [Jeffrey, Charles. Edward, Peter]
- **Nicknames:** Ärret, Fladdermusen, Psykot, Nisse [Freaky, Commie, Ghost, Rat]

RIKSENERGI

**57**

## AGE

In this game, your character is between 10 and 15 years old. Choose your age freely. Your age affects your attribute score and the amount of Luck Points you have, but also how you picture the Kid in your mind and how you play the character.

**YOUR BIRTHDAY:** Determine freely what the date of your birthday is.

## ATTRIBUTES

Your Kid is defined by four attributes that tell you what you are good at and how you can cope with Trouble. The attributes are: **BODY**, **TECH**, **HEART** and **MIND**. The attribute scores range from 1 to 5, and correspond to the number of dice that you roll when you try to overcome Trouble.

- ■ BODY is the ability to jump high, run fast, fight, sneak, and climb.
- ■ TECH is the ability to understand machines and robots, program technological things, open locked doors, and build things.
- ■ HEART is the ability to make friends, lie, know the right people, create a good atmosphere, and persuade others.
- ■ MIND is the ability to find weak points, understand people, situations and creatures, solve riddles, understand clues, and have the right knowledge at the right time.

---

### CHOOSING YOUR AGE

As you have noticed, being older means higher attribute scores but fewer Luck Points. Higher attribute score mean you will always be better at certain actions, while more Luck Points make you more versatile.

---

**STARTING SCORES:** Distribute points equal to your age in the four attributes. Your starting score can be no higher than 5 in any attribute. You need to take at least 1 in each attribute.

**GROWING OLDER:** When you turn a year older, you gain another attribute point to spend. You can spend it on any attribute you like, but no attribute score can ever go above 5.

When you turn 16 years old, you are no longer a Kid for the purposes of this game. Time to make a new character.

## LUCK POINTS

The so-called Luck Points are something you can use to overcome Trouble more easily – they give you the chance to re-roll dice. This is explained further in Chapter 5.

In this game, younger Kids are luckier than older ones. You start the game with a number of Luck Points equal to 15 minus your age. Your Luck Points are replenished at the beginning of every session. You cannot save Luck Points from one session to another and you can never go above your starting number.

When you turn a year older, your maximum number of Luck Points is permanently reduced by one.

## SKILLS

Each attribute has three connected skills. These are areas where the Kid can be well trained. The level of a skill varies between 0 and 5, and corresponds to how many dice you can add to the dice roll when you try to overcome Trouble, in addition to the dice from your attribute. At the start of the game, you distribute 10 points among your skills. You may take up to level 3 in the three *key skills* of your Type. For other skills, a starting skill level of 1 is the maximum.

### BODY

- ■ SNEAK is the ability to hide and sneak.
- ■ FORCE is the ability to lift heavy things, fight, and endure in physically stressful situations.
- ■ MOVE is the ability to climb high, balance, and run fast.

### TECH

- ■ **TINKER** is the ability to build and manipulate machines and other mechanical items.
- ■ **PROGRAM** is the ability to create and manipulate computer programs and electronic devices.
- ■ **CALCULATE** is the ability to understand machines and other technical systems.

### HEART

- ■ **CONTACT** is the ability to know the right person.
- ■ **CHARM** is the ability to charm, lie, befriend, and manipulate.
- ■ **LEAD** is the ability to make others work well together, and to help them when they are scared, sad or confused.

### MIND

- ■ **INVESTIGATE** is the ability to find hidden objects and understand clues.
- ■ **COMPREHEND** is the ability to have the right piece of information or to be able to find it at the library.
- ■ **EMPATHIZE** is the ability to understand what makes a person, an animal or any kind of conscious thing tick, and how to find its weak spot.

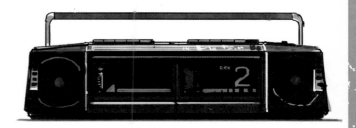

## ITEMS

Some Items can be useful to overcome Trouble. Items can give a bonus to the dice roll, from 1-3 extra dice to roll.

To get a bonus from an Item, it must be obvious how it is of use to you. A skateboard gives a bonus to **MOVE** when you're fleeing from a bully in the street, but not when climbing a tree. The Gamemaster should disallow unreasonable attempts to use Items.

Most objects that you encounter during the Mysteries are props, everyday things that are described to give atmosphere but that don't affect dice rolls. This can be a stick in the woods, a Coke bottle or a notepad. The Gamemaster decides which objects are Items that give a bonus and which are just props.

### ICONIC ITEM

You start the game with one Iconic Item; it works just like other Items, but it also says something about who you are.

This Item gives two bonus dice in a situation where it can be used to help you to overcome Trouble. The Iconic Item will not disappear or break whatever happens, unless you want it to. If it gets stolen or lost, you'll find it before the end of the Mystery. The Iconic Item cannot be used by other Kids.

### GAINING NEW ITEMS

You may find or build things, or train Creatures, to get new Items during a Mystery. The Gamemaster gives the Item a bonus of +1 to +3, depending on how powerful it is deemed to be. Often, Items that can be encountered are described in the Mystery.

### LOSING ITEMS

Between Mysteries, all Items are lost except the Iconic Item. Inventions break, domesticated animals run away or die, the police collect a runaway robot. If you want to keep an Item, you may choose to replace your Iconic Item. The new Iconic Item gets a bonus value of +2 no matter what value it had previously. If you play a Mystery Landscape (Chapter 7), the Gamemaster decides if the Items are deleted at the end of every session or on special occasions that mark a transition from one part of the story to another.

## PROBLEM

All Kids have a Problem. You may have kept yours to yourself or told the other Kids. The Problem is a part of Everyday Life, something that worries you. During the game, the Gamemaster will use the Problem to put you in Trouble. If you solve the Problem, then you must pick a new one before the next Mystery.

You should choose a Problem that you want to explore during the Mysteries. It's a signal from you to the Gamemaster: put my Kid in this kind of Trouble!

## DRIVE

Your Drive is the reason why you expose yourself to dangerous and difficult situations to solve Mysteries with your friends. It helps you to understand your Kid, and makes it easy to start a new Mystery; whatever happens, the Kids will want to figure it out. You may change your Drive between Mysteries.

## PRIDE

Every Kid has a Pride, something that makes you feel strong, important, and valuable. Pride may be well known to the group, or a secret. The Gamemaster should use the Pride to put you in Trouble by setting up scenes that highlight or threaten the Pride. A classmate turns out to be as good or better than you at school. Dad is losing his job at the fire station. An animal is tormented.

Pride is also a tool for you to understand and play your Kid. Problem and Pride may interact, and Pride can even become a Problem, but it may also be two separate things. You can change your Pride between Mysteries.

Once per Mystery, you may check your Pride to get one automatic success in a dice roll. You can check your Pride after a failed roll, or even after a successful roll in order to get an extra success (page 66). You must explain how your Pride helps you. If the Mystery takes several sessions to play, or if the group plays the Mystery Landscape, Pride may be checked once every session.

### EXAMPLE

**The Gamemaster:** *The hole in the ground is dark and damp, and you hear something echoing down there. When you lean in over the hole, it sounds like laughter. Mad mechanical laughter. What do you do?*
**Player 1 (Olle):** *I back away from the hole. "I think we should find another way in."*
**Player 2 (Anita):** *"No way." I stare at you with firm eyes, but I'm really scared. "We are going down there, and we are going to stop that thing." I slowly sneak down into the hole trying to move as quietly as possible.*
**The Gamemaster:** *Roll* SNEAK.
**Player 2:** *I failed, but I check my Pride, "Nothing scares me," so I make it anyway!*

## RELATIONSHIPS

You should define your Relationships to the other Kids in the group. This is best done together with the other players. If one Kid has the Relationship "Older sister" to another Kid, the players need to agree that their Kids are, in fact, siblings. None of the Kids should be enemies, but it's fun to have some tension in the group; love, envy or mistrust. The Relationships can be changed between Mysteries as the Kids are affected by what happens.

You should also choose two Relationships to NPCs. The NPCs that are mentioned in the Type descriptions are part of the Mystery Landscape (Chapter 7). If you want to write your own Relationships and NPCs, you need to do it together with the Gamemaster, so that those NPCs can easily be connected to the Locations in the Mystery Landscape. The NPC Relationships are meant to be a connection between the Kids and the strange things that will start happening as the game is played.

If the group has decided to play only pre-written Mysteries and not use the Mystery Landscape, the

RIKSENERGI

Gamemaster can let the players create NPC Relationships that are part of Everyday Life and not connected to Locations. These Relationships are used to set scenes from Everyday Life. It's also possible to let the Kids have two NPC Relationships with connections to Locations and one or two NPC Relationships from Everyday Life.

## ANCHOR

All Kids have an Anchor, a person that you can go to for support, comfort and care. It can be a friend, a parent, a teacher or a neighbor. It cannot be another Kid.

If you suffer from one or more Conditions (below), you can spend a scene with your Anchor and heal all Conditions. You must allow the Anchor to take care of you, and there must be a physical or mental closeness between you. The Gamemaster is not allowed to put you in Trouble in this scene. If you put yourself in Trouble, you don't heal any Conditions.

**TYPICAL NPC RELATIONSHIPS RELATED TO EVERYDAY LIFE**

- Tim wants to knock me down.
- Ulla doesn't trust me with her secrets.
- Mattias bullies me.
- Greta is a parasite in our home.
- Lisa is out to make life difficult for me.
- Whatever I do is wrong in Tina's eyes.
- Marie was a true friend but she betrayed me.
- I'll get my revenge on Mimmi.
- Anna took my virginity.
- I admire Patrik, but he ignores me.

RIKSENERGI

*EXAMPLE*

**The Gamemaster:** *Does anybody want a scene?*

**Player 1 (Olle):** *I need to heal my Conditions.*

**The Gamemaster:** *Cool, what do you do?*

**Player 1:** *My Anchor is my father, so I seek him out.*

**The Gamemaster:** *What do you usually do to get close to each other?*

**Player 1:** *We talk sports.*

**The Gamemaster:** *What are your conditions?*

**Player 1:** *Upset and Scared.*

**The Gamemaster:** *Okay, your father is sitting in front of the TV watching a game when you find him. He sits slouched, with a beer in his hand and a stern look on his face. He nods without looking away from the TV. "Hello son!"*

**Player 1:** *"Hello." I sit down beside him, close to him.*

**The Gamemaster:** *What makes him understand that you are Upset and Scared?*

**Player1:** *Probably my posture.*

**The Gamemaster:** *He turns off the TV and looks at you. "What's the matter?"*

## CONDITIONS

The Kids cannot die, but they can suffer from Conditions. When you try to overcome Trouble but fail, or if you push a dice roll (Chapter 5), you may be forced to take a Condition. There are five Conditions, and the first four are mild: Upset, Scared, Exhausted and Injured. The exact interpretation of a Condition can vary, and may need to be adapted to the situation at hand.

You decide what Condition to take in a given situation, and you get a -1 on all dice rolls until it is healed. Additional Conditions are cumulative; two Conditions give -2 on all dice rolls. If all four mild Conditions are marked and you take another Condition, you are Broken.

If you get Broken, something really bad has happened. You are mentally or physically hurt, and you will automatically fail all dice rolls until healed.

### CONDITIONS

| Condition | Modifier |
|-----------|----------|
| Upset | -1 |
| Scared | -1 |
| Exhausted | -1 |
| Injured | -1 |
| Broken | Automatic Failure |

The Conditions are also an indicator for how to play the Kid. You decide how much you want to play out your Conditions in the scenes. The Gamemaster can help you by asking questions: How do you feel? In what way are you Upset? You should never be forced to play your Condition if you don't want to do so.

## EXPERIENCE

At the end of the session, the Gamemaster will distribute Experience Points (XP) to the Kids. These can be used to raise skills. It costs five XP to raise a skill by one level, and 5 is the maximum level in any skill. Read more about XP in Chapter 6.

## NAME

Give your Kid a name, choosing from the premade options or coming up with your own.

## DESCRIPTION

Write down something about what your Kid looks like, and what she is like as a person. You should also write down things that you find useful when you are going to play the Kid in game, such as how she talks and moves, what clothes she wears, and so forth.

## FAVORITE SONG

Choose your favorite song from the 1980s. Try to pick a song that says something about who your Kid is. You can also use the song as a "theme" to play at the gaming table when appropriate. Your choice of favorite song has no mechanical effect.

## HIDEOUT

The Kids have a Hideout together, where they can be alone and safe. The players should agree on what their Hideout is, and where it is located. The Gamemaster may not let NPCs find the Hideout unless the Kids show it to them. The Gamemaster may not put you in Trouble while you are in the Hideout, but you can put yourself into Trouble there, for example by arguing with another Kid.

You can heal your Conditions in the Hideout in the same way as with using the Anchor. This requires that two or more of the Kids are present, and that they are physically or mentally close to each other, for example, hugging, telling secrets or stories or comforting one another. If the Kids put themselves in Trouble during the same scene, they don't heal any Conditions. All Kids share the same Hideout.

## QUESTIONS

After all players have created a Kid, and before the game starts, the Gamemaster will ask a number of questions of you. You should answer them as honestly as you can, and from the perspective of your Kids.

The Gamemaster chooses 4-6 questions from the list directed at the Kids, and distributes them one at a time, and 2-3 from the list of questions addressed to the whole group. It is the responsibility of the Gamemaster to ensure that all players get to answer questions and gets roughly the same amount of focus.

### QUESTIONS TO THE KIDS

- In what way has your Problem gone from bad to worse lately?
- What do your parents do for work?
- What do you think about school?
- What is your favorite food?
- Do you have siblings? What do you think about them?
- What does your room look like?
- What do you dream about at night?
- What makes you angry?
- What do you want to work at when you grow up?
- What do you think about sports?
- What is your experience with robots?
- What is the furthest you have traveled from your home town?
- How are you affected by your Pride?

### QUESTIONS TO THE GROUP

- Who in the group has the most to say?
- When did you get to know each other?
- What makes you laugh?
- What secrets do you have?
- Who dislikes you?
- Who wants to be in the gang?
- What are you fighting about?
- Who among you is most mocked?
- Who is the leader?
- Who is in love with whom?
- What sets you apart from other kids?
- What are you not talking about?
- What do you like to do?

RIKSENERGI

# CHAPTER

# 05

RIKSENERGI

# TROUBLE

*"Foxhound requesting permission to return to ba…" I was interrupted by a sudden snap among the twigs on the slope behind the robot. In terror, we watched as the robot twirled around with shocking speed, and we saw how it moved across the entire glade in a second, like a lightning-fast spider. A frightened pheasant flew out of the shrubbery, cackling in terror, and narrowly avoided the robot's pincer, which snapped through the air behind the bird's tail.*

*Lo stared at me, terrified, and hissed: "Request granted, return to base, over and out." Then we ran.*

Trouble is something that prevents Kids from doing something; it can be a bad thing about to happen or a possibility fraught with danger. It is the Gamemaster's job to create Trouble, but the Kids can also get themselves into Trouble. Trouble is woven into the conversation and described by the Gamemaster as people and creatures doing things, or as something happening. The Gamemaster asks you how you react, and you may try to overcome it somehow, or ignore it and let it happen.

RIKSENERGI

## TYPICAL TROUBLE

- Someone is standing outside the entrance and will see you if you try to enter.
- One of the bullies throws a bottle at you.
- The old man's dog is chained to a tree in the garden; it seems to be sick and is frothing at the mouth.
- Mom refuses to let you go out tonight.
- Your parents start to argue again.
- The car drops you off at the southern part of the island; it's a long way to walk home in the middle of the night.
- Your classmates don't believe you.
- He looks at you as if he sees you for the first time. Now you have the chance to tell him how you really feel about him.
- The robot attacks you with its claw.
- The portal opens with a deafening roar, and everything in the room is sucked towards it, including you.

## SUFFERING CONDITIONS

Sometimes the Gamemaster will tell you that you will suffer a Condition (see Chapter 4), if you don't overcome the Trouble. This should happen only when it's obvious that you will take a beating. If you get a Condition that is already checked, you must choose another one to check.

## THE DICE ROLL

You describe how you try to overcome the Trouble, and what you're trying to accomplish. The Gamemaster may ask for more details if she thinks the situation is unclear, or may ask you to change your mind if you are trying to do something that is impossible.

Grab a number of dice equal to your score in the attribute you use. Then add more dice equal to your level in the corresponding skill. If there isn't any suitable skill, only roll for the attribute. Every six rolled is a success. In most cases, only one success is needed to overcome Trouble.

## ITEMS AND PRIDE

You may use your Iconic Item for a dice roll, when appropriate (the Gamemaster has final say). It gives you two extra dice to roll.

You can also use your Pride, once per Mystery. It gives you an automatic success. You can activate the Pride after a failed roll, or even after a successful roll to add a success.

*EXAMPLE*

**The Gamemaster:** *At the bottom of the hole lies a stone tablet with strange figures and characters on it.*

**Player 3 (Dennis):** *I pick it up. Do I understand what it says?*

**The Gamemaster:** *Not without studying it at the library.*

**Player 3:** *Okay, I place it in my backpack and bicycle over to the school library. A while later, I sit at a table covered in books.*

**The Gamemaster:** *Roll* COMPREHEND.

**Player 3:** *I have* MIND *4 and* COMPREHEND *3, for a total of seven dice. (Rolls the dice.) I get a 6, which means success!*

**The Gamemaster:** *When you open a book about Pharaohs, you realize that these are Egyptian hieroglyphics. The tablet must have traveled through some kind of portal from another time. It tells about a monster with shiny, hard skin and long, two-fingered hands that can easily lift a grown man.*

**Player 3:** *Do I get what that means?*

**The Gamemaster:** *No more than you've already figured out.*

## LUCK

You can spend a Luck Point after a failed dice roll. A Luck Point lets you reroll failed dice, without needing to push. You cannot go back to the earlier result. You cannot spend more than one Luck Point on a single dice roll. Your maximum number of Luck Points is equal to 15 minus your age. Your Luck Points are replenished after each play session. You cannot save them between sessions.

## DOING THE ALMOST IMPOSSIBLE

In rare cases, more than one success is needed to overcome Trouble. You might be trying to do something almost impossible, such as persuading your mother to let you go outside even though the garden is full of crazy robots, or jumping from a bridge down onto a car passing at full speed. This may require two or even three successes. The Gamemaster should only demand more than one success in the most extreme cases.

RIKSENERGI

## NO TURNS OR INITIATIVE

In many roleplaying games, conflicts and combat are divided into segments of actions that are resolved one at a time. This is not the case in *Tales From the Loop*. Instead, each action or intention is resolved with one single dice roll. This doesn't mean there can't be more than one roll in a conflict. Let the dialogue decide what happens and what seems reasonable. Don't forget to describe actions before rolling dice. In the end, the Gamemaster has the final say about what seems plausible.

RIKSENERGI

| Trouble | Successes Required |
|---|---|
| Difficult (Normal) | 1 |
| Extremely Difficult | 2 |
| Almost Impossible | 3 |

## ANSWERING QUESTIONS

Some skills let you ask questions of the Gamemaster. The Gamemaster must answer them truthfully, and with as much detail as seems possible in the situation. You have overcome Trouble, and should not be given vague or half-truth answers.

*EXAMPLE*

**Player 1 (Olle):** *Dad, have you been cheating on mom?*
**The Gamemaster:** *"How can you even ask that question, of course not! Go to your room! Not one more word of this nonsense." He looks really mad.*

**Player 1:** *I try to see if he´s lying.*
**The Gamemaster:** *Roll* **EMPATHIZE**.
**Player 1:** *Success. Let´s see... I want to know if he´s lying, and I want to know what he feels.*
**The Gamemaster:** *Oh, he is absolutely lying. He´s mad, but also ashamed and, you suddenly realize he's very, very scared.*

## BUYING EFFECTS

If you roll more successes than you need, leftover success can sometimes be used to "buy" beneficial bonus effects. Such effects are described for each skill. The same effect can be bought several times. The Gamemaster decides which effects, if any, are suitable in any given situation. If there isn't any risk of collateral damage, you can't choose "You avoid any collateral damage."

You shouldn't need to buy Effects to achieve what you set out to do. They are a means of getting more than you asked for.

*EXAMPLE*

**Player 2 (Anita):** *I roll* **FORCE** *to wrestle my brother to the ground. Three sixes! Can I buy effects?*
**The Gamemaster:** *Of course.*
**Player 2:** *I can buy two effects, let´s see... He is humiliated, and I don´t have to roll again for the exact same Trouble.*
**Gamemaster:** *Okay, remember it's the exact same Trouble; if he attacks you in front of others you will beat him without rolling the dice. Now, tell me how you wrestle and humiliate your brother!*

## NON-PLAYER CHARACTERS

The Gamemaster never rolls dice for the NPCs. When they try to overcome Trouble, the Gamemaster decides if they succeed or fail. If their actions cause Trouble, the Kids may try to prevent or overcome them.

RIKSENERGI

When an NPC helps you, the Gamemaster may decide to give you 1, 2 or 3 bonus dice. This only happens in rare cases. The Kids need to rely on each other.

### SPECIAL NPCS

Some NPCs are significantly harder to beat. They will have one or more *special attributes*, with a score of 2 or 3. Trouble that is directly tied to a special attribute is particularly hard to cope with – to overcome the NPC, you need to roll a number of successes equal to the attribute score. The Gamemaster has final say as to whether a special attribute is applicable for a roll.

> *EXAMPLE*
>
> *A strange underwater storm with the special attribute* WILD CURRENTS *2 means that Kids who try to swim through the water must get two successes to make a* MOVE *roll. Kids trying to wrestle or outrun a raptor with* FEROCIOUS BEAST *3 need three successes. If they try to outsmart the raptor or beat it in some other way that isn't physical, only one success is required.*

## FAILED ROLLS

If you roll no or too few successes, your action fails. An unsuccessful attempt to overcome Trouble must never mean that nothing happens. Somehow the situation changes, probably for the worse. What happens is up to the Gamemaster to decide. You might need to check a Condition, you might end up in new Trouble, or you might suffer a Complication (see the boxed text). Some examples follow:

- You are caught or detained.
- The robot you built becomes hostile.
- Your parents get angry and give you a curfew.
- A time machine sends you thousands of years back in time, instead of forward.

## PUSHING THE ROLL

When you fail a roll, you may choose to immediately retry the task, by mentally or physically pushing yourself to the limit of your abilities.

### COMPLICATIONS

A failed test shouldn't be a roadblock. To progress the Mystery even if a dice roll fails, the Gamemaster can use Complications. Suffering a Complication after a failed result, you still succeed with the most crucial part, but something goes wrong along the way. The Gamemaster decides what happens. The word "but" is often helpful.

Complications may lead to new Trouble, present a risk for new Trouble, provide a partial clue (forcing the Kids to investigate further), or force the Kids to change their plans. Examples:

- You climb over the fence and into the scrapyard, but the guard dog heard you.
- As you row out into the lake, the boat's owner comes running from the parking lot.
- You grab the scientist's notebook and run, but it gets torn in half.

This is called pushing the roll, and can only be done once, immediately after the failed roll. You must describe what you do to push yourself. You may push a successful roll to be able to buy more Effects.

When you push a roll, you must first check a Condition. Choose any Condition that you feel fits the story. Then you reroll all the dice except those showing sixes. If the reroll is successful, the Gamemaster describes what happens. If the reroll also fails, you may not push again (but you can use a Luck Point or your Pride).

If the Trouble came with a threat of a Condition, you may have to check two Conditions if you pushed the roll but still failed after the reroll. You can push a dice roll before or after using a Luck Point.

*EXAMPLE*

**Player 2 (Anita):** *I look her in the eyes and try to look sad. "But please mom, if you don't drive us we'll miss the party."*

**The Gamemaster:** *Roll* CHARM.

**Player 2:** *Damn, I miss.*

**The Gamemaster:** *She looks stern and is about to say something, do you push?*

**Player 2:** *Yes, of course. I look away and say with a cold voice, "If dad was alive he would have done it."*

**The Gamemaster:** *What Condition do you check?*

**Player 2:** *I'm getting really Upset now.*

**The Gamemaster:** *Ok. Reroll all dice.*

**Player 2:** *No successes this time either.*

**The Gamemaster:** *She doesn't say anything, just looks at you.*

**Player 2:** *I start crying for real, with shame, and go to my room. I feel horrible.*

## CHANCE TO SUCCEED

| Number of dice | Chance to succeed | Pushed roll |
|---|---|---|
| 1 | 17% | 29% |
| 2 | 31% | 50% |
| 3 | 42% | 64% |
| 4 | 52% | 74% |
| 5 | 60% | 81% |
| 6 | 67% | 87% |
| 7 | 72% | 90% |
| 8 | 77% | 93% |
| 9 | 81% | 95% |
| 10 | 84% | 96% |

## HELPING EACH OTHER

One Kid may help another overcome Trouble if it seems plausible in the situation. To help, you describe what you do, and then your friend gets one extra die to roll. A Kid may never get help from more than one of her friends for a single dice roll. The Gamemaster has final say on when helping is possible.

When you help someone, you are bound to the outcome of the roll. If it fails, you suffer the same effects as the Kid who rolled. In some situations, all of the Kids need to overcome the same Trouble at the same time. You are trying to walk home through a blizzard or sneak past the headmaster. In these cases, you cannot help each other as noted above. You can, however, give each other successes from Bonus Effects (below).

## KID VERSUS KID

When two or more Kids fight each other, wrestle, haggle, hide from each other, or come on to the same guy, you all say what you want to do and roll the dice at the same time. The one with the most successes wins and gets to say what happens.

You can all push your rolls. If you get equal numbers of successes after the push, you may buy extra successes by checking Conditions, one success for each checked condition. You can make yourself Broken to win if you want to. If there still isn't a winner, something happens that interrupts the situation – a parent walks in, the rain starts falling, or the lunch break is over.

## EXTENDED TROUBLE

Sometimes, at a crucial moment of a Mystery, Trouble can be so climactic that the Kids have to come up with a plan and work together – a single dice roll is not enough to portray the Trouble they are in. Each Kid will have their part to play in the plan's final success or failure. This is called Extended Trouble.

### 1. SET THE STAKES

The Gamemaster declares what is at stake; what will happen if the Kids fail.

### 2. THREAT LEVEL

The Gamemaster declares the total number of successes that the Kids need to beat the Trouble. A Threat Level of twice the number of Kids is normal, three times the number of Kids is hard, and four times the number of Kids is almost impossible.

Don't use NPC special abilities (previous page) in Extended Trouble – it's included in the Threat Level.

### 3. MAKE A PLAN

The Kids decide what they want to do, agree on which skill each one will use, and in what order they will then act to make their roll. The Kids get to choose which skills to use, but the Gamemaster can disallow any clearly unreasonable skill uses.

### 4. PLAY THE SCENES

Each Kid gets a scene to act and rolls for their chosen skill. Successes go towards reaching the Threat Level, but can also be used for bonus effects. If there is time, a Kid may roll for **LEAD** to create a dice pool (below) instead of adding towards the Threat.

### 5. OUTCOME

Each Kid rolls once, pushing rolls if they want to, and when all scenes are over the total number of sixes is compared to the Threat level of the Extended Trouble.

- If the final sum of sixes are less than half of the Threat Level, the Kids have failed completely.
- If the number of successes reaches half or more of the Threat Level, the Kids can check additional Conditions to get more sixes, in order to reach a compromise. Each added Condition counts as an extra success. The Kids can make themselves Broken to succeed if they want to. If the Kids reach the Threat Level this way, they will achieve a part of their goal. Details are up to the Gamemaster.
- If the Kids reached the Threat level, without checking extra Conditions, the Kids achieve their goal, and overcome the Trouble.

### DESCRIBE HOW YOU DO IT

It isn't enough for you to say you use a skill. You need to say what you do in order to get to roll. This could be done by having a conversation in-game or by describing your actions; how you study a dinosaur with the binoculars, or how you open the top of a robot with a hammer and a screwdriver and then telling the other players what it looks like inside.

RIKSENERGI

**71**

# THE SKILLS

## SNEAK (BODY)

The ability to hide, sneak or steal.

**BONUS EFFECTS:**

- Give a success to another Kid.
- You find something unexpected, or more of what you were looking for.

## FORCE (BODY)

The ability to lift heavy things, fight, and endure physically stressful situations.

**BONUS EFFECTS:**

- Give a success to another Kid.
- Impress, frighten or humiliate.
- Pin your opponent.
- Take something from your opponent.
- Your opponent is knocked unconscious.
- You don't need to roll to overcome the exact same Trouble in the future.
- You avoid any collateral damage.

## MOVE (BODY)

The ability to climb high, balance, run fast, and chase someone or get away.

**BONUS EFFECTS:**

- Give a success to another Kid.
- Impress someone.
- No one notices you.

## TINKER (TECH)

The ability to build and manipulate machines and other mechanical items.

### BUILD

The Gamemaster will tell you what it takes to build something. Some examples of what might be needed:

- You need a certain Item.
- You need to successfully **CALCULATE**.
- You need to successfully **COMPREHEND**.
- You need to successfully **PROGRAM** something.
- You need a lot of time.
- You need new tools.

When you have what you need, you roll to overcome the Trouble of actually making the thing. If the roll is successful, you write down the object as an Item with a bonus of +1.

**BONUS EFFECTS:**

- The thing is more durable than expected. Add +1 to the bonus (up to +3).
- The thing can do more than expected. Add +1 to the bonus (up to +3).
- The thing is more discreet than expected. Add +1 to the bonus (up to +3).

### AVOIDING ATTACKS

Sometimes, an NPC tries to hurt or manipulate you. In such a situation, describe how you try to avoid the Trouble, and roll for the relevant skill. If it's a physical attack, like a punch to the face, **MOVE** is most often used. If the NPC is doing something relational like seducing you or telling you lies, use **CHARM**. In situations where you need to rely on wits to understand something in time to avoid it, roll **COMPREHEND**, and in situations where a sharp eye is required, like when you are walking into an ambush, roll **INVESTIGATE**.

If you aren't aware of what is about to happen, like when someone has put a sleeping pill in your breakfast cornflakes, the Gamemaster can decide that you don't get to roll to avoid it or that it is Extremely Difficult or even Almost Impossible.

### MANIPULATE

The **TINKER** skill can also be used to break, use or jury-rig mechanical things, to pick locks, and drive motor vehicles. Sometimes you have to use **CALCULATE** first to figure out how to do it.

#### BONUS EFFECTS:

- Give a success to another Kid.
- You don't need to roll to overcome the exact same Trouble in the future.
- You do it quickly.
- You do it quietly.
- You show off.

## PROGRAM (TECH)

The ability to create and manipulate computer programs and electronic devices. This is a sister skill to **TINKER**, but used for electronic things rather than mechanical.

### CREATE

The Gamemaster will tell you what it takes to create something. Some examples of what might be needed:

- You need a certain Item.
- You need to successfully **CALCULATE**.
- You need to successfully **COMPREHEND**.
- You need to successfully **TINKER** first.
- You need a lot of time.
- You need new tools.

When you have what you need, you roll to overcome the Trouble of actually creating the thing. If the roll is successful, write down the object as an Item with a bonus of +1.

#### BONUS EFFECTS:

- The thing is more effective than expected. Add +1 to the bonus (up to +3).
- The thing can do more than expected. Add +1 to the bonus (up to +3).

### MANIPULATE

The **PROGRAM** skill can also be used to manipulate electronic items. Examples include infecting a computer with a virus, disabling an alarm or electronic lock, confusing or controlling robots, and operating strange objects like time machines or transformation globes. Sometimes you have to use **CALCULATE** first to figure out how to do it.

#### BONUS EFFECTS:

- Give a success to another Kid.
- You don't need to roll to overcome the exact same Trouble in the future.
- You do it quickly.
- You get new or unexpected information.
- You show off.

## CALCULATE (TECH)

The ability to know how technical objects work and how to use them. It could be robots, machines, magnetrine ships, cyborgs, or an alarm clock. If you succeed, you get to ask two questions:

- What is its purpose?
- How does it work?
- How can I use it?
- Who built it?
- What problems could it cause?
- Is it illegal?

#### BONUS EFFECT:

- Ask one additional question and take +1 die on one roll when you use the information (up to +3).

## CONTACT (HEART)

The ability to know the right person and can get a hold of her. You tell the Gamemaster who the person is, and roll to overcome the Trouble of finding her. If you succeed, you find her, or she finds the Kids ready and able to help. If you fail, the person doesn't want to help you or maybe she even wants to hurt, humiliate or make life difficult for you, and will come looking for you.

#### BONUS EFFECTS:

- The contact has all the right tools with her.
- The contact may heal one of your Conditions.
- The contact brings more people, also ready to help.
- You don't have to roll to get a hold of the contact again during this Mystery.
- The contact knows something important.
- You may use the contact once as an Item with bonus +1 (up to +3).

RIKSENERGI

**73**

## WHEN TO KNOW WHAT

There are four skills to get information: **COMPREHEND**, **INVESTIGATE**, **CALCULATE** and **EMPATHIZE**. In some cases, they will overlap. The Gamemaster and the players should decide together which skill is appropriate in any given situation, and in some cases you may choose the better of two skills. The Gamemaster has final say.

**COMPREHEND** is the broadest skill. It is used to know things that can be learned in school, to crack riddles, and to find information in libraries. **INVESTIGATE** is only used to look for things, finding a hidden door, or to examine a corpse or a crime scene. **CALCULATE** is used when you examine, study or want to figure things out. Maybe you want to know how to destroy an alarm, or you want to know what the strange device on the roof is. **EMPATHIZE** is used to figure out things about conscious creatures, what they are feeling, planning to do, how to make them do something or what they like or dislike. The skill applies whether they are human, animals or robots, as long as they are conscious.

RIKSENERGI

### EXAMPLE

**Player 1 (Olle):** *Do I know anybody who could help us get to the body?*

**The Gamemaster:** *Do you?*

**Player 1:** *Eh… yes, my dad's friend is a cop. He likes to play with me when he visits.*

**The Gamemaster:** *What is his name?*

**Player 1:** *He is called Salmon because he loves to fish, but his real name is Oskar.*

**The Gamemaster:** *Roll* **CONTACT**.

**Player1:** *Miss!*

**The Gamemaster:** *Suddenly a police car parks outside the school. All the kids go to the windows to look. You can see that it's Salmon, and he walks right towards your classroom and he looks mad. Maybe he heard what you did at the robot factory?*

# CHARM (HEART)

The ability to charm, lie, befriend, and make people do what you want. As always, the Gamemaster decides what can plausibly be achieved.

**BONUS EFFECTS:**

- She keeps believing you.
- You have formed a lasting relationship.
- She will take risks to help you.
- She will try to persuade others to believe you.
- She's frightened, confused or impressed.
- She's infatuated.

# LEAD (HEART)

The ability to make your friends work together, to help them focus on the task at hand in difficult situations, and to soothe them when they are scared or confused.

If you have time with the other Kids, you may inspire and prepare them for a difficult situation. You roll to overcome Trouble, and your successes become a dice pool (see the table below). You may, in the upcoming scenes, distribute bonus dice to the other Kids when they roll to overcome Troubles – but only if they do as you say. You cannot give these dice to yourself.

If you fail to **LEAD**, you must check a Condition, and ask the other Kids how the relationship has been hurt. There may only be one dice pool active at a time – the group cannot have more than one leader.

### LEADING OTHER KIDS

| Successes | Dice Pool |
|-----------|-----------|
| 1 success | 2 dice |
| 2 successes | 4 dice |
| 3 successes | 6 dice |

If you spend time privately with another Kid, giving her advice and comfort, you may heal one of her Conditions. You roll to overcome Trouble, and if you succeed, the Condition is healed. If you fail, you suffer the same Condition. You cannot heal Broken Kids using this skill.

BONUS EFFECTS:

- Heal an additional Condition.
- Heal one of your own Conditions.

## INVESTIGATE (MIND)

The ability to find hidden objects, understand clues, break puzzles or survey a place or a situation. You get to ask two of these questions:

- What is hidden here and where is it?
- What does it mean?
- What has happened here?
- How can I get into/out of/past something?
- What threats can I perceive here?
- Where is it?

If the roll fails, you have misunderstood something, someone has found out something about you, or you suffer a Condition. The Gamemaster decides.

BONUS EFFECT:

- Ask one additional question and get +1 die on one roll when you use the information (up to +3).

## COMPREHEND (MIND)

The ability to have the right piece of information or to be able to find it at the school library or a similar location. The Gamemaster will give you the information, or ask you to come up with something on your own. If you fail the roll, the Gamemaster gives you bad news or the wrong information (the Gamemaster doesn't say which it is).

BONUS EFFECT:

- You get additional information and +1 bonus die to one roll when you use the information (up to +3).

## EMPATHIZE (MIND)

The ability to study what makes a person, an animal or a conscious robot or cyborg tick, and how to find its weakness. You need time to study or talk to the creature or person to be able to roll for the skill. If you succeed, you get to ask two questions.

- What is her weak spot?
- How can I make her do something?
- What does she feel?

- What does she want?
- What will she do?
- Is she lying?

If the roll fails, the Gamemaster either gives you bad news or the wrong information (the Gamemaster doesn't tell which it is) or makes something bad happen.

BONUS EFFECT:

- Ask one additional question and take +1 die on one roll when you use the information (up to +3).

### EXAMPLE

**Player 2 (Anita):** *I want to know what he is thinking, so I roll* EMPATHIZE, *with four dice.*

**The Gamemaster:** *Wait, wait, wait! You have to study him or talk to him before you can understand him.*

**Player 2:** *Okay, I do that. I talk to him.*

**The Gamemaster:** *What do you say?*

**Player 2:** *I walk up to him in the schoolyard, and ask him what he was doing on Adelsö yesterday.*

**The Gamemaster:** *He looks at you for a long time. "I wasn't there."*

**Player 2:** *"Strange, I'm sure I saw you there."*

**The Gamemaster:** *"You're mistaken." He looks confused or scared. Roll the dice.*

RIKSENERGI

RIKSENERGI

# THE MYSTERY

*Stories were told of something huge and horrible living down there in the water. Maybe a water spider, or some amphibian, had nested in one of the reservoir's many dark crevices and given birth to something malformed, a lifeform changed by heavy metals and chemicals that had leaked into the water. Maybe it was something that had arrived from another dimension through a tear in space-time, caused by the experiments down in the Loop.*

A Mystery is a scenario for the Kids to play. Like a comic book or a TV show episode, a Mystery has characters and a plot for the players to uncover. Unlike these, a Mystery has no set chain of events – which turns the story takes and how it ends depends on the choices the Kids make, and, to some extent, on chance.

There are four complete Mysteries ready for play in Chapters 9-12 of this book. Most Mysteries take a couple of hours to solve. Each Mystery has a structure that includes six phases that will help you as a Gamemaster to set scenes and put the Kids into Trouble.

Using a Mystery is the primary way to play this game, preferably for one-shots or shorter campaigns. An alternative method of play uses something called a Mystery Landscape – read more about that in Chapter 7.

This chapter will explain the structure of a Mystery, and guide you, as a Gamemaster, in writing your own scenarios. The structure is also an aid for you to write your own Mysteries.

## FOR THE GAMEMASTER'S EYES ONLY

This chapter, as well as the rest of this entire book, is for the Gamemaster's eyes only. Players should not read past this point, as it will spoil the fun for everyone to know the hidden truths of the game beforehand.

## INSPIRATION FOR MYSTERIES

You can get a lot of inspiration from books and movies. The car from Stephen King's Christine could be a mad robot or a magnetrine ship, the clown in It could be a murderous cyborg and the bullied girl in Carrie could get her powers from advanced technology. The adventures of The Famous Five by Enid Blyton could be set in the land of the Loop.

Many technological oddities found in Doctor Who and Star Trek can be placed by the Loop in the Eighties, and cause all kinds of Trouble. Time machines, compression fields, 3-D glasses, the "defabricator" from Doctor Who or the shrinking ray from Honey, I Shrunk the Kids are all possibilities that can be introduced.

The Mysteries should have the same tone as movies and TV series like E.T., The Goonies, Stranger Things, Super-8, and Scooby Doo.

# THE TRUTH OF THE MYSTERY

The first thing you need to do when you write a Mystery is to create the Truth of the Mystery. What is the story about? Most Mysteries in this game can be divided into three categories: Human Error, Conflicts and Mischief.

HUMAN ERROR MYSTERIES are about people's inability to manage the great things they have created.

- A scientist has created a time machine that he has lost control of, and he has been thrown back to the Stone Age. The hole in the fabric of time is open, and creatures wander in and out.
- A gravity dissolver has accidentally fallen from an airplane, and landed nearby.
- The result of an unsuccessful animal experiment has been flushed down the drain, and has grown to become a monster in the lake.
- Three different experimental buildings randomly create a force field that makes people grow old very quickly.
- A scientist puts his brain into a robot, which then flees and refuses to come back.
- A machine comes to life and decides to wake more of its "species."
- A creature from another time or place is stranded by the Loop, and needs help to return home.

CONFLICTS are about the tension between two or more parties that want opposite things, and are willing to fight to get what they want.

- Soviet or American industrial spies try to steal the secrets of Riksenergi or DARPA.
- A student who hates her teacher decides to take revenge by using her tech skills.
- A robot is on the run, and its "owners" want to catch it.
- Criminals use technology to steal from the town residents.
- A scientist tries to use runaway kids as human tissue samples in her cyborg factory.
- A dinosaur hunter and a Tyrannosaurus Rex use the forest as their battleground.
- Workers at a Loop facility try to sabotage a new machine that will make many of them unemployed.
- Environmentalists want to sabotage the fusion reactor.
- Afghan Mujahedeen come to the Loop to steal or buy technology to help in the fight against the Soviet invasion.

MISCHIEF is about other kids who create problems for fun.

- Teenagers steal a robot and bring it to a party, but things go off the rails, and someone is badly hurt or even killed.
- A kid finds a gap in the ground, which leads down to a maze of underground tunnels where he gets lost.
- Some teens use an invention to cheat on their tests.

## THE MYSTERY AND EVERYDAY LIFE

The narrative of the game actually consists of two parts: the Mystery and Everyday Life. In one scene, the Kids chase a runaway robot, and in the next, they try to stop a drunk dad from driving his car to work. Some scenes could be about both the Mystery and Everyday Life.

It is your job as Gamemaster to mix scenes related to the Mystery and scenes related to Everyday Life. The Mystery is the main story, and usually more scenes are related to the Mystery than to Everyday Life.

What can happen in the Mystery – the people and locations the Kids may encounter, and how it begins and could end – is described in the Mystery. To set scenes related to Everyday Life, you need to know the Kids well.

### PLAYING EVERYDAY LIFE

To come up with scenes related to Everyday Life, you should consult the players' character sheets or talk to the players to get a picture of their Kids' Problems, Prides, and Relationships.

---

## EVERYDAY SCENES WITHOUT APPARENT TROUBLE

- Dad is sitting in the kitchen with soot on his face, and speaks proudly of fighting a fire during the night.
- Dad wants to throw Jacob's sneakers away and buy new ones.
- Mom asks Jacob to come in and sit on the bed and tell her about his day.
- Jacob gets to read his homework about firefighters in front of the whole class.
- Jacob and his mother sit in the kitchen eating porridge, when the radio plays their favorite song.

RIKSENERGI

RIKSENERGI

## EVERYDAY SCENES WITH TROUBLE

- It's the middle of the night. Mom has disappeared into the forest in just her nightgown, and dad is at work.
- Tony is waiting on the path to the beach, with a baseball bat and a wide grin.
- Dad is angrily knocking on the door of Jacob's room. He has found out what happened down at the dock.
- Mom is mad and believes that Dad is cheating on her. She throws things all over the house, and Dad has locked himself in the garage.
- Dad wants Jacob to stop seeing his friend Sarah, because she is too weird.
- Jacob finds out that his dad is cheating on his mom with the mother of one of the other Kids.

RIKSENERGI

You should also bear in mind what they answered to the questions you asked when the Kids were created. Write down some ideas of what can happen when you do come up with them.

Scenes related to Everyday Life can be everyday scenes with no obvious Trouble. They illustrate normal suburban life, as a contrast to the stunning events of the Mystery, and give each player a chance to get to know her Kid better. You can also set scenes from Everyday Life with more apparent Trouble. In sidebar, there are examples of typical scenes from Everyday Life.

Sometimes there is a link between the Mystery and Everyday Life. The uncle who comes to visit is also the scientist who has let the strange creatures loose in the forest. Mom has been infected by the mind virus. It turns out that an older brother stole the robot.

## AN OVERVIEW OF THE MYSTERY

The Mystery is played in six phases: Introducing the Kids, Introducing the Mystery, Solving the Mystery, Showdown, Aftermath, and Change. The Gamemaster decides if she wants to keep strictly to these phases or improvise. Some players want the Gamemaster to clearly mark when going from one Phase to the next, while others want the Gamemaster to keep the structure to herself to get a sense of being part of a narrative where anything can happen.

## INDIVIDUAL VERSUS GROUP SCENES

Scenes of Everyday Life tend to focus on individual Kids, rather than the whole group. For that reason, keep Everyday Life scenes short and succinct, and don't draw them out. Also, whenever possible try to find ways to have several Kids present in the same scene of Everyday Life. Otherwise, players have to wait and listen a lot, which could be fun for a scene or two, but not for long. A Kid can follow another to play at her house after school. The other Kids can be present when one of them gets bullied. Parents invite all of them to supper. An easy way is to let two Kids be siblings or live together for some reason.

If it's not possible to have several Kids present in a scene, you can let the players play NPCs for this scene only.

### PHASES OF THE MYSTERY

1. Introducing the Kids — Each Kid gets a scene of her own from Everyday Life, with or without Trouble.
2. Introducing the Mystery — The Kids encounter or discover something that they start to investigate.
3. Solving the Mystery — The Kids visit Locations, discover Clues, and overcome Trouble while at the same time having to manage Everyday Life. This is the core of the Mystery, where most scenes take place.
4. Showdown — The Kids have solved the Mystery, and must now try to stop what's happening, often in a dramatic scene where everything is at stake.
5. Aftermath — The Mystery has been solved, and even if the Kids are successful, their lives are mostly the same as before. Each Kid gets one scene from Everyday Life.
6. Change — The players may, if they like, change their Kids' Problems, Iconic Items, Prides, and Relationships. The Kids gets experience points which can be used to increase skills levels.

## PHASE 1 – INTRODUCING THE KIDS

The Mystery always starts with each of the Kids playing a scene from Everyday Life, with or without Trouble. This scene helps a player to get to know her Kid, and shows the other players what her Kid is like. The Gamemaster may set a scene up on her own, or ask the player for a suggestion. The GM can get inspiration from the Kid's Problem, Pride, and Relationships. A general piece of advice is to choose the most obvious scene. Don't overthink it.

The Gamemaster will cut the scene when it feels done, and move on to the next Kid. These scenes should be kept rather short. After this phase, most scenes will be played with all the Kids present, acting as a group.

### EXAMPLE

**The Gamemaster:** *Ok, let's start the game! It's a damp and rainy weekend in late October. Rumors are spreading about cut-backs at the Loop, and many of the adults are irritated and quiet. Outside, it is muddy and dark. Leaves cover the ground, and the cold from the lake blows in over the island with the smell of water and fish. Who gets the first scene?*
**Player 1 (Jacob):** *Let me have it.*
**The Gamemaster:** *Do you have an idea, or do you want me to give you a scene?*
**Player 1:** *I have one. I am sitting in my room, grounded by mom, waiting for my father to come home and give me a scolding.*
**The Gamemaster:** *What have you done?*
**Player 1:** *She found me looking through her medicine bottles.*
**The Gamemaster:** *You hear your mom walking around on the ground floor. Suddenly, she stops and at the same moment, you hear the familiar sound of your dad's car as he parks out front. A moment later the door opens, and you hear your mom and dad talking, but you don't hear what they're saying. What are you doing?*
**Player 1:** *I'm sitting on my bed sorting my Garbage Pail Kids cards and I'm mad. She totally overreacted.*
**The Gamemaster:** *You hear your dad coming up the stairs.*

## PHASE 2 – INTRODUCING THE MYSTERY

Next, the Mystery is introduced. You let the Kids encounter or hear about something that arouses their curiosity. This usually happens in a single scene, where all the Kids are present, but it can be stretched out for several scenes.

If the Mystery was introduced without all the Kids being present, you should set up a scene where everyone is present and able to talk to each other, before moving on to the next phase.

You can use the Truth of the Mystery to figure out how to introduce it. Let the Kids get a little glimpse of what's wrong or different, but they shouldn't be shown the whole picture. Something has disappeared, something has been added that shouldn't be there, a rumor of some kind or a problem has appeared that needs to be solved.

If the Kids don't seem interested in solving the Mystery, you should remind the players of their Drives.

## PHASE 3 – SOLVING THE MYSTERY

This is the biggest part of the Mystery, where most of the scenes will take place. The Kids visit Locations and talk to people looking for Clues, overcoming Trouble, and trying to solve the Mystery.

You set scenes about the Mystery and Everyday Life, alternating between the two. In most scenes, all Kids should be present if possible. If the Kids have been split up for one or more scenes, you should set up a scene where everyone is present. You can simply ask the Kids, "Where do you meet up, and what do you do?"

You may improvise new Trouble in a scene. A caretaker shows up, or a guard dog spots the Kids.

### THE MAP

A core feature of Phase 3 is usually a map that depicts the part of the Loop area where the Mystery takes place. The map should be put on the table for everyone to see. Most often, there is one map for the players and a secret map for the Gamemaster, with all Locations marked.

## TYPICAL WAYS TO INTRODUCE THE MYSTERY

- A child has disappeared.
- Rumors spread about a runaway robot that wanders the land.
- Lumps that look like eyes grow on the bodies of the Kids.
- A strange house appears in the middle of town, and the adults behave as if it has always been there.
- One of the Kids finds a gap in the ground, leading down to a huge network of paths.
- A strange girl starts in school.
- A cyborg is hiding in the woodshed.
- The Bona Towers flicker and disappear for a few seconds.
- Someone spreads fake money.
- Cats disappear.
- Rumors spread of strange fires.
- Someone has left an ancient map of the area in a Kid's school desk.
- A man with a rifle is hiding in the forest, speaking into a walkie-talkie in a foreign language.

In most Mysteries, there will be three Locations to visit during this phase. This is a good number of Locations for a one-evening Mystery. When you write your own Mysteries, you may plan for more or fewer Locations.

### LOCATIONS

At each Location, there are usually some sort of Clues and/or suggestions of possible Trouble. Locations can be mundane or fantastic – it can be anything from a garbage dump or a school cafeteria to a robotic factory or a portal to other parts of the world.

It does not matter if the Kids don't visit all the Locations, as they can be saved for later Mysteries. In some Mysteries, it is obvious which Locations to visit and how to get to them. In others, it is Trouble to get to know where to go and how to get there. **CONTACT** and **COMPREHEND** can be used to get help and information.

### CLUES

A Clue may be something that someone knows – a thing, a diary, a drawing, tracks in the gravel or an event that reveals something. The clue reveals something about the Mystery. Clues can be connected to each other, so that the first Clue leads to the second, that that leads to the third, which finally solves the Mystery. They can also be three Clues that all point in the same direction. Another variant is that all three Clues are necessary to understand the big picture, but the Kids may find them in any order.

**CLUES CAN REVEAL:**

- Where to go next
- What will happen
- Who is involved
- Where to find more information
- What has happened
- How to solve the problem
- How to use a strange machine or communicate with a creature
- What is threatening the Kids
- How to get to a certain place or time
- Or something else.

**TYPICAL LOCATIONS WITH TROUBLE AND CLUES:**

- "Sloppy" Lundqvist is a twenty-year old former hockey player who lives in a ramshackle house in the woods at Mörby. He knows that it was a brother of one of the Kids who stole the robot, but he will not say it voluntarily. Sunken eyes, aggressive, and often drunk.
- On the sandy beach of the lake, there are tracks in the sand from a quadruped creature that seems to have come up from the water. One of the giant lizards is hiding in the bushes, guarding its eggs. It will attack if the Kids come too close.

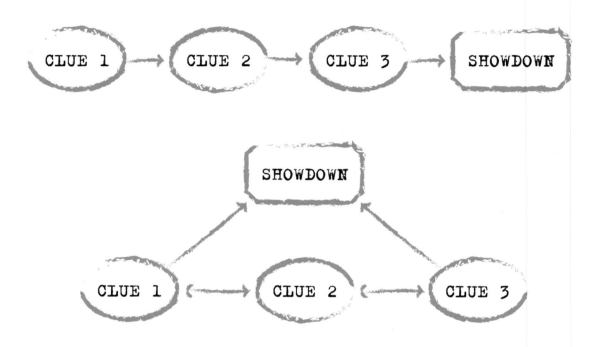

In a rusty magnetrine ship, tools for cyborg maintenance lie neatly stacked. Someone clearly lives here, and that person appears to cooperate with the fugitive cyborgs. The tools' owner has connected a car battery to the tools, and electrified them. The rust in the magnetrine ship makes it dangerous to move around; the Kids risk falling straight through the decks down to the rocks below.

Down in the underground passages, there is a room where the abducted boy was kept hidden. Here, the Kids find a chair with rope, empty food containers, and bags of candy, but also a hidden note that the boy left behind. With his nails, he has smeared "uncle" in dirt on a dropped handkerchief. The passages are dark and labyrinthine, and it's easy to get lost.

At the missing scientist's desk inside the laboratory, there is a blueprint that is difficult to understand. It reveals that the scientist is trying to construct a huge battle robot. Among the scientist's things there is an address book with only one address, to "Sweet Maya, Kungsberga." It is difficult to get past the guards and scientists to get to the desk.

## TYPICAL COUNTDOWN

1. Another group of kids steal a robot.
2. They are found out.
3. The police try to arrest them, but the kids make the robot attack the police.
4. They use the robot to rob a kiosk.
5. Principal Larsson tries to stop them, but gets badly hurt.
6. The kids hide on the northern parts of Svartsjölandet.
7. One of the kids tries to sneak away to tell his mother, but the others spot him, and tell the robot to capture him.
8. The kids use the robot to rob a bank, but it fails and hurts many people before fleeing into the woods.

RIKSENERGI

RIKSENERGI

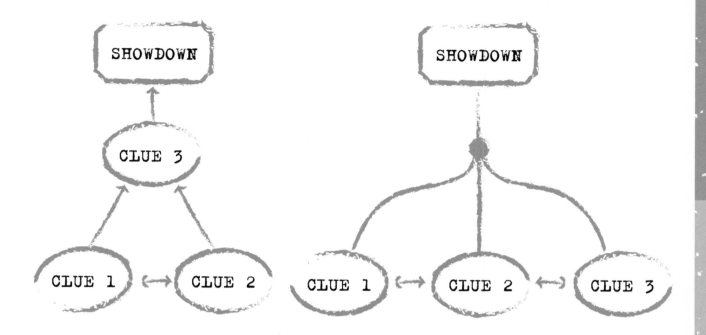

## TOOLS FOR PHASE 3

Phase 3 is the meat of the story, and you can employ many useful methods during this phase.

**LUCKY BREAK.** Some Mysteries have a "divine intervention" event that can be used if the Kids can't solve the Mystery or run out of time. Something helps them solve the Mystery, and makes it possible for them to move on to the Showdown. *A letter falls out of a book. The scientist's colleague calls the parents of a Kid and tells them something important. Someone is seen driving through the village.* You should be careful not to use this trick too much, as players can feel cheated because they didn't solve the Mystery themselves.

**PUZZLES & RIDDLES.** Some Mysteries have puzzles and riddles to be solved by the players themselves, rather than by the Kids. Examples of this are texts written in code or pieces of a map that must be assembled correctly. You tell the players that this Trouble cannot be solved by using skills. Often, these puzzles are presented as a handout, a document or an object that is given to the players.

**MORE MAPS!** You should draw new maps (often quick sketches) during the Mystery, depicting houses and other locations where scenes take place, so that the players can get an overview of what's happening.

**COUNTDOWN.** Mysteries may have a Countdown. Things will happen step by step, if the Kids don't prevent it from happening. The last step in a countdown is often something catastrophic for the community, for the Kids or for someone else.

### TYPICAL RETRIBUTION COUNTDOWN

1. The robbers spy on the Kids.
2. The robbers call the Kids' parents, and lie to them to make them force the Kids to stay at home.
3. The robbers threaten the Kids.

RIKSENERGI

You advance the countdown one step at regular intervals without telling the players, and then describe the results in a scene. *If the next step is that the pyromaniac sets fire to another house, you tell one of the Kids that she wakes up in the middle of the night to cries and the smell of smoke. When she looks out the window, she sees the neighbor's house on fire.*

**RETRIBUTION COUNTDOWN.** Mysteries can also have a countdown of how the antagonists, those responsible for the Truth of the Mystery, try to prevent the Kids from finding out about the Mystery. They may try to stop the Kids, perhaps even attacking them. This is called a Retribution Countdown, and it usually advances one step for each Clue the Kids find.

The antagonists can cause problems for the Kids, spy on them, threaten them, or even attack them. *After the Kids find the gangsters' hidden stash of cash, you set a scene where one of the Kids is called to the headmaster. Something illegal was found in her school desk. The gangsters are trying to frame her.*

THE TILT is when something unexpected happens that changes the situation in a fundamental way. This often happens towards the end of Phase 3, and is often what leads to the Showdown. The Tilt can be linked to a Location, a Countdown, or the Lucky Break.

## PHASE 4 – SHOWDOWN

The Showdown is the finale of the Mystery. It could be a Location, a person, an event or all of them at the same time. The Kids have solved the Mystery, and now they must stop bad things from happening, maybe free a kidnapped child, close a portal or capture a robot or a dinosaur.

Sometimes the Kids will need help from the police or other adults, but usually they need to handle the Trouble themselves. You should make sure that all the Kids are present during the Showdown, so that no player misses out on the most important scenes of the Mystery. The Showdown will often involve Extended Trouble (page 70).

If the Kids fail in the Showdown, sometimes they can try again. Otherwise, the Showdown ends and the game moves on to the Aftermath. Even after the Showdown, there may be things that the Kids don't understand about the Mystery. Use those things to create new Mysteries.

## PHASE 5 – AFTERMATH

Life moves on. After the Showdown, you should set one scene from Everyday Life for each of the Kids. The scenes take place minutes, hours or days after the Showdown. Despite the Kids' heroism, things haven't changed – parents are still fighting, and math tests aren't any easier. Nobody believes the Kids when they talk about the strange things they have seen. All the evidence is destroyed, or can be explained away.

These scenes usually don't contain Trouble. If the group is short on time, you can skip the scenes, and instead let the players briefly describe a snapshot of their Kid in an everyday situation.

### TYPICAL TILTS

- The kidnapper is actually a good guy. He is trying to save the lives of people who will die in a horrible storm, which he has foreseen with his Future Goggles.
- The old lady unexpectedly gives the Kid the reward, and asks them to go home without having found the missing necklace. The old lady has been brainwashed by her son, who is a thief and an inventor of strange devices.
- The uncle visiting one of the Kids' families is, in fact, a robot.
- The stargazing student must have been lying! It's her blood on the knife, and now she is alone with the person she wants to murder.

### TYPICAL SHOWDOWNS

- The mad scientist is in his hideout, and he is just about to open a black hole. Two mechanical bulldogs guard the hideout.
- The electrical storm sweeps across town, and destroys all electronic devices. The Kids have to stop it with the Items they have built or found.
- The ape-like creature is standing on top of the huge cooling tower, and is about to transport the building to its home world.
- The Kids finally find the corpse, half-submerged in the swamp. The killer watches them through binoculars; she will not let them leave to tell the police.
- Stenhamra Church crackles with energy and floats up into the air. The Kids must prevent it from dissolving into atoms.

RIKSENERGI

**87**

## PHASE 6 – CHANGE

After the Mystery, you and the players should discuss whether the Kids have changed or learned something new from the experience. Each player reads her Kid's Problems, Pride, Iconic Item, and Relationships out loud, and changes what she likes.

Most often these aspects stay the same, but if the player is bored of some aspect of her Kid or if something happened during the Mystery that demands change, it should be changed. If the Kid solved her Problem, she chooses a new one. Use what happened in the Mystery as inspiration.

All Conditions are healed between Mysteries. If time has passed and the Kid has missed her birthday, she increases an attribute rating by one (page 58) and loses a Luck Point. A Kid who turns 16 moves on in life, and stops solving Mysteries. The player creates a new Kid.

The player may stop playing her current Kid and create a new one between Mysteries. There should preferably not be more than one Kid of the same Type.

### EXPERIENCE POINTS

After the Mystery, or after the session if the Mystery continues, the Kids get Experience Points (XP) that the players can use to increase skill levels. Read five questions out loud to the Kids, and let the players answer them. Each Kid gets one experience point for each question answered with a "yes."

To increase a skill by one costs five XP. A skill level can never go higher than 5. The Kid can at most save 10 XP. They may only be used before or after a session, never during play.

## SETTING THE MOOD

The mysterious environments and the mood are key parts of *Tales From the Loop*. You and the players should try to create a feeling of being inside Simon Stålenhag's images.

To set the tone, players can describe what their Kids look like, what they eat for breakfast, how they fix their clothes or hair, or what they read before they turn off the lights before bed. You can describe how the waves crash against the rugged cliffs, or the cooling towers that rise over the town like pillars of doom. Three themes should be emphasized: Nostalgia, Everyday Life, and the Machines.

QUESTIONS FOR EXPERIENCE POINTS

1. Did you participate in the session? (Each Kid present always gets at least one XP.)
2. Have you been in Trouble because of your Problem or your Relationships?
3. Did you use, or struggle with, your Pride?
4. Did you put yourself at risk for the other Kids?
5. Have you learned something new? (What is it?)

NOSTALGIA is the world seen through the eyes of the Kid, and childhood seen through the eyes of the players. Freedom, opportunities for discovery, to catch your first fish, climbing to the top of a tree or driving with dad to buy a hamburger.

EVERYDAY LIFE is boring and tedious. Adults set rules and limitations, not letting the Kids decide for themselves. The ugly cap your mother compels you to wear, sweaty socks, math class every Monday morning.

THE MACHINES are both part of everyday life and fantastic. They are always there, with the smell of oil and ozone, squeaky movements and heavy strides. At the same time, they are scary and enchanting. How can they even exist? The grown-ups live in the delusion that they can control the machines.

**TIPS FOR SETTING THE MOOD**

- Set the mood early in the Mystery. Then, everyone will remember it, and you don't need to spend much time on descriptions later on. Everyone at the table gets the same feeling.
- Look at Simon Stålenhag's art together.
- Describe (a few) details. You rarely need to describe everything that can be seen or heard, but it's always good to describe a couple of details. The Kid's blond hair that refuses to lie down at the back of his head, a seagull on a rock, the eyes of the cyborg.
- Use all of the senses. Describe what the Kids see, hear, smell, taste, and feel.
- Don't forget the seasons and the weather. Is it summer, with golden fields of rapeseed, or fall with muddy fields? Coltsfoot growing in the sun, or a garden covered with snow? Is it windy, does it rain on the abandoned factory?

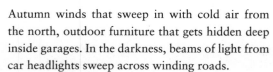

Autumn winds that sweep in with cold air from the north, outdoor furniture that gets hidden deep inside garages. In the darkness, beams of light from car headlights sweep across winding roads.

■ Home is where the heart is. If the parents are fighting, the house feels cold and unsafe. If there is a celebration and joy, the windows are open and the rooms feel inviting and friendly.

■ The Mälaren Islands are surrounded by water. Wherever they are, the Kids can see or smell the lake. The wind whips up waves, the smell of freshly caught fish, and fishing boats visible in the distance. There is always an island or a rock to swim to. This tip only applies to the Swedish Loop setting.

■ Share the responsibility. You should not describe everything. Ask questions of the players, let them decide how something looks or feels. Make sure that everyone gets a chance to contribute.

■ The adults are remote and detached. Their conversations are uninteresting or confusing. They look at you with weary eyes when they pretend to want to listen. Restrained emotions, parties with too much alcohol, suspicious questions about your friends and activities.

■ Use similes. The wreck of the cargo ship is lying on its side like a wounded moose, the headmaster's house is towering on the hill like a huge toad, the punch to your face sounds like a heavy book being dropped.

Sometimes, there is an antagonist behind the Truth of the Mystery, someone who deliberately has caused the problems and certainly doesn't want to be stopped. Try to make these people nuanced. There are very few purely evil people – most have a reason to do what they do. They might feel offended, rejected or misunderstood.

## ITEMS

Sometimes, the Kids find Items that are so special that they give bonus dice (Chapter 4) in certain situations. The bonus tells the players that the Item is an important part of the Mystery. All Items disappear or break between Mysteries, if not made into an Iconic Item.

### TYPICAL ITEMS

| Item | Bonus |
| --- | --- |
| Hover Vehicle | +2 |
| Hallucinatory Soft Drink | +1 |
| Trained Dinosaur | +3 |
| Baseball Bat | +1 |
| Flying Shoes | +3 |
| Skis | +1 |
| Wrench | +2 |
| Truck | +1 |
| Gun | +3 |
| Ladder | +2 |

You should be careful with letting NPCs have guns that they use against the Kids. The players may feel compelled to arm their Kids too, and soon the Mystery is turned into a shootout.

## NPCS – HUMANS, CREATURES, AND MACHINES

All Mysteries contain a couple of NPCs that will either attempt to thwart the Kids, ask them for help or help them. It's good to mix ordinary people and creatures, like a journalist or a guard dog, with robots and dinosaurs. The NPCs are described briefly with their name, what they look like, how they behave, what they want, what Trouble they can cause, and if they have a Clue. Try to give each NPC a detail that stands out, so that the players can keep track of them – a stutter, a red cap, angry eyes or a broken tail. Some NPCs have special attributes – this is described further in Chapter 5.

**Mindmap of the Mystery Dreams Come True.**

**Secret Government Laboratory**
Scientists trying to control
dreams to make a weapon

**"Micke"**
Abusive father

Wants her back

Scared

**Anette**
Peter's mother
has moved

Feels abandoned

**Peter**
Dream-hacking
teen

In a relationship

Hates and hurts
through dreams

**Niklas**
The Kids' teacher

Teacher
suddenly
very ill..

**Kids**

**Niklas**
House

**Hospital**
Niklas in
tormented
dream-coma

RIKSENERGI

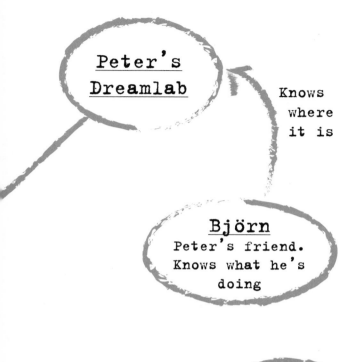

## BIGGER MYSTERIES AND CAMPAIGNS

You can create bigger Mysteries that take several nights to play by expanding Phase 3, Solving the Mystery, with more Locations and NPCs. It may be helpful to draw an overview (see the example of one, to the left) of all Locations, NPCs and Clues, and allow the Kids to move around freely.

Several Mysteries can be linked together by an underlying Truth to form a Campaign, a longer story arc played out over many sessions. The first Mystery may serve as an introduction, where the Kids only get to know a small part of what is going on. Then, they can solve one or more Mysteries that reveal more about the Truth, while the overall situation gets more dramatic and serious. More is at stake than first was believed. The final Mystery should be extra grandiose, dangerous, and contain spectacular Locations and NPCs.

In the Campaign, a couple of NPCs and Locations should be recurring to create a sense of the stories being connected. It is important that the actions of the Kids in one Mystery have repercussions in the next Mystery. A Campaign often has a clear antagonist, someone that the Kids must find and stop, and who will likely try to stop the Kids. A Campaign can have a Retribution Countdown stretching over several Mysteries.

### PRIDES IN BIGGER MYSTERIES

In Mysteries that takes several sessions to solve, you can let the Kids use their Prides once every session instead of once every Mystery.

**MALTEMANN MEASUREMENT STATION D1400.** A common sight around the Loop are these measurement stations that are dotted around the landscape. Often called "penguins" by locals because of their shape.

**SERVICE MODULE PAARHUFER RE-15.** A rare design only built in a few copies. The Service Module RE-15 was commissioned by Riksenergi and specifically built for maintenance of flux stations in bodies of water.

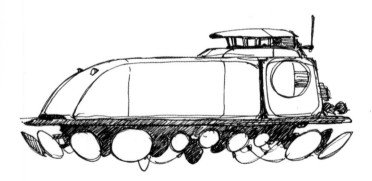

**LIEBER-ALTA LOCOMOTIVE SHIP M60 OCH M75.** These classic workhorses are common sights in the landscape surrounding the Loop. They often serve in basic service roles or as light transports.

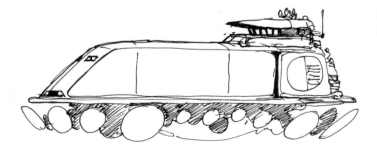

RIKSENERGI

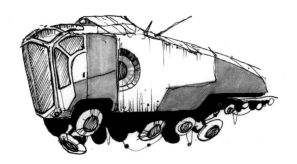

**LIEBER-ALTA CABLE MAINTENANCE VEHICLE 12.**
A true workhorse that is held in high esteem among the cable technicians at Riksenergi. The CMV 12 can often be seen in action on the Mälaren Islands. Neither nimble or quick, the CMV 12 is known for its reliability and high driver comfort.

**IWASAKA SPIDER PROBE ROBOT.** The Japanese spider robots are sometimes seen in or around water or along coastlines. Being amphibious, they are capable swimmers. Constructed to measure radiation levels and monitor chemical leakage around The Loop.

**CORSAIR DELTA.** The elegant design of the Delta turns heads wherever it's flown. Built by the English company Corsair and with a characteristically long nose cone, the Delta is one of the most beautiful magnetrine ships in use today. A handful of these ships are operated by the Defence Forces and the Coast Guard.

**IWASAKA SBR-71.** An early model originally constructed for the Japanese Self-Defense Forces. The SBR-71 was adapted for civilian use in the mid 1970s and a handful were operated by Riksenergi as service vehicles well into the '80s.

RIKSENERGI

PAARHUFER AUTONOMOUS PATROL UNIT MK.82. **Commonly known as the "Fire Watchers". These tall robots are primarily used for guard and patrol duties around the Loop and other restricted areas. It has become a sport among kids in the area to try to lure the robots with hand-held flares and torches.**

VECTRA ATV SERIES 2. **A version of Vectra's popular all-terrain vehicle, adapted to colder climates. The ATV 2 is used by Riksenergi, as well as various emergency services.**

VECTRA LAND TRAIN. **A modular design often used for civilian as well as military purposes. The Land Train can be customized with freight and service modules. Because of it's shape, it has earned the nickname "the Centipede."**

RIKSENERGI

TRICERATOPS. **Three horns, nine meters tail to nose, eight tons of muscle and bone. The Triceratops is one of the most classic dinosaurs to have walked the Earth. That was 65 million years ago. But why does Mrs. Eriksson's garden look like a battlefield? And what are those strange footprints in the soil?**

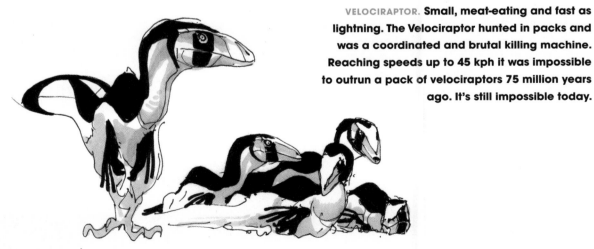

VELOCIRAPTOR. **Small, meat-eating and fast as lightning. The Velociraptor hunted in packs and was a coordinated and brutal killing machine. Reaching speeds up to 45 kph it was impossible to outrun a pack of velociraptors 75 million years ago. It's still impossible today.**

RIKSENERGI

**97**

**RIKSENERGI**

# THE MYSTERY LANDSCAPE

*It truly was an enigmatic house. My father used to say it was just a regular house that a giant had lifted and flipped over on its side. Tons of old things towered along the walls, almost all of them things that had no place in a home. A big, shaggy German Shepherd strolled along the paths among all that junk, and somewhere in the middle of the clutter, always busy disassembling something, was the dog's master: my uncle, Alf. To say that it was messy would be wrong. There was an order here, and a feeling of recycling—sort of like a compost heap.*

The Mystery Story is not the only way to play *Tales from the Loop*. Another way is to use a Mystery Landscape – a sandbox environment with strange locations, exciting creatures and constructions, and people with dubious agendas.

In this method, the Kids are allowed to move about freely without a pre-written plot, and they seek out Mysteries to explore. A Mystery Landscape can be used in combination with regular Mysteries, and several Mysteries could even be played simultaneously. If the Mysteries described at the end of this book are used in a Mystery Landscape, the season indicated may have to be changed to fit the game.

The basis of a Mystery Landscape are mysterious Locations. Two things can make the Kids want to explore a Location: Hooks and Relationships. Hooks are

events that you, as the Gamemaster, can use to make the Kids interested in a Location. The Kids have Relationships to NPCs connected to the Locations, and these Relationships should be interesting enough to make the Kids want to investigate.

Scenes from Everyday Life and scenes related to Mysteries and Locations should be mixed as in normal play, and you should alternate between setting scenes yourself and letting a player do it. There is no clear end to the story in the Mystery Landscape. It can be continued indefinitely, as you keep inventing new Locations and the players come up with new Problems.

This chapter presents one Mystery Landscape. It is based on the Swedish Mälaren Islands, but includes suggested tweaks for using it in the Boulder City Location as well.

RIKSENERGI

## TIPS FOR THE GAMEMASTER

- **Roll with it.** Let the Kids loose and rely on the players. Sooner or later, they will find a way to move the story forward. Do not take responsibility for the players' fun. Your task is to make sure that there are exciting things to do, not to decide what the Kids do.
- **Let things get worse if the players are passive.** Let the Kids' Problems accelerate and advance the Countdowns. Turn up the heat until the Kids can no longer sit still.
- **Recycle Locations and NPCs.** Let NPCs develop unexpected and exciting relationships to each other. Show new sides of the NPCs, such as perhaps the callous policeman is a weepy dad?
- **Speed up and slow down.** Increase the tempo at times. Let things happen that force the Kids to act fast. Slow down the tempo at times, and let tranquil scenes drag on for a bit.
- **Do not be afraid of loose threads** or that you do not know the Truth behind a Mystery. The answers will come to you as you continue playing.
- **Use the Kids' Relationships** with NPCs, with each other and their Problems as much as you can. Push things to the extreme, but do it step by step, so that the players have time to act and adjust.
- **Let the NPCs act while the kids are doing something else.** Enemies hit back, they ally themselves with each other or dig out the Kids' embarrassing secrets, and show them to everyone in school.
- **Talk directly to the players** when it feels like the game doesn't work. Perhaps they have misunderstood what is expected of them, or you have done something that does not feel right for them. Sometimes you simply have a bad day.
- **The adults must never know.** Whatever the Kids find out, it will never be public knowledge. Somehow the evidence is destroyed or disappears, or no one believes it. The rest of the world stays ignorant.

### THE MYSTERY LANDSCAPE MAP

When the Kids start to take interest in a Location, its Countdown starts and things begin to happen. All Locations are marked on the Mystery Landscape Map, and the players should have access to it. You will find two Mystery Landscape Maps (one for the Swedish Loop and one for the US one) at the back of this book. You can also download them from the Free League website.

### PLAYING THE MYSTERY LANDSCAPE

A Mystery Landscape is best suited for long-term play. The Gamemaster's task is mainly to have an overview of what is happening, and the timing of Hooks, Countdowns, and Trouble. Since it is difficult to prepare for the game, the Gamemaster needs to rely more on improvisation, and roll with the players' own ideas.

When playing in a Mystery Landscape, the Kids' Iconic Items and Drives may be used once every session. Items that are not Iconic are lost at the appropriate times, like when summer break is over or when the Kids have finally overcome Trouble at a difficult Location. The Gamemaster has the final say.

At the end of each session, the Kids get XP and the players may alter their Drive, Iconic Item, Problem, Anchor, and Relationships.

For the Mystery Landscape to work well, the Kids need to have Relationships with NPCs, as well as Problems and Drives, that encourage them to start investigating. When a player feels that a Relationship to an NPC has played out its course and wants to change it, she should work together with you to create a new NPC, which will be a basis for you to create a new Location in the Landscape.

There is no obvious way to resolve a Location in the Landscape, and no pre-written Showdown. Some Locations may exist in the Landscape for the entire game. The Kids can revisit Locations they encountered and NPCs they met earlier.

> *EXAMPLE*
> **Player 1 (Olle):** *I don't think I have any use for my Relationship with the Mad Hunter Roland any more, since he's dead. Or should I keep it?*
> **The Gamemaster:** *No, it's fine, so change it.*

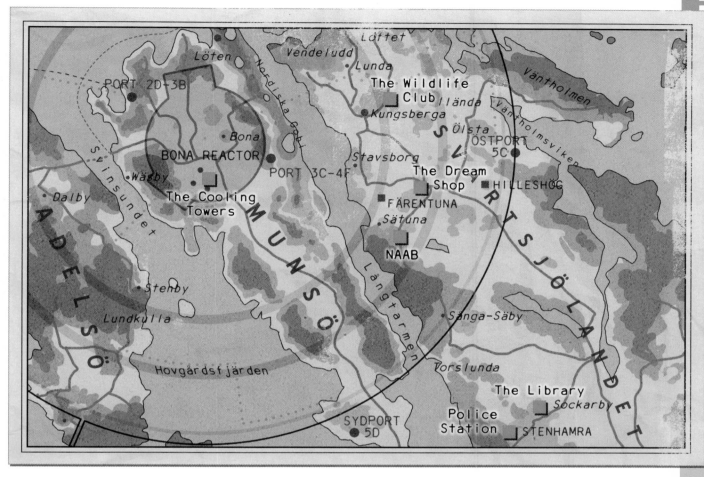

**Example of Mystery Lanscape Map**

**Player 1:** *Do you have any ideas?*
**The Gamemaster:** *It would be nice if it involved the young girl working for the undertaker. Her name is Jennifer. Maybe you could have a reason to check her out?*
**Player 1:** *How about, "Though I haven't spoken to her yet and she's older than me, I am madly in love with Jennifer?"*
**The Gamemaster:** *Great stuff!*

## THE SCHOOL LIBRARY

The school library in Stenhamra [Boulder City] is known for its vast collection of odd books, and the caretaker, Per "Prutte" Äng [Jeffrey "Farty" Allen]. He works both as a janitor and as a school librarian, since the former librarian, Mona Eriksson [Mary Walker], disappeared last year.

Prutte has huge problems with flatulence, and one can often hear and smell him from afar. There are wild rumors among the students that "Prutte" has killed kids who behaved badly.

### THE TRUTH

Few people know that Per has been living secretly at the school for years. He moves through the corridors with a wolf-like agility, constantly licking his dry lips, prepared with a wrench in hand to fix leaks and chase brats.

Per and Mona had a secret love affair for several years, drawn together by a common interest in art and books about cyborgs and transcendence of the human intellect. The pair used the school library to buy rare books, and built a laboratory in a closed part of the school basement.

RIKSENERGI

With machine parts and tissue from animals, the couple built a cyborg that looked like a monstrous copy of Per with cables, flesh, and entrails hanging out. Unfortunately, the copy was created with too much intellect and almost no empathy. It hated its makers for its hideous appearance, and secretly decided to build its own copy, but this time without flaws. The copy of Per killed Mona and Per to get the parts it needed and built another copy, this time almost impossible to tell apart from the original. The new copy of Per took on the role as both caretaker and school librarian. One of its flaws, a broken pipe, makes it leak smelly gas in the corridors that it walks day and night.

The original copy wasn't satisfied with the result, and decided to build yet another copy. It attacked and killed a jogger in the woods to get the material it needed, and tried again. The original copy has since built three copies of Per, each of whom take turns walking the halls of the school and guarding the school library. The original copy still isn´t satisfied. It plans to kill students and teachers to get more raw material. Since it cannot leave the locked part of the basement because of its appearance, it commands its creations to get the things it needs. But some of the copies are getting restless, and want to break free.

On the floor in the big laboratory, several dead bodies lie wrapped in plastic. The room is filled with mechanical parts, things stolen from chemistry class, and several freezers with human body parts. There are two entrances to the room, one from the rear of school and the other through a door from the school library and down a staircase. The original copy has hidden explosives in the room, in case it risks getting caught.

### HOOKS

- A student at school disappears.
- One of the Kids sees two copies of Per at the same time.
- Per dates one of the Kids' parents, and the Kids see Per adjust a cable.
- One of the copies make contact with one of the Kids, to tell them "an awful secret." When they meet again, another copy has taken its place and says that there's nothing to be worried about. But the second copy needs to know how much the Kid has found out.

### COUNTDOWN

1. A student reports being hunted in an empty corridor by an adult with a black mask.
2. A student disappears, and the only thing left is a large stain of blood.
3. Someone close to the Kids disappears. Can they find him before he is turned to spare parts?
4. One of the Kids is picked as the next victim.

## TIPS FOR THE PLAYERS

- Your task is to explore the world, look for mysteries, and try to solve them. Do not be afraid to put your Kid in danger. The other Kids will help you, and it will be exciting and fun. Remember that Kids cannot die.
- You create the game that you want to play. Don't let anyone else take responsibility for your experience. Make sure your Kid is interesting and that you invest emotionally in her.
- Don't be afraid of slow or emotional scenes. These scenes often make you get to know the Kid. A dramatic scene, like being chased by a murderer or hiding from killer robots, becomes more interesting if you know that the Kid wants to get home to comfort her mother who has cancer.
- Don't be afraid of loose threads. In a Mystery Landscape, there will always be things to do, and you will never get to a point where you have all the answers.
- Use your Relationships with the other Kids to create drama. Be angry, fall in love, be jealous. Let your Kid lose control.

## PER ÄNG (JEFFREY ALLEN)

*"It's a classic Van Gogh, but you wouldn't know, would you, brat?"*

Per is a short man with a stocky body. His almost white hair is held in place by a torn red cap. Per seems clumsy, but is actually quite agile. He speaks with a slow, toneless voice and never looks anyone in the eyes. He can often be seen reading books, and is very well educated. He loves art and classical music, but he really dislikes students – now even more than before he was turned into a cyborg. The best part of the day is when they go home and stop sabotaging the building. The original copy has the special attribute INHUMAN STRENGTH 2 (see page 69). The other copies have the special attribute FEELS NO PAIN 2.

## THE DREAM SHOP

When the outcast teenager Peter Månsson [Peter Dale] quit school, nobody missed him. The other students were tormented by his nasty remarks, the teachers could not stand him, and the girls hated his dirty looks and creepy suggestions. Even the nerds didn't like him. As a matter of fact, Peter's only friend, Björn [Bryan], felt it was a relief to stop being associated with him. Peter quit school because he felt hated, and he blamed it on everyone but himself.

Peter's mother has run a shop called the Dream Shop for a few years now, where she sells dream catchers, crystals, self-help books, and other New Age related items. Because she suffers from both electrical hypersensitivity and fibromyalgia, she is mostly bedridden at home in the cottage where she lives with her son. It is now Peter who runs the store.

### THE TRUTH

Peter devotes his free time to building a dream machine in the shop's basement, which he now calls the Dream Lab. For a while now, people all over the area have had strange dreams. Peter has managed to build a machine that allows him to break into other people's dreams and control them. With the help of the machine, he has started to give his enemies terrible nightmares, and entered the private dreams of the girls he desires.

Recently, Peter has discovered that he can give instructions to the dreamers. The dreams follow them into their waking lives and in this way, Peter has started to enslave three of his former schoolmates, who occasionally visit the Dream Shop to give him compliments or gifts. So far, nothing serious has happened. Peter is still testing his machine, but he plans to use it to get the things he wants and the appreciation he has always been denied.

Meanwhile, a secret group of scientists with links to the army has discovered that someone is manipulating dreams. They themselves have tried to invent a similar device, and are now trying to find out where on the islands the dream machine is. They are prepared to send in a team of commandos to steal the device and kidnap its creator.

### HOOKS

- The Kids overhear Björn [Bryan] talking to himself about Peter controlling dreams, and how this must be stopped.
- The Kids' teacher, Niklas [Neil], has been in a relationship with Peter's mother for some time. Peter feels infringed upon and hates Niklas, and uses his Dream Machine to put Niklas into a coma.
- A sibling of one of the Kids becomes a victim of Peter's machine.
- One of the Kids is accused by mistake of being the dream manipulator, and the scientists try to kidnap her.

RIKSENERGI

**103**

### COUNTDOWN

1. Someone else the Kids know becomes a victim of Peter.
2. Someone gets seriously hurt through her waking dreams.
3. Peter finds out that the Kids are looking for him, and starts sending them warnings in their dreams to back off.
4. Peter attacks the Kids with nightmares.
5. Someone kills herself because of the dreams.
6. Peter's friend Björn tries to physically stop him, but is seriously beaten by Peter's dream slaves.
7. Peter is kidnapped by the scientists but escapes.
8. Peter builds an even larger Dream Machine to get back at all the people on Svartsjölandet.

### PETER MÅNSSON (PETER DALE)

*"It's only fair, after all I've had to endure, that I get the love I deserve."*

Peter has grown up with a father who physically and mentally abused both him and his mother. It filled Peter with a sense of being useless, stupid, and disgusting. Peter does not understand that these are his own feelings about himself. Instead, he thinks that everyone else is against him, and he behaves in a way which confirms just that.

The only people who have managed to reach him are his mother and his friend, Björn. Maybe Peter can still be saved if he will experience a moment of true compassion and warmth?

Peter is a tall, sixteen-year-old boy with black hair and intense eyes. He smokes constantly, and never seems to stand still. He talks all the time with a nasal voice about all the wrongs he has experienced.

# THE WILDLIFE CLUB

Until a few months ago, the Wildlife Club was run by field biologists and boy scouts who met to watch birds and go on excursions, playing guitar in front of an open fire. That changed when Lisa Tengby [Lisa Tanner] moved to the area and took over the club. Now, most of the club members have quit, leaving an inner core strictly controlled by Lisa. Club activities are kept secret, and anyone who reveals them is at risk of exclusion or worse. At the same time, a number of nightly attacks have been reported in the area, and there are whispers that a pack of wolves have somehow made their way down through the country and settled here.

### THE TRUTH

Lisa Tengby's parents moved from Stockholm [Las Vegas] when they discovered that their daughter not only used drugs but also was a member of a sect that hung around in the city at night and attacked people. What they did not understand was that Lisa and her friends had discovered a way to use chemical substances to absorb animal minds and abilities – or at least, so they thought. They tried to let themselves be possessed by the spirits of the city's rats and wild dogs to heighten their senses and increase their strength.

When Lisa moved to the Loop area, she took the drugs with her, and made herself the leader of the Wildlife Club. She got rid of all those who didn't want to participate in her experiment. The Club now consists of a dozen teenagers who get together on weekends to go out to the woods and be filled with "wolf-souls." It is said that the group of wolves now living in the area have been drawn there by Lisa.

The clubhouse is a two-story building made of wood, filled with pictures of animals, framed maps, and books about famous explorers and animals. Lisa likes to light candles and incense, play psychedelic music, make the club members play painful games, use drugs, and tell each other their secrets.

If Lisa's experiment really works or if it's only dangerous adolescent games with drugs, and if there really are wolves in the area is up to the Gamemaster to decide.

RIKSENERGI

### HOOKS

- One of the Kids' older brothers joins the club and is changed. He becomes quiet, keeps to himself, and comes home with strange wounds on his chest and back.
- One of the Kids sees the Club members running naked through her backyard, howling, with a dead and bloody animal in their hands.
- One of the Kids' dogs is found dead, and the vet examining it says that the bite marks on its body are human.
- Lisa's sister asks the Kids to join the Wildlife Club to spy on Lisa.

### COUNTDOWN

1. One night, those attending a student orienteering training night are attacked by the Club, and seriously injured. The next day, everyone at school is talking about werewolves.
2. The Club members kill someone.
3. Hunters go out to shoot the wolves, who are believed to have attacked humans.
4. One of the Club members is shot dead by a hunter, and found naked in the woods.
5. Lisa gathers her flock in an abandoned cottage, and forbids them to contact their families. She plans for them to fight the humans who attacked them.

### LISA TENGBY (LISA TANNER)

*"For thousands of years, humans have become weak because of inventions and machines. But the wild animals have never lost their strength and the ability to see the world clearly. Somewhere deep inside us, we are still creatures of the wild."*

Lisa comes from a family of alcoholics, many of whom died young. Though her parents have managed to save themselves and Lisa's older sister from this fate, they didn't reach Lisa in time. She lives for the rush of the drugs, and doesn't see how they've affected her. Lisa has become a cold-hearted liar who does anything for the kicks.

RIKSENERGI

Sometimes, she believes what she tells the Club members about gaining the strength of animal spirits, but mostly she just enjoys the drugs and manipulating others.

Lisa is a blonde teenager with a winning smile, cool hairstyle, and the latest fashion in clothes. She knows what is cool in the city, and uses it to impress and take control of the local teens. She is a gifted leader and knows what to say to stir emotions.

## THE COOLING TOWERS

Visible from anywhere in the Loop area, the three cooling towers are a constant presence for the locals. Every evening at 6 pm, a siren is heard all over the area. This is the result of the daily reset of the Towers' fifteen huge demister valves.

The priest in Wäsby [St Christopher], Hans-Erik Thelin [Joseph Harold Sullivan], has always been a strong supporter of the Loop, and often says in his sermons that the knowledge to build the accelerator comes from God. During the past year however, Hans-Erik has suffered a series of disasters. His two children died in a car accident, which resulted in his wife leaving him and moving away. A group of parishioners accused him of stealing money from the church, and he discovered that he is suffering from incurable cancer.

Until a few months ago, none of this seemed to affect Hans-Erik's good mood. But one day, rumors started that the signal from the Cooling Towers made something snap inside his head. Hans-Erik stormed out of his house without jacket and shoes, shouted and cursed the Cooling Towers, and has neither worked nor seen his friends since then.

RIKSENERGI

### THE TRUTH

Hans-Erik is convinced that the Loop is not a creation of man, but something made by God or the Devil. In recent months, he has used his technical knowledge from his previous career as an engineer to break into the Cooling Towers, and build a home in a storage space. He has explored the Towers' interiors and made his way down to the huge underground tunnels, reaching the Gravitron to examine whether the creation is a gift or a punishment.

In the depths Hans-Erik, influenced by lack of food and sleep, has had a number of revelations that led him to the conclusion that the Gravitron is connected directly to Hell, and will serve as a portal for the Devil. The Loop must be destroyed, and the easiest way to do that is to blow up the Cooling Towers.

Over a period of a few weeks, Hans-Erik bought explosives and transported them to the Towers at night. He has also equipped himself with a hunting rifle, and built a number of robots meant to warn him of intruders and to attack people trying to stop him. Soon, he will have enough explosives to stop the influence of the Devil of the Loop.

### HOOKS

- One of the Kids spots Hans-Erik as he transports explosives to the Cooling Towers.
- The Kids see someone moving on top of one of the Cooling Towers, but no one believes them.
- Hans-Erik's wife comes looking for him. She has gotten a disturbing letter in which he stated that he will end the Devil's influence. She wonders if the Kids have seen him, and she is worried that he might do something stupid.
- Someone says that she looked through one of the windows at Hans-Erik's house, and saw that he had written strange things about the Loop and the Gravitron all over the walls.

### COUNTDOWN

1. Someone sees Hans-Erik close to the Cooling Towers, and starts a rumor that he has become a madman living in the forest nearby.
2. A technician who works with maintenance at the Cooling Towers finds Hans-Erik, but is attacked by one of his robots, and beaten unconscious.

Hans-Erik ties him up in a storage room. The technician is the father of one of the Kids or the father of a classmate.

3. Hans-Erik shoots at someone going towards the Towers. No one sees where the shot came from.

4. A huge explosion is heard as some of Hans-Erik's explosives go off too soon. Firefighters, medics, and police race to the Cooling Towers, while Hans-Erik flees down into the Gravitron tunnels.

### HANS-ERIK THELIN (JOSEPH H. SULLIVAN)

*"This is the work of the Devil, who will drag us all down to Hell if we do not stop him!"*

It was a revelation that made Hans-Erik quit his job as a robotics engineer, leave his family in the big city, and become a priest. He found work at the community in a small church in the Loop area. There, he met the love of his life, they married, and had kids. Hans-Erik was certain he and his family were watched over by God. He believed that he had been given this chance to leave his earlier destructive marriage, and start again so as to fill the people of this small town with the love and power of God. He is now a broken and confused man, who is about to do things he will regret for the rest of his life.

Hans-Erik still wears his priest outfit, though neither he nor it have been washed for months. His chestnut brown hair is uncombed, and his eyes are filled with panic and grief.

## THE POLICE STATION AT STENHAMRA

A new inspector has recently started working at the police station in a small town in the Loop area. Her name is Ing-Marie Blankäng [Karen Richards], and her colleagues already want to get rid of her. Though she has tried to hide it, it has become public knowledge that Ing-Marie is a believer in a great number of occult things, such as alien abductions and a monster living in the lake. Her colleagues think that she's weird, and they don't trust her as a partner.

Ing-Marie has her desk in a corner of an open office. Her table is covered with papers, books, and photos from various investigations. Ing-Marie is a methodical and very talented investigator, who solves more crimes than most.

On the wall behind her desk, her colleagues have posted mocking newspaper clippings about crazy UFO enthusiasts and mental illness. No one at the station looks at or talks to Ing-Marie, who goes by the nickname ET. The house that Ing-Marie has rented is filled with notes and newspaper clippings related to the search for and about information on strange creatures.

In the last few weeks, Ing-Marie has been seen during her free time watching the surface of the lake with binoculars. She has rented a fishing boat to go on long trips out on the lake, where she's said to use strange devices to look for something in the water.

### THE TRUTH

Ing-Marie took the job here because she is convinced that a prehistoric sea creature is living at the bottom of the lake. She has built a number of devices to try to spot it and force it to surface, so that she can photograph it. Ing-Marie is a very lonely person, and would love to share her findings and her work with someone – even a bunch of Kids.

The gigantic sea creature that Ing-Marie is looking for probably doesn't exist, but her devices that pick up strange signals from deep down in the lake aren't giving false information.

A group of secret agents from another country have constructed a base in an abandoned cottage, where they store a number of highly advanced mini-submarines.

RIKSENERGI

They plan to use them to kidnap scientists from the Loop, and bring them home to steal their knowledge and make them invent new things. The agents don't use their real names, but call themselves names based around fish species. The leader of the group calls herself Pike.

### HOOKS

- A scientist related to the Kids disappears.
- The Kids see something coming up from the water and going back down again, perhaps a gigantic creature?
- One of the Kids finds Ing-Marie crying in her police car, because of the harassment at work. When they talk to her, she tells the Kid of her findings in the lake, and asks if the Kids want to help her.

### COUNTDOWN

1. Ing-Marie sees something at night, and takes a photograph of a blurry shape in the water.
2. Several scientists disappear, all of them close to the water. One of the scientists is somehow related to the Kids, or they see it as the disappearance occurs.
3. An old woman reports strange men hiding in the forest, speaking a foreign language.
4. The agents find out that Ing-Marie is looking for them, and sink her boat.
5. The agents attack Ing-Marie in her home.

RIKSENERGI

## ING-MARIE BLANKÄNG (KAREN RICHARDS)

*"You remind me of my brother. I hope you get to meet him someday."*

Ing-Marie came into contact with supernatural events early in life, when at the age of eleven, she witnessed a group of Aliens who entered her home and abducted her parents and brother. It didn't matter that everyone tried to get her to realize they were robbers who murdered her family. Ing-Marie decided to dedicate her life to finding out what the government was trying to hide. She became a police officer, but spends all of her free time investigating strange phenomena. Ing-Marie is a member of a large number of UFO groups, but has no real friends. She is used to being ostracized and teased, but she does not want to lose her job. She moved to Mälaröarna because she believes that a gigantic prehistoric animal is living in the lake. Ing-Marie's home and car are full of notes, newspaper clippings and photographs.

Ing-Marie is a twenty-five-year-old woman with blonde hair and a watchful gaze. She dresses in a police uniform, or jeans and a T-shirt. She has a raspy voice, curses constantly, and drinks coffee.

# NAAB (NAI)

A year ago, scientist and businesswoman Olivia Martinez bought land in the countryside east of the Loop, and built a research facility that now goes by the name Neuro Ascension Aktiebolag or NAAB [Neuro Ascension, Inc - NAI]. The company collaborates with researchers at the Loop, to use knowledge from the Gravitron for the development of medicines for dementia.

The NAAB facility is surrounded by electric fences with cameras, and the area is patrolled by armed guards with dogs. Those who work at the company have signed strict confidentiality agreements, and many of them are researchers who have been flown in from other parts of the world. During the past few weeks, the guards from NAAB have been seen patrolling outside the area and even around the villages, as if they were looking for something.

## THE TRUTH

Olivia Martinez has headed up companies at various locations all over the world for many years, but she has always had to move on because of violations of the law and ethical principles of research. Her goal has always been to find ways to stimulate the human brain to transcend, and gain access to abilities like telepathy and telekinesis – abilities that Olivia claims humans had thousands of years ago but have forgotten. At the research station, there are several young people who are, more or less voluntarily, participating as human test subjects.

Recently, one of Olivia's experiments led to a serious explosion in the basement, where the most secret and dangerous experiments take place. Several people were killed, and the explosion opened a portal to another world. This world can be another dimension with dark forces which shouldn't be allowed to roam the earth, a passage into the human collective unconscious, or mass hallucinations created by the gases leaking in the explosion.

Something came through the portal and managed to escape out of the research station. Olivia calls the creature OW-1 because it's the first contact with the Otherworld. She describes the OW-1 as a tall and thin humanoid without skin, with big round eyes and a predator's jaws. Arms and legs seem to have too many joints, and the hands and feet have claws with barbs.

RIKSENERGI

Olivia has seen that OW-1 can move in and out of the Otherworld through temporary portals. The creature can only move over a limited part of the Loop area, and seems to be looking for something.

Recently, people have been attacked by OW-1 and killed or been kidnapped to the Otherworld. Olivia has instructed the guards to seek out and kill OW-1, and silence anyone who tries to find out what's going on.

The former rock star Niklas "Nille" Landgren [Mikey Hayes] lives in a cottage nearby. He met Olivia several years ago when he lived with his wife, Liz, in Seattle, and Olivia had a research facility in the area. Liz, who was pregnant at the time, participated in Olivia's experiments and disappeared. Nille has since followed Olivia around the world to find out what she is trying to do, and to have her prosecuted for her crimes.

Liz actually fell in love with Olivia during the experiments in Seattle, and left Nille without telling him. She has travelled with Olivia all over the world as her lover, friend, and research assistant. Liz doesn't want Nille to find out he has a son named Alex, and that she and Olivia are raising him together.

It's up to the Gamemaster to decide if there is indeed a creature that has broken out of NAAB, or if there is a gas leak and the people who have disappeared will be found unconscious near the facility. No matter what, there will not be any evidence giving the public proof of any supernatural events. If OW-1 is used as a creature from another plane, it has Strength 3.

## HOOKS

- The Kids see Nille watching the NAAB facility with binoculars.
- Alex, one of the human test subjects, has managed to escape from NAAB, and has now found shelter in the basement of one of the Kids' houses. There is something odd about him – he seems to have the ability to read minds, but can't remember anything from before he escaped the research station, though he is very scared of going back.
- A classmate disappears near NAAB.

## COUNTDOWN

1. Someone the Kids know disappears near NAAB.
2. With the help of a contact in Military Intelligence, Olivia Martinez takes over the local police station and begins to interrogate people who live in the area around NAAB.
3. A person is found killed. The newspaper says that it was an attack by an animal, probably a bear, but there are no bears in the Loop area.
4. The guards from NAAB break into Nille's home, to find out what he knows and kidnap him. Nille manages to flee, but NAAB steals all his notes and films and starts looking for him.
5. OW-1 attacks one of the Kids.
6. OW-1 finds and kidnaps the human test subject Alex, who fled from NAAB. With the help of Alex, OW-1 manages to return to the Otherworld and close the portal to earth.

## NIKLAS "NILLE" LANDGREN (MIKEY HAYES)

*"Learn to love the darkness Kid, you are going to spend a lot of time together."*

Niklas "Nille" Landgren became a famous artist in the Seventies with his rock band Tangle. When he quit his music career to focus on his art and writing, he met the country singer, Liz, and they moved to Seattle where they lived happily for several years. When Olivia Martinez convinced people in the area to participate in her experiments, Liz was one of the test subjects. She disappeared overnight, and Nille blamed Olivia and has since then hunted her down all over the world, trying to obtain justice and learn the truth. Nille now lives alone in a cottage, which he fills with notes, photos, and articles about Olivia Martinez. Nille has managed to make contact with the police officer Ing-Marie Blankäng, and convinced her that something strange is going on at NAAB.

Nille is a lonely man with a grey beard, a cowboy hat, and a hollow stare. He is often seen sitting outside his cottage playing the guitar and singing. He smokes a pipe, drinks too much, and never goes anywhere without a revolver.

RIKSENERGI

# 08

**RIKSENERGI**

# THE FOUR SEASONS OF MAD SCIENCE

*A scientist scorned by the establishment. A failed experiement. A lust for revenge. These four Mysteries will take the Kids through a tumultous year of strange happenings, weird creatures and even gates to the timespace itself. Welcome to the four seasons of mad science.*

The remaining chapters of this book contain four Mysteries that can be played individually or as a coherent campaign, named *The Four Seasons of Mad Science*.

The first three Mysteries each take about 3-5 hours to play. The Gamemaster can extend them by adding more Locations or setting more scenes from Everyday Life within them. The fourth Mystery, *I, Wagner*, is longer, and will take 2-3 sessions to play. It is intended to be played as the finale of the campaign and not as a standalone Mystery.

The Kids are expected to be living somewhere near Kungsberga on Svartsjölandet [near Boulder City]. The Mysteries have examples of how the Kids may overcome Trouble, but the players may solve the Mysteries in any fashion they like.

## BACKGROUND

The scientist Lena Thelin [Diane Petersen] was a child genius. She excelled at advanced mathematics, won international chess competitions, and managed to breed new varieties of flowers and insects. As a teenager, she was one of the few who understood the principles of the magnetrine effect, and she could grasp some aspects of how the Gravitron works. When the Loop was built by Riksenergi [DARPA], she was one of the first scientists hired. She has since worked in a number of different fields of science, but mainly focused on the link between genetics, neurology, and robotics.

Lena's weakness is her personality, which makes it hard for her to put her intellect to practical use. Because of her inability to finish what she starts and her carelessness and self-absorption, she has never completed any of her often ingenious projects.

RIKSENERGI

A few months ago, she tried, against her manager's direct order, to use the Gravitron to create a black hole. The experiment failed, and was revealed by her superiors. The lead researchers at the Loop decided to evaluate Lena's performance. After they studied her failures, conflicts with colleagues and managers, and inability to follow directives, they decided to offer her compensation in exchange for her resignation. Lena refused, and was eventually fired.

Lena is very bitter, and thinks she was forced to quit because of colleagues who felt threatened by her superior talent. To some extent, she's right – several of her colleagues felt threatened by her and tried to discourage her, but it was not the reason she was released from her job. Lena lacks the ability to see her own shortcomings.

Lena has decided to remain in the Loop area, and use her intellect and knowledge to take revenge on her former bosses and the colleagues who got her fired. She has sold her house in Stenhamra [Boulder City] and settled in an old farm on Adelsö [north of Canyon Point Road], where she has collected a large number of technological devices that she stole during her years at Riksenergi [DARPA]. People who knew her assume that she has left the area and moved somewhere else.

## THE KIDS AND THE CAMPAIGN

As a Gamemaster, you should try to find links between the Kids and Lena. If a parent works as a scientist, she worked with Lena, and may even have been the manager who fired Lena. One of the Kids may be a relative of Lena. Put conversations and rumors about Lena in the background of scenes throughout the campaign. Lena has become a laughingstock among the locals.

The campaign takes place over the course of a year, and each Mystery is set during one of the four seasons.

Keep in mind that the Kids grow older and their lives change. The Four Mysteries are called *Summer Break and Killer Birds, Grown-up Attraction, Creatures From the Cretaceous* and *I, Wagner.*

---

### SETTING THE MOOD

In each Mystery, there is a text about the Mood of the Season. The text is not meant to be read out loud, but to inspire you when you set the mood and set scenes related to the season.

RIKSENERGI

# SUMMER BREAK AND KILLER BIRDS

*Summertime. Neverending days spent roaming the countryside look-ing for something to do. Boredom and bliss in equal measure.  But underneath the sweet Swedish summer, something stirs. Something is wrong. It begins with a talking bird, and soon the Kids are involved in a nefarious plot. Can they solve the Mystery before it is too late?*

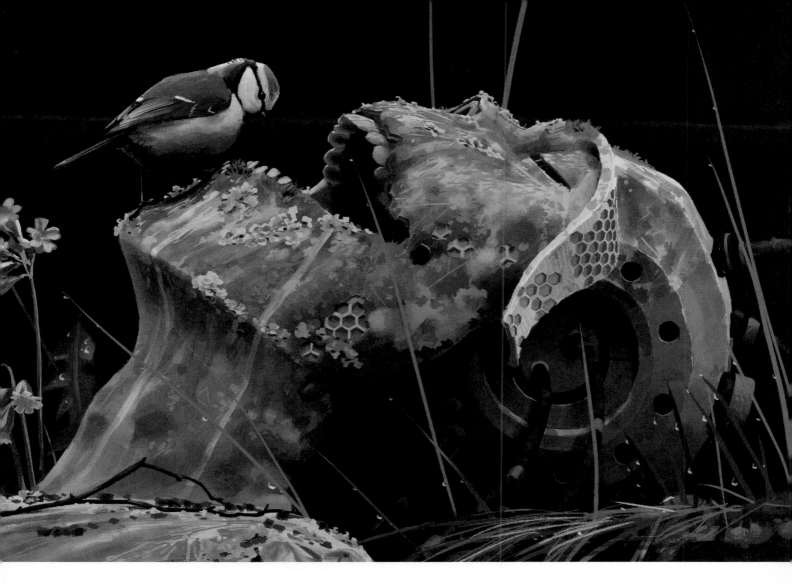

This is an introductory Mystery that is designed for newly created Kids.

## THE TRUTH OF
## THE MYSTERY

The disgraced scientist Lena Thelin has decided to take revenge on her former colleagues and managers at Riksenergi [DARPA]. She has captured wild birds and enhanced them with cybernetics so as to train them to attack people at her command. Lena has made her former sidekick at Riksenergi, Gunnar Granat [Donald Dixon], resign and help her with her plans.

Gunnar is hopelessly in love with Lena, and she has convinced him that Riksenergi has treated her horribly. Gunnar moved out of his house on the outskirts of Kungsberga [Boulder City] and, much to Lena's displeasure, moved in with her at her farm on Adelsö [north of Canyon Point Road]. Rumors are spreading that he quit his job and left home to go on a long romantic vacation abroad with Lena.

Gunnar and Lena found the wreck of a magnetrine ship on an island in the Nordiska Gobi [Sentinel Island] and made it their workshop. Here, they caught the birds and implanted chips in their heads with the help of a machine.

At first, both Lena and Gunnar thought their work with the birds would not only lead to revenge, but also to scientific advances that would make both of them famous. However, the experiments did not turn out as planned. Lena's carelessness and impatience led to some of the birds gaining a form of human intelligence and the ability to engage in simple speech,

RIKSENERGI

while others became aggressive, and attacked Lena and Gunnar. Lena gave up the experiment and left the workshop in the old ship, so as to allow the manipulated birds to die of hunger. She also told Gunnar to stay on the ship and watch over the workshop, with the true purpose to get him out of her life and not disturb her anymore. To make sure he doesn't follow her, she blocked the door with a metal beam.

The birds in the magnetrine ship didn't die. Instead, Gunnar fed them and let them out into the wild. He is obsessed with Lena and continues their experiment, in the hope of proving his worth to her. By now, he is quite insane. He continues to catch birds and implants microchips in them, creating even more manipulated birds using the machine that he and Lena built, waiting for Lena to return. Which she never will.

The birds have begun to spread across northern Munsö and Svartsjölandet [Boulder Beach]. The birds that have become aggressive are seagulls, black-headed gulls, great cormorants, and a goshawk. The Goshawk is the leader of these Killer Birds, which have started to attack animals. It is only a matter of time before they begin attacking humans. The only birds manipulated by the machines that haven't become aggressive are pigeons. Instead, they have development rudimentary intelligence and the ability to speak with a human-like voice. Because they refuse to submit to the Goshawk, they have been driven away by the other birds, and started to build their own nests in northern Svartsjölandet.

If the Kids somehow show the birds or Lena's machine to adults, such as their teachers or the police, the adults won't believe that the implants made the birds attack, and the machine won't work anymore. The Kids are on their own.

The Mystery is about the Kids finding out what has happened to the Birds, and stopping Gunnar from creating more Killer Birds.

## SUMMER ON THE MÄLAREN ISLANDS

It's summer break, the sun is up almost around the clock, and it's very hot. Birches, pines, ferns, and blackberry thickets cover the landscape. Mosquitoes plague those who venture out into the thickets and woods where rabbits, foxes, and deer attend to their newly born. Along the shore, one can see small fish and flies that thrive in the seaweed. Children pick flowers and sorrel, swim and play tag. Teenagers stay up all night, drink beer and race souped-up mopeds, try snuff for the first time, and make out in badly pitched tents. The gardens smell of barbecues and fresh paint on the picket fences. The Swedish flag flies from flagpoles, and the radio program *Summer* can be heard from the verandas at 1 pm every day. Freshly caught fish from one of the fishermen down at the harbor, home-grown new potatoes, and strawberries are eaten in large quantities. At the kiosk, the GB-clown tempts young and old with ice cream, Storstrut, and Lakritspuck.

## (SUMMER IN BOULDER CITY)

Most smart people don't go out into the heat of Boulder City in the dead of summer. The average high temperature on such days reaches over 100°F (38°C), and it can spike much higher. That's how it works in the desert, which sees less than six inches of rain all year long. It is, as people like to say, a dry heat, but once you can fry an egg on the sidewalk outside your home, it doesn't matter if the heat's dry or wet.

In the '80s, many people don't have air conditioning in their homes, and just have to tough out the heat with electric fans or swimming pools. Some escape to the comfort of shopping malls or supermarkets for the air conditioning. In the evenings – after dusk, once the temperatures begin to drop – folks emerge from their homes, and drink in the cooler air for a bit of relief. Until then, though, it's far better to stay inside and play games.

## INTRODUCING THE KIDS

Set a scene for each of the Kids in their Everyday Lives with or without Trouble. You can ask the players for ideas, or look at their character sheets. Use these scenes to set the mood. In the background, an adult mentions

or makes a joke about Lena and Gunnar and their alleged "love vacation."

You should ask the players a lot of questions before and during the scenes. Let the players describe what things look like, and how the Kids perceive people in their surroundings. Don't try to control the scenes, but let them play out naturally. The players should be given space to describe and play their Kids. The scenes don't need Trouble, but if it comes up, the Kids may try to overcome it, and the players can roll the dice for a skill.

### EXAMPLE

**The Gamemaster:** *Okay, let's start the first session of Tales From the Loop. You all have your Kids. It is the first of four Mysteries in a campaign, so if we want to we can keep on playing when this one is finished. It's summer break, and the weather is very hot. You eat a lot of ice cream, and get to roam the island as you please. Today, there is no wind and it's baking hot. Who wants the first scene?*

**Player 1 (Olle):** *I can go first, but I don't have any idea for a scene.*

**The Gamemaster:** *No problem. (Looks at the character sheet.) Okay, Olle, it's one of those days when your mom seems almost normal. Your father is at work. The smell of freshly baked cinnamon buns fills the house as she calls your name. I guess you are on the second floor.*

**Player 1:** *No, I'm in the garden practicing penalty shots at the wall. I put down the ball, take off my shoes, and go into the kitchen. "That smells good, mom."*

**The Gamemaster:** *She smiles at you. "Do you want milk or soda?"*

**Player 1:** *"Soda."*

**The Gamemaster:** *She puts down the book in a foreign language that she's reading, probably about something complicated like Italian renaissance painters, and opens the fridge and gives you the can.*

Typical scenes when introducing the Kids:

- A Kid is having supper with her family.
- A Kid is talking on the telephone with her boyfriend, who seems to be sad but doesn't tell her why.
- A Kid is told to mow the lawn, and gets a chance to sneak away from the chore.
- A Kid is caught in the middle of an argument between her parents.
- A Kid is riding her bike to the beach with another Kid.
- A Kid finds her older sister drinking beer.
- A Kid is talking to a friend who wants them to shoplift from the supermarket.

RIKSENERGI

## INTRODUCING THE MYSTERY

One or more of the Kids will hear pigeons talking to each other or to the Kids. The pigeons talk with mechanical bird voices. Although they have become more intelligent, they are still dumb animals driven by urges. They ask for food, discuss how to steal shiny trinkets for their nest, look for a good breeding place, or argue about a partner. The Kids can hear the birds while playing in the garden, hanging out in the Hideout or riding their bikes. Make sure that no adult is present. Wait for the players' reactions. If they do nothing, the birds fly away. Remind the players of their Kids' Drives.

If a Kid catches and examines a pigeon and rolls **CALCULATE**, she sees small stitches on the head of the bird, and signs of a microchip having been inserted.

A Kid studying the pigeons and making a **COMPREHEND** roll realizes that the pigeons seem to be working in groups in a way that is very unusual for birds. They help each other carry off heavy branches, and they seem to work together to look for food. The Kid also understands that an ornithologist or a good library is needed to understand more. The ornithologist Mats Tingblad [Christopher Boyd] lives in a secluded house nearby.

RIKSENERGI

It's rumored that he has gone mad, and once broke his legs when he tried to jump off a cliff wearing a bird costume. Some say he tried to take his life. The Kids can follow the pigeons if they make **MOVE** rolls, and will then find the Pigeons' Nest, described below.

*EXAMPLE*

**The Gamemaster:** *All of the Kids have been introduced, so let's move on. Where are you when you start to find out about the Mystery?*
**Player 2 (Anita):** *Could we be in our Hideout, under the bridge?*
**The Gamemaster:** *Sure! Tell me about the Hideout.*
**Player 1 (Olle):** *I guess it's an old bridge that's not used anymore, except by us kids. It goes over a small creek that has almost been completely overgrown. We can sneak in under the bridge without being seen, and there we have built a hut.*
**The Gamemaster:** *You are all sitting in the Hideout under the bridge when you hear a funny voice from above you. (Makes her voice sound funny.) "I found some corn, I found*

*some corn, happy me, I found some corn." And then another darker, but still strange, voice. "Lucky you, lucky you. I never have no luck. Poooor me, poooor me!!!"* What do you do?

### THE KILLER BIRDS ATTACK

During the Mystery, the Killer Birds become more aggressive. You should advance the Countdown one step when it feels appropriate. The first step should come quickly, perhaps even the scene after the Mystery is introduced. You can let the Kids hear about the events, or be there to see them and be given a chance to help or even be attacked.

You can create tension by letting birds that have not been manipulated gather in the trees. These birds are stressed by the Killer Birds, screaming from the treetops, and circling in large flocks in the sky. It may be a mystery in itself as to which birds are dangerous.

## SOLVING THE MYSTERY

The Mystery takes place in northwestern Svartsjölandet and Nordiska Gobi on Munsö [in and around Lake Mead]. When the Kids travel between the Locations, it can be Trouble to get hold of a boat or you can simply move on to the next scene, assuming the Kids made it there somehow. While the Kids are investigating what happened to the birds and visit different Locations, the Killer Birds start attacking people.

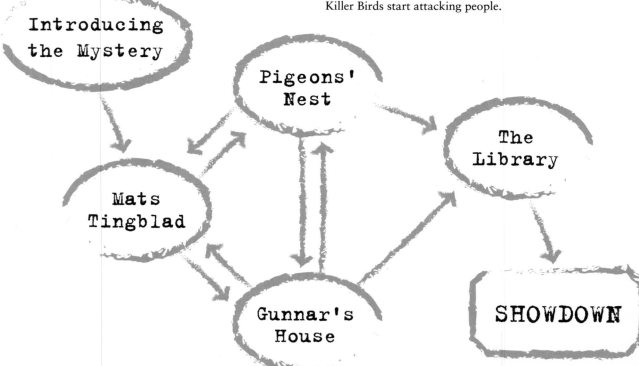

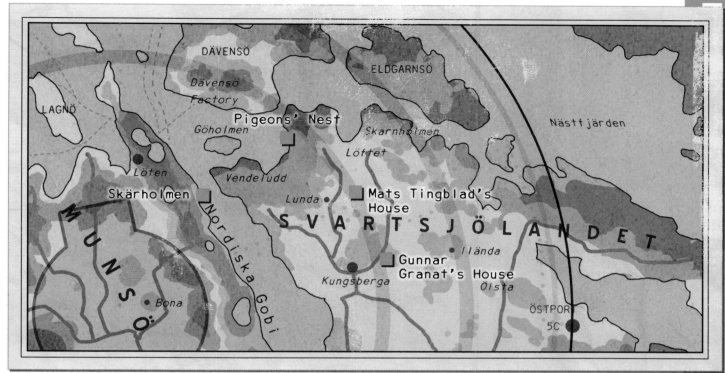

The Countdown (see the boxed text) shows what happens step by step. You should mix scenes where the Kids investigate with scenes where they see or hear about the birds' attacks and scenes from Everyday Life (the Kids have to go home to eat, or meet people as they move through the area).

### EXAMPLE

**The Gamemaster:** *So, you fail your* **MOVE** *roll, which means the birds get away and you can't keep up with them. What do you do?*

**Player 2 (Anita):** *Can I roll* **CONTACT** *to get in touch with someone who knows about birds?*

**The Gamemaster:** *Sure.*

**Player 2:** *(Rolls the Dice.) Success!*

**The Gamemaster:** *You've heard of this strange man, Mats Tingblad. He was once a celebrity on TV talking about birds, until he had an accident. He was bitten by a swan. Afterwards, he became afraid of birds. He is a loner, living isolated in a house close by.*

**Player 2:** *Can we go there?*

**The Gamemaster:** *Of course. You ride your bikes to his house, and park them out front.*

## COUNTDOWN

1. A large number of dead birds are found. They are common birds without microchips, seen as competitors by the Killer Birds. Even some dead dogs and cats are found. Maybe one of the Kids' pets?

2. A young person, perhaps someone the Kids know, is attacked by seagulls, and badly hurt. She takes refuge in a phone booth and the Birds try to get in until a farmer shoots at them with a shotgun, chasing them off.

3. A large group of Killer Birds gather in a playground. The children flee into their houses. The birds attack the houses through open windows and chimneys. Several people are injured, maybe even killed.

4. A large group of Birds attack the Kids or their families.

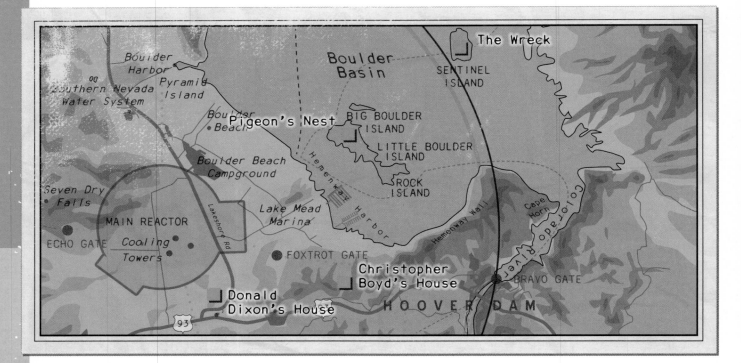

*The house is next to a meadow, with high grass and a lot of flowers. The house is dark and two stories high. It is surrounded by a high metal fence with a gate. A lot of birds sit on the house, and the windows seem covered by bird droppings. What do you do?*
**Player 1 (Olle):** *I open the gate and go inside.*
**The Gamemaster:** *It's locked.*

# LOCATION 1: THE ORNITHOLOGIST'S HOUSE

Mats Tingblad [Christopher Boyd] lives in a solitary wooden house east of Lunda [Lakeshore Road]. The house is hedged by a high metal fence with a locked gate. The garden is overgrown, and everywhere there are birdhouses and bird feeders. The house is two stories high, narrow and tilted alarmingly. At the top, there is a balcony. The roof has a variety of perches for birds. All the windows have lockable shutters. It smells of bird droppings and mould. The house is full of old newspapers, birdcages with parrots, cockatiels, budgies, and a free-flying crow that often lands on Mats head.

It is common knowledge that the ornithologist Mats Tingblad lives here. He was previously a celebri-ty on a nature program on Swedish Television [NBC], but has now become a recluse. The players can roll **COMPREHEND** or **CONTACT** to find him, or you may let the Kids already know about him or hear someone mention him. If they fail a roll to find him, they still find him, but he's in an extremely bad mood, and certainly doesn't want to help the Kids.

### TROUBLE

To get into the house, the Kids have to climb the fence or open the locked gate somehow. Mats is inside the house, but will not open the door if they knock. He has recently been attacked by the Killer Birds, and has dried blood all over his upper body and gaping wounds on his face. He is chasing his pet birds around the house to kill them with an axe. Mats thinks that the time has come when all birds will attack humans. The Kids can see him moving around through the windows on the upper floor. The front door is locked, but it is possible to open the windows on the top floors from outside. If the Kids climb up the wall of the house, they need to roll **MOVE**.

Mats is very worried about the aggressive birds. He sees no reason to help the Kids if they don't somehow persuade him, which they can do with **CHARM**. A Kid who makes an **EMPATHIZE** roll understands that

Mats is very worried about what will happen when the birds become legion and spread. The simplest way to reach him is to make him understand that the Kids can stop the Killer Birds from spreading. It is impossible to persuade Mats to leave his house, as he is terrified of the birds.

## CLUES

Mats understands that someone has tampered with the birds, and made them aggressive and intelligent. He has noticed that pigeons seem to have developed speech instead of aggression. Mats has counted the birds and seen that they are steadily increasing in number, and that they seem to be organizing themselves into increasingly larger groups that are taking control of the wildlife in the area. It is only a matter of time before they attack people and animals. Mats believes that there must be a person or a machine that is manipulating the birds. If this isn't stopped, the Mälaren Islands [Boulder] are facing a disaster that will soon spread and potentially threaten the entire country.

Mats has met the scientist Gunnar Granat [Donald Dixon] on several occasions, and knows that Gunnar is an expert on the neurology of birds.

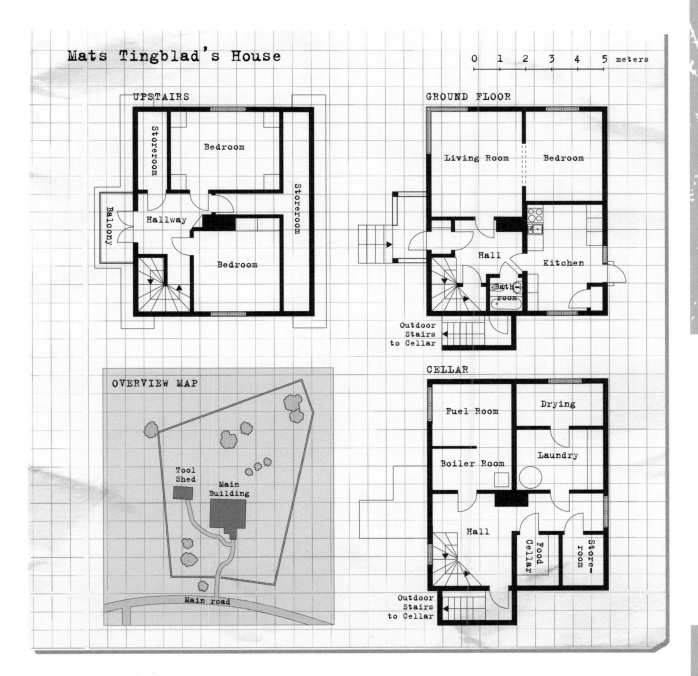

RIKSENERGI

Mats also knows that Gunnar recently left his house on the outskirts of Kungsberga [Boulder City] and disappeared. Mats suspects Gunnar of somehow being connected to the Killer Birds.

Mats has noticed that many of the pigeons are moving north, and he suspects they are building a great nest there. He also noted that several of the aggressive birds are flying out over the water, and believes they have their nest on Munsö or on one of the smaller islands north of Svartsjölandet [Big Boulder Island]. Mats has seen a goshawk hovering over the other Killer Birds, and believes it to be the leader. He thinks that it can lead the Kids to the birds' habitat.

## LOCATION 2: THE PIGEONS' NEST

The Kids can find their way to the Pigeons' Nest by pursuing a pigeon, or by talking to the ornithologist Mats Tingblad [Christopher Boyd] or with Majsan [Stacey] at Gunnar Granat's house.

A hundred pigeons have settled on the northern part of Svartsjölandet on a cliff overlooking Spånviken [Big Boulder Island]. They are building a huge nest of branches, pieces of metal, and glass shards, and will defend it in large numbers against other birds, predators, and humans. The pigeons constantly talk to each other about the quality of the building materials, and they fight over mating and food. Their voices are metallic, and their words interspersed with chirping.

The nest is being watched by groups of gulls, black-headed gulls, and great cormorants that attack unwary pigeons, pecking them to death. With a successful **COMPREHEND** roll, a Kid understands that the Killer Birds are trying to take control over the pigeons who are working together to protect the nest and each other. If the Kids study the Killer Birds, they suddenly fly away, as if they heard a command, and disappear out over the water.

### TROUBLE

It is a hard to climb up to the nest. The Kids need to pass sharp rocks and tall cliffs. They have to roll **MOVE** or **SNEAK** to get close to the nest without being seen. If the pigeons spot the Kids, they become quiet and gather around the nest. Groups of pigeons begin to circle in the air above the Kids. If the Kids continue forward, the pigeons attack them. The Kids have no choice but to leave, and must roll **FORCE** or **MOVE**, suffering a Condition if they fail.

### CLUES

The nest is constructed of a variety of branches and objects stolen from the north of Svartsjölandet and Nordiska Gobi [Sentinel Island]. In the nest, there are also several rusted metal pieces from the magnetrine ship where Lena and Gunnar created the birds. Kids who successfully **INVESTIGATE** will find a piece of metal that is labeled IEX-4Z32. With a successful **COMPREHEND** or **CALCULATE** roll, the Kids will understand that this is the identification number of a magnetrine ship. With the help of a library, they can find out which ship and where it is.

When the Kids leave the Pigeons' Nest, they see a young woman several hundred meters away watching the birds through binoculars. She gets up, and rides off on a bike heading south. This is Maja "Majsan" Sivertsson [Stacey Johnson]. If the Kids follow her, she will lead them to Gunnar Granat's [Donald Dixon's] abandoned house near Kungsberga [near Boulder Beach].

## LOCATION 3: GUNNAR'S ABANDONED HOUSE

The Kids can get to Gunnar's [Donald's] house by listening to adults talk about his animal experiments, by talking to the ornithologist Mats Tingblad [Christopher Boyd] or by following "Majsan" [Stacey] from the Pigeons' Nest. They can also be saved by Majsan and her dog when they are attacked by birds, and invited to "her" house.

The House is a two-story, yellow brick house with red roof tiles. Gunnar was bewildered by Lena's invitation to help her with her experiments with birds, and left his house immediately without cleaning or emptying the fridge or taking out the garbage. The house is messy and dirty. Everywhere, there are cables, tools, and strange drawings. The bookshelves are filled with books about birds, neurology, and animal behavior, but also books about love, courting, and how to make that special someone notice you.

The living room walls have a dozen framed photographs of famous scientists. Next to Einstein hangs a photo of Lena [Diane], a middle-aged woman with curly blonde hair, white clothes, and a proud gaze. On her lab coat, there is a pin with the Yin and Yang symbols. On a VHS player lies a copy of Alfred Hitchcock's movie *The Birds*. All over the house, there are framed photographs of Lena and Gunnar, with Gunnar often in the background, smiling insecurely and looking at Lena.

For the last few months, 15-year-old "Majsan" has been secretly living in the house. She comes from central Stockholm [Las Vegas], and has run away from home because of her controlling and intrusive stepdad. Majsan has brought her dog, the wire-haired dachshund Bullen [Ham], who is fat and happy, and protects Majsan with great zeal. Bullen is limping on one leg after being beaten by the stepdad.

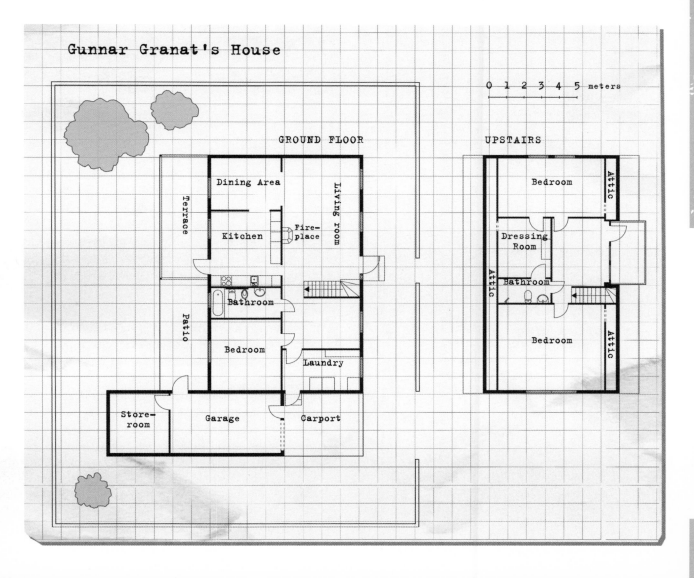

Gunnar Granat's House

0 1 2 3 4 5 meters

GROUND FLOOR

Dining Area

Terrace

Kitchen

Fireplace

Living room

Bathroom

Patio

Bedroom

Laundry

Storeroom

Garage

Carport

UPSTAIRS

Bedroom

Attic

Dressing Room

Attic

Bathroom

Bedroom

Attic

RIKSENERGI

## THE LIBRARY

If the Kids want to get more information, they can go to the school library. The public library in Stenhamra [Boulder City] is closed for the summer. The school is also closed for summer, but there are several doors and windows that can be opened by the Kids without much effort. The School Library is described in The Mystery Landscape (page 101).

In the library, the Kids can get information with a successful **COMPREHEND** roll. They can find out that the magnetrine ship with ID code IEX-4Z32 was previously used to transport ore in northern Russia, but it was scrapped a few years ago, and is now located on an island in the Nordiska Gobi [Sentinel Island]. A map indicates that the island is called Skärholmen and is located in the middle of Nordiska Gobi.

If the Kids try to get information about the birds or the microchip, they learn that the Killer Birds are behaving very abnormally. They should not cooperate, talk, or attack other animals and humans. However, the bodies of the birds should sooner or later reject the microchips, killing the birds.

If the Kids fail their roll, they still get the information, but they are detected by "Prutte" (page 103), and must escape or explain themselves. Caught by Prutte, he will keep them in school and call their parents, asking them to pick them up. He will explain his presence at the school as being due to broken pipes in the basement.

Another way to find the magnetrine ship IEX-4Z32 is to use the **CONTACT** skill to talk with someone who has knowledge of ships and ID numbers. Let the players decide who it is and roll the dice.

Majsan has paid attention to the Killer Birds since she was attacked by a group of gulls. She has killed a bird which she has examined with a knife, a pair of pliers, and some scissors on Gunnar's kitchen table. Majsan is related to Gunnar. He is her uncle, and she used to visit him as a child. She suspects him of somehow being responsible for the Killer Birds, but she doesn't know where he is.

Majsan misses her little sister. If things turn out well with the Kids, she may consider becoming a pretend sister to one of them, and may well be included as an NPC in future Mysteries.

### TROUBLE

If the Kids try to get into Gunnar's house, they have to sneak past a couple of neighbors who, after seeing Majsan sneak around, have taken it upon themselves to keep the area safe. They take turns patrolling on bike paths and trails. The front door of the house is locked. It is possible to get in through the high fence at the back of the house, so as to prevent people seeing into the garden or the house. The patio door has been left unlocked.

Majsan will hide at first, but if the Kids go into the house she lets Bullen loose, who comes rushing in with loud barks. She steps forward with a kitchen knife, and screams at them to leave or she will hurt them.

She tells them to keep quiet about her living there, if they know what is best for them.

The Kids can make her change her mind with a successful **CHARM** roll. Using **EMPATHIZE**, they realize that she is very lonely, and scared of being discovered and sent home. She would really like to get to know other people. "Majsan" doesn't, under any circumstances, trust adults. She will not follow the Kids to Nordiska Gobi [Sentinel Island] for fear of being seen by adults.

### CLUES

Majsan knows about the Pigeons' Nest and understands that the pigeons are not dangerous. Majsan knows about the ornithologist, Mats Tingblad, and thinks that he knows more, but she has not talked to him.

Among Gunnar's things, there are drawings of birds and microchips. Those who manage to study them and roll successfully on **CALCULATE**, see that they are meant to be used to build a machine that will attract birds automatically, and modify them. The chips

are supposed to let a person control the birds, but the blueprints seem to be missing details on how that control will work – as if the person who made the drawings stopped in the middle of the work.

Hidden under Gunnar's bed can be found his diary. He writes about his work at the Loop facility. In many places in Gunnar's notes, he writes about his love for the amazing Lena, who is not only beautiful but also a genius scientist who will one day win the Nobel Prize. He writes about the colleagues who don't understand Lena, and work against her and treat her badly. Gunnar describes his monumental sadness when she was forced to quit her job. But a couple of weeks later, he is overwhelmed with happiness as Lena has asked him to work with him on a new experiment in a place called "IEX-4Z32." A Kid who makes a **COMPREHEND** or **CALCULATE** roll knows that it is the ID number of a magnetrine ship, but she must study at a library to get more information.

## THE SHOWDOWN

Nordiska Gobi is an area of islands in the northeastern part of Munsö [Boulder Basin] with a large amount of debris and remnants of various technological marvels. The water is full of rusty pieces with razor sharp edges, ships half-submerged in the water, and strange domes, circular towers, and magnetrine disks. A rich wildlife previously lived here, but when the Kids enter this area, it is quiet and still. In the distance, the Killer Birds can be seen patrolling the skies.

The wreck of the magnetrine ship IEX-4Z32 lies on the small island of Skärholmen [Sentinel Island]. The Kids must either swim (requires a **MOVE** roll) to get there or find a boat of some kind (rolling for **TINKER** or **CONTACT**).

IEX-4Z32 is a 25-meter-long wreck, lying tilted to one side. The ship was previously painted black, but is now largely rust-colored. Rainwater can be seen collected in the magnetrine discs. On the old antennas, birds sit looking out over the water. On the side of the ship, close to the ground, there is a door that is blocked from the outside by a metal beam. If opened, it slides to the side revealing stairs leading up. Birds fly in and out of the wreckage through vents. Machine fans and bird chirping can be heard from inside the ship.

Just inside the door, there is a machine room and storage facilities. The Kids have to climb up through the tilted ship to the cockpit at the top of the vessel, where Lena and Gunnar have built a machine with multiple bird feeders filled with bird food. The machine looks like an arcade game, with blinking lights and long metallic arms. The machine is powered by a large generator with a battery. There are hundreds of birds here, and every surface is covered by bird droppings, feathers and carcasses of dead birds. There are also a number of tools to be found in the room that can be used as weapons (+1 bonus).

RIKSENERGI

## LUCKY BREAK

If the players get stuck in the scenario, and don't know what to do or where to go next, you can use this Lucky Break (page 85): One of the Kids sees the Goshawk chasing and killing a rabbit. It then flies towards Nordiska Gobi. The Kids may follow it to the Showdown.

RIKSENERGI

Gunnar lives in a small storage room, close to the cockpit with a half-eaten package of Mariekex [crackers] and an almost empty bottle of Trocadero [soda]. This is where he spends his time when he's not using the machine to transform more birds. If Gunnar spots the Kids, he will stay hidden and spy on them until they reach the cockpit. Then he will appear, threatening to kill them if they don't leave. Gunnar is very dirty and his body is covered by small wounds from the birds' pecking. His hair and beard are unkempt and his eyes are glazed over with an insane stare. He looks like – and is – a madman. He expresses both love and hate for Lena, his "beloved," but does not reveal her name.

### EXAMPLE

**The Gamemaster:** *You manage to haul the metal beam off to the side, and open the door without being seen. The door opens, gliding to the side with a soft sound. From inside, comes the smell of bird droppings. The ladder inside leads up at an angle because the ship is lying tilted on the ground.*

**Player 2 (Anita):** *I slowly climb inside, listening to hear where the machine is, but also taking care not to be heard.*

**Gamemaster:** *Roll* SNEAK. *In fact, all of you should roll, since I guess all of you will be climbing inside, right?*

**Player 1 (Olle) and 3 (Dennis):** *Yes.*

**Player 2:** *Success, and one extra success.*

**Player 3:** *Can I get help from your extra success? My roll failed.*

**Player 2:** *Sure!*

**The Gamemaster:** *How do you help him?*

**Player 2:** *Dennis is about to trip on a wire sticking out from the wall when I hiss at him, "Watch it!"*

**The Gamemaster:** *Okay, you all succeed, and you crawl and climb up inside the ship. You hear sounds from the top of the ship, in the cockpit. There are several birds, and one that sounds like a bird of prey. What do you do?*

### TROUBLE

To avoid being spotted by patrolling birds on the way to Skärholmen [Sentinel Island], Kids need to make **SNEAK** rolls. Failing this roll requires them to make **MOVE** rolls to get away, and if they fail again they will suffer a Condition. They will also suffer a Condition if they fail a roll for **FORCE** in order to haul away the metal beam from in front of the door.

Sneaking through the ship to the cockpit without being spotted by Gunnar requires a **SNEAK** roll for each Kid. If any of the Kids fail their roll, Gunnar will notice them. He will call for the Goshawk using the machine, and he will be waiting for the Kids in the cockpit. If all of the Kids make their **SNEAK** rolls, Gunnar will be caught by surprise and emerge from the storage room only when the Kids have reached the cockpit. Then he will call for the Goshawk, which arrives after a few minutes to attack the Kids. Lots of smaller Killer Birds will follow the Goshawk in battle. The confrontation with Gunnar and the Goshawk counts as Extended Trouble (page 70). The Threat Level is normal (twice the number of Kids) if Kids surprise Gunnar, but hard (three times the number of Kids) is they failed their **SNEAK** rolls.

Gunnar can be handled in several different ways. The Kids can **CHARM** him to make him see the error of his ways, they can use **FORCE** to wrestle him to the ground, or **TINKER** or **PROGRAM** to break the bird machine. To deal with the Goshawk and the rest of the Killer Birds, the Kids can, for example, use **MOVE** to outrun them, or **FORCE** to fight the birds' onslaught. Reward players who think up creative ways of dealing with the threat.

## Magnetrine Ship IEX-4Z32

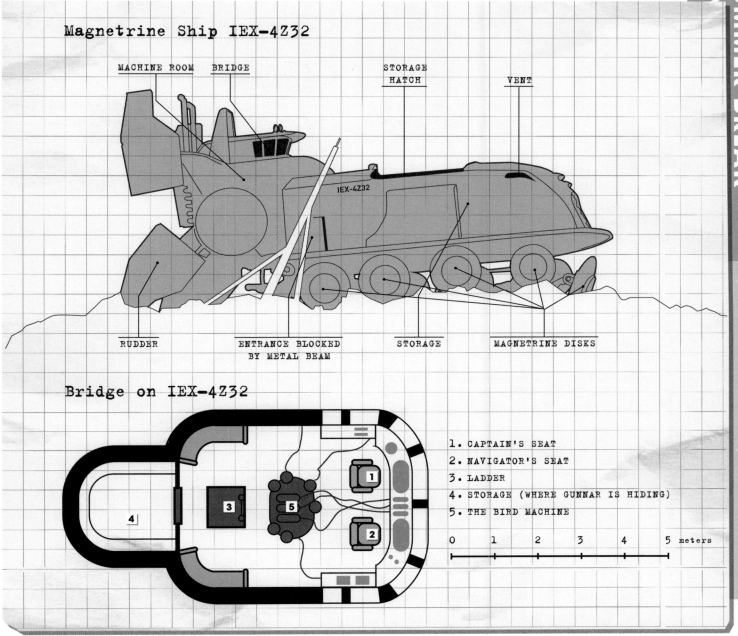

MACHINE ROOM    BRIDGE                STORAGE
                                      HATCH              VENT

IEX-4Z32

RUDDER          ENTRANCE BLOCKED      STORAGE         MAGNETRINE DISKS
                BY METAL BEAM

## Bridge on IEX-4Z32

1. CAPTAIN'S SEAT
2. NAVIGATOR'S SEAT
3. LADDER
4. STORAGE (WHERE GUNNAR IS HIDING)
5. THE BIRD MACHINE

0    1    2    3    4    5 meters

If the Kids succeed, Gunnar will break down in tears, the machine will break down, the birds will be chased off, or a combination of the above. In any case, the scourge of the killer birds is over. The Kids have stopped the production of Killer Birds, and those that exist will soon die of infections caused by the microchips.

If the Kids didn't kill the Goshawk, it will be seen soaring over the Loop area in future Mysteries, and it might even nest near the Kids' homes.

If the Kids fail to overcome the Extended Trouble, they will be chased off the ship by Gunnar and the birds. A wave of Killer Birds will haunt the area for the entire summer, causing severe problems until the machine eventually breaks down by itself.

### THE GOSHAWK

The Goshawk has the special attribute SHARP BEAK 2 (see page 69), but this is only used if a Kid confronts it outside of the Extended Trouble.

RIKSENERGI

## AFTER THE SHOWDOWN

Even if the Kids manage to stop Gunnar, he will never admit to what he has done. The technology of the bird machine is strange, and even if the Kids show it to some adults, they won't believe it had anything to do with the bird attacks.

Most of the birds with implants will escape. Even if the Kids manage to catch one and show it to the police, they won't connect it to the bird attacks.

Gunnar will not tell anyone about Lena or her part in what has happened. His love for her is strong, but he has finally understood that she will never love him back. Gunnar will, in the coming months, leave his house and move away from the area. He will let Majsan live in his house as long as she wants to.

## AFTERMATH

The Kids now get a scene each from Everyday Life, with or without Trouble. The player may choose a scene, or ask the Gamemaster to set up a scene. If the group is short on time, each player can give a brief snapshot of a moment in the Kid's everyday life instead.

> *EXAMPLE*
> **The Gamemaster:** *I'd like to set a last scene for Olle, in which his mom is not feeling well, but I don't have any ideas.*
> **Player 1 (Olle):** *She is waiting for me when I come home, mad at me for plotting against her with dad. In her mind, we hate her.*
> **The Gamemaster:** *Ah, great... Okay, it's getting dark as you bike to your house knowing you have done a great thing. You can see your mother waiting in the driveway, dressed in winter clothes. When you wave at her she doesn't respond, as if she hasn't seen you.*
> **Player 1:** *"Hi mom!" I try to hug her gently.*
> **The Gamemaster:** *She doesn't let you. "Where have you been?" She doesn't let you answer. "I know what you've been doing! You and your father hate me, you hate all women because we are smarter than you! You want me locked up in that house, washing your dirty underwear and cooking your food!"*

## CHANGE

You and the players should go through the character sheets together, and figure out if the Kids have changed in some way. The players may, if they want to, change their Problem, Pride, Iconic Items and Relationships. Ask questions about Experience out loud (page 88). Remember, each Kid gets 1 XP for each affirmative answer. If they get 5 XP, they may raise a skill one level.

## NPCS

This section describes the NPCs that the Kids might meet in this Mystery.

**MATS TINGBLAD (CHRISTOPHER BOYD)**

*"The woodpecker strikes with its sharp beak eight to ten times a second. It can make holes in cement. Imagine what would happen if it attacked your skull."*

Mats Tingblad has loved birds since he was a child. He became a well-known figure on a nature program on television, but was bitten by a swan. No one knows if it was fear after the bite or the wound infection that changed Mats, but he became introverted, paranoid, and terrified of the birds he once loved. He lost his job, his wife, and lost touch with his children and friends.

Mats is still obsessed with birds, and surrounds himself with birdcages, LPs with bird calls, posters with birds, and books about birds. But instead of studying them with love, he looks at them with horror. Mats is convinced that sooner or later, the birds will join forces and attack mankind. He wants to be as prepared as possible and know his enemies.

Mats is a large bald man with a big beard. He has huge hands but a thin, almost girlish voice. He is dressed in dirty wildlife clothes, and has a pair of binoculars and a notepad ready at hand.

### "MAJSAN" SIVERTSSON (STACEY JOHNSON)

*"Don't tell your parents, they will send me home."*

15-year-old Majsan grew up with a single mother working two jobs and a little sister in central Stockholm [Las Vegas]. She is tough and hard to scare. Yet that's exactly what happened. The mother's new boyfriend is a violent man, who took the opportunity to come on to Majsan as soon as they were home alone. Very soon, Majsan couldn't take it any longer. She took her dog, the dachshund Bullen [Ham], and fled to the Mälaren Islands [Boulder City] where her uncle Gunnar [Donald] lives, whom she used to visit on summer vacations as a child. Now, she hides in Gunnar's abandoned house, and lives on what she has found in the pantry. She suspects that her uncle Gunnar is somehow connected to the Killer Birds. Majsan was attacked by a group of gulls, and she has taken up the fight against the birds. She avoids talking to adults; she doesn't want to be sent home. At night, she screams in her dreams.

Majsan is a tanned and wiry young woman, with her blonde hair full of hairspray. She wears colorful sun-glasses, a shirt with Minnie Mouse on it, and constantly chews gum or smokes. She misses her little sister, Tove, and might "adopt" one of the Kids.

### GUNNAR GRANAT (DONALD DIXON)

*"She is the most brilliant scientist ever born!"*

Gunnar is a man shaped by a childhood filled with bullying, violence, and loneliness. He has always been shunned by other people, and expects nothing else. Only in science has he found a safe and welcoming haven. Gunnar is a biologist who specializes in bird neurology. He has worked many years at the Loop, constructing cyborg brain implants. When he met Lena, he instantly fell in love with her, and started to follow her around like a puppy. She used him, but never gave him any sign of appreciation. Gunnar thought she had finally fallen in love with him when she asked him to quit his job and work with her on her bird experiments. Now, he's realizing that yet again, he's been used. Gunnar hasn't had any contact with Majsan for years. He loves her like his own child, but doesn't really know how to show his feelings to her.

Gunnar is a thin, middle-aged man with untidy, long, blond hair. He dresses in an extremely dirty science lab coat and lisps when he speaks.

RIKSENERGI

**131**

RIKSENERGI

# GROWN-UP ATTRACTION

*The autumn wind is brisk and chilly. The calm of everyday life settles over the area. But something else is in the air. A taste of something forbidden, something unnaturally tempting. The Kids notice how adults behave strangely, becoming victims of desire. Can the nefarious plot be stopped in time or will the grown-ups go willingly to their own doom?*

This is a Mystery that can be played over the course of one session. It can be used as the second part of the *Four Seasons of Mad Science* campaign.

## THE TRUTH OF THE MYSTERY

The scientist Lena Thelin [Diane Peterson] has wanted to take revenge on her former colleagues and managers at Riksenergi ever since she was fired because of her inability to complete projects and her unwillingness to obey instructions.

Lena has invented a machine that has the ability to attract people, making them want to stay close to it and protect it, and arousing their most primitive instincts, aggression, hierarchical thinking, and sexuality. Lena's plan was to place her invention, which she calls the Artificial Attachment Node (the ArAN), on Svartsjölandet [Boulder Beach], so all the adults on the Mälaren Islands [in Boulder City] would be drawn to it. Then she would enter the research facilities and take what she wanted, destroying the rest.

The ArAN requires huge amounts of energy. Lena needed to connect it to the Gravitron. She managed to find and enter an underground tunnel near the access tunnel P-1 on Väntholmen on Svartsjölandet [near Hemenway Pass]. She placed the ArAN on Väntholmen, linked it to the Gravitron, and started it. It immediately began to attract adults. Lena realized her mistake too late, as she is also an adult, and was instantly imprisoned by her own creation.

RIKSENERGI

## AUTUMN ON THE MÄLAREN ISLANDS

It is cold and windy on the islands, and the rain seems to fall sideways. Dark clouds blow across the sky, and mighty thunderstorms rage in the area. The leaves are colored red, yellow, and orange, and lie in banks on the ground. There are puddles everywhere with earthworms and frogs contained therein, and the birds fly south in arrow-shaped formations.

The classroom smells of wet clothes, and the lessons seem to never end. During breaks, students stand in groups shivering or go exploring on muddy paths between bare trees. In gym class, children are forced outside to practice orienteering or running. Everyday life goes on – work and school, breakfast and supper, brushing of teeth, and alarm bells ringing. The days become shorter and darker, and the cold makes everyone don caps and gloves. Spinning bike wheels spray up mud and rainwater.

## (AUTUMN IN BOULDER CITY)

The baking heat starts to cool down in Boulder City once school starts up again. Fortunately, the schools are airconditioned, so they're tolerable, if dull. Kids often find reasons to hang around for after-school activities, rather than having to haul themselves home during the hottest part of the day. Football players often wind up practicing in the morning to avoid heat stroke.

By October, though, temps have cooled to tolerable levels, and people wander about a lot more. There's a crisp snap in the air. It's good fishing weather, and it's finally cold enough to fire up the barbecue for some outdoor cooking, too.

## INTRODUCING THE KIDS

Each Kid gets a scene from Everyday Life. The Gamemaster should try to include adults in the scenes, so that they can be attracted by the ArAN and disappear later in the story. Dad taps on the door, and offers cookies. An aunt stays at the house because she's on vacation (but everyone knows that she recently gambled away all her money and had to sell her house).

## INTRODUCING THE MYSTERY

An adult disappears. It can be a teacher, a parent or an older sibling. The person is 16 years of age or older, and has slipped away without being seen. The Kid wakes up in the morning, and her mother is gone. The teacher doesn't turn up to class. The older brother's room is empty in the morning, and the bed is still made.

A successful **INVESTIGATE** roll lets the Kid discover that the adult left in the middle of whatever she was doing, and that she made an effort to leave unseen. There are no signs of the adult having been abducted against her will, and there are no traces of other people helping or following her. If the Kid follows the adult's tracks, she loses them somewhere on the way to Väntholmen [Hemenway Pass].

The Library

ArAN → The Echo Sphere → The Service Engineer

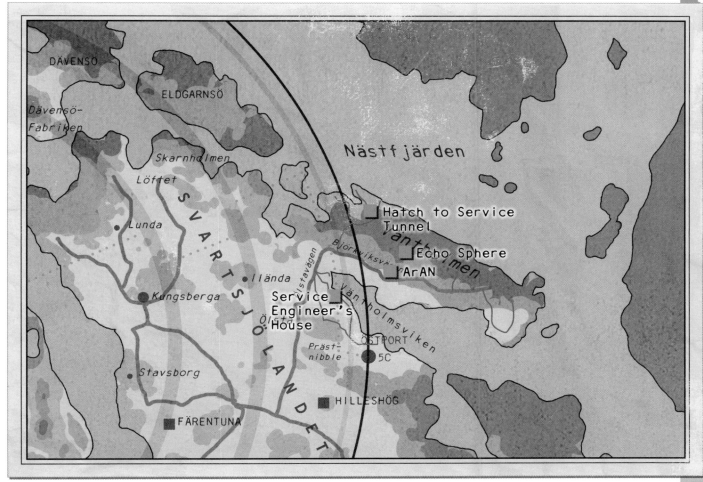

Don't forget to set one scene where all the Kids are present before proceeding to the next section. Only after that will the Kids get an opportunity to pursue an adult to Väntholmen and the ArAN.

SHOWDOWN

## SOLVING THE MYSTERY

The Mystery unfolds on and near Väntholmen [Hemenway Pass] on Svartsjölandet [outside Boulder City]. Mix scenes where the Kids try to solve the Mystery with scenes from Everyday Life, and scenes linked to the countdown of how The ArAN affects the islands' population.

More adults disappear, one by one. This affects each Kid's Everyday Life. If mom disappears, dad will obviously get upset and worried. Maybe he tries to comfort the Kid, or gently find out if the Kid knows something about mom having a love affair. Perhaps he sends the Kid to hear if the neighbors have seen something?

If the Kids met Majsan [Stacey] in the Mystery Summer Break and Killer Birds, she can be one of the people affected by the ArAN.

RIKSENERGI

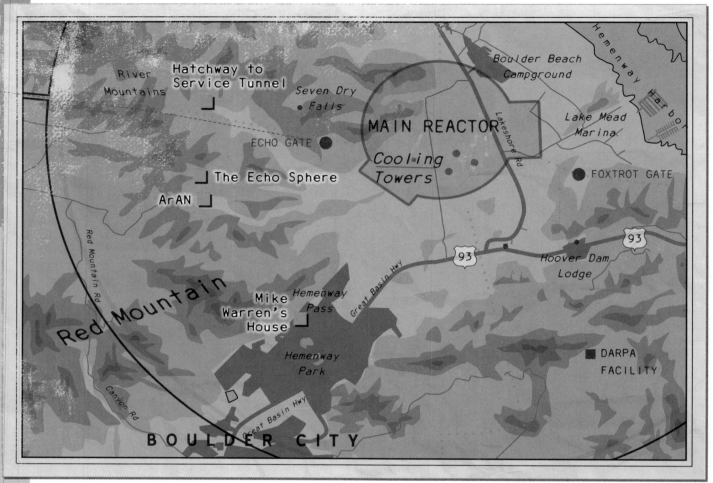

## LOCATION 1: THE ARAN

The ArAN machine has been placed in the middle of a fenced meadow, between the forest and the beach on the southern side of Väntholmen, next to a farm [close to Hemenway Pass]. The Kids can find it by following an adult who tries to sneak away unseen. This requires a successful **SNEAK** roll. If the roll fails, the Kids have lost the adult somewhere on the way, and must find some other adult who sneaks away from home.

The ArAN consists of a shiny metal cylinder on the ground, one meter high and two meters wide. Black letters on the side of the cylinder form the words ArAN.

The first time the Kids see the ArAN, it is surrounded by twenty adults sitting and standing, talking and looking out into the distance, seemingly at peace. One of them is Lena Thelin. She is a middle-aged woman

with curly blonde hair, white clothes, and a proud gaze. If asked what she is doing in the meadow, she says she's studying insects modified by radiation from the Gravitron.

If the Kids approach, they are stopped by the adults who say that this is not a good place for Kids, and ask them to go home. If asked what they are doing here, the adults have reasonable explanations – they are looking at the beautiful view, having a moment to themselves for thinking, or they are looking for a place to build a country house. If the Kids press the issue, the adults become aggressive and then use force to make the Kids leave.

The ArAN affects adults in the northern part of Svartsjölandet [Hemenway], but it is getting stronger and its influence reaches further every hour that passes. If the Kids bring other grown-ups to the ArAN,

such as parents or cops, they too fall victim to its influence and join the group in the meadow. The next time the characters visit the place, there will be significantly more adults present.

### TROUBLE

If the Kids try to get to the ArAN by force or cunning, they will be stopped by the adults. To pass them is impossible, and the players may not even roll to try. Let the players describe what the Kids are trying to do, and then tell them what happens as they fail.

Provided with some kind of battering ram or a tractor from a nearby farm, the Kids may try to get to the ArAN using **FORCE** or **TINKER**. The crowd has the special attribute **DENSE CROWD** 3, which means that it requires three successes for the Kids to **FORCE** their way through the crowd using that skill.

If the Kids manage to get to the ArAN it has **STEEL HULL** 2, which means that the Kids need two successes to destroy it. The adults will continue to attack the Kids until the ArAN is destroyed. When it is finally destroyed, the adults immediately cease to attack and head home. Their minds unconsciously create a more or less reasonable explanation for what has happened. No one will believe the Kids if they talk about what has happened.

### CLUES

If the Kids examine the surroundings using **INVESTIGATE**, they see that heavy cables lead from the ArAN into the ground. The Kids cannot reach these without getting to the ArAN. There are other, thinner cables leading from the ArAN north into the woods. If the Kids follow these, they come upon an Echo Sphere (below) lying on the ground. If they fail the roll to **INVESTIGATE**, they see the cables anyway but don't get to roll to try to discover the robot hiding in the woods next to the Echo Sphere (below).

A Kid who makes a **CALCULATE** roll understands that the ArAN affects the grown-ups with some kind of subliminal vibrations. This requires huge amounts of energy, which probably means that the metal cylinder is connected to the Gravitron. If this connection is broken, the machine will lose its influence. A Kid who makes an **EMPATHIZE** roll realizes that the adults are becoming more bestial as time goes by.

---

## THE ARAN MAKES ADULTS:

- Want to get close to it. Its effect is reinforced by the Moon, which makes most adults sneak away during the night.
- Want to hide its existence from other people, thus the reason for sneaking away to it.
- Prevent others from getting near or damaging it. They are prepared to sacrifice their lives for the ArAN.
- Act more like animals or primitive Stone Age people. They become more aggressive, sexually active, and uninhibited. They form tribal hierarchies, where some lead and others follow.
- Ignore their own needs for food, drink, sleep, and medical treatment, which will eventually lead to health problems and death.
- Forget the ability to speak, and start communicating with grunts and gestures.
- Not understand that it is the ArAN that affects them. If asked, they will find an excuse for being on the site, and believe it themselves.
- The ArAN only effects people of ages 16 and up.

RIKSENERGI

RIKSENERGI

## COUNTDOWN

Advance the Countdown each time the Kids visit the ArAN, or when it feels right and the story needs more energy.

1. The influence of the ArAN is increasing, and more adults are being drawn to the site. The adults are becoming more aggressive, primitive, and sexually active. The meadow smells of excrement, and several adults are bleeding after violent fights.

2. Even more adults are drawn to the site, from as far as southern Svartsjölandet and Munsö [Hemenway]. A police car arrives at the site to find out what is going on, and the policemen become victims of the ArAN, too. The adults have a clear hierarchy within the group, and fight amongst themselves. All the adults are naked and walk with a crouched posture. Hideous things are happening.

3. Yet more adults are drawn to the site, now even people from Adelsö [Boulder City]. An ambulance and a group of journalists have been drawn to the site, and join the others in the meadow. The adults have stopped using words, some are walking on all fours, and people suffer from fluid loss and hunger. Soon, people will start dying.

RIKSENERGI

## THE ECHO SPHERE

Cables buried in the soil lead from the ArAN to an Echo Sphere, located in a forest glade about a hundred meters to the north. Lena has used the abandoned Echo Sphere to program and control The ArAN. She hid it so no one will see it, and attempted to bury the cables leading to it.

The sphere is brown and somewhat rusty, two meters in diameter, and weighs 800 kilograms. Besides the cables running from the ArAN, there is an open hatch on the Sphere where thick cables lead into the ground.

Lena has placed a robot in the woods near the Echo Sphere. It has been instructed to guard the Echo Sphere, and chase away anyone who approaches. Lena has dressed the robot in clothes, so that it will be mistaken for a person if anyone sees it. The robot is named Isaac.

### TROUBLE

Tell the Kids that they feel like they are not alone when they approach the Echo Sphere. They must make **INVESTIGATE** rolls to spot Isaac in the woods. If they fail, Isaac approaches them unnoticed.

Isaac has been instructed to scare people away from the Echo Sphere, and, if necessary, to attack them. He will step out of the forest, stare at them, and with a mechanical voice ask them to leave this place. If the Kids try to talk to him, they may roll **EMPATHIZE** to understand his motives. If they succeed, they realize that Isaac doesn't want to hurt anybody. Even though he has been ordered to protect the Echo Sphere, he suspects that it is there for a bad reason.

The Kids can **CHARM** Isaac to come with them to the ArAN. If they do, Isaac realizes that something has gone wrong, and lets them investigate and shut down the Echo Sphere. He warns them of trying to cut the cables.

If the Kids manage to **CHARM** Isaac, he can also tell them that the ArAN is connected to the Gravitron through underground service tunnels. He doesn't know where the entrance is, but he can tell the Kids that the service engineer responsible for the area must know. Isaac refers to Lena as his "master," but will not betray her name. He tells the Kids that his master has placed two dangerous robots in the underground tunnels to guard the cable connecting the ArAN to the Gravitron. If the Kids cooperate with Isaac, he can become a recurring character in future Mysteries.

If the Kids don't talk to Isaac, and start examining the Echo Sphere or the cables leading to it, he will attack them. He uses his electrical shock grips. If the Kids fail to defend themselves (by rolling **MOVE** or **FORCE**), they suffer the Injured Condition, and get chased away. Isaac will not prevent them from leaving.

RIKSENERGI

If the Kids cut the cables to the Echo Sphere with an axe or similar tool, the Sphere will explode and all Kids close by must roll FORCE. If they fail, they are immediately Broken. A Kid who studies the Sphere with CALCULATE realizes that this will happen, and that it is possible instead to turn off the Sphere. This requires some time and a successful PROGRAM roll.

If the Kids succeed in shutting down the Echo Sphere, it slows down the increase of the ArAN's power of attraction. It also eventually leads to the ArAN self-destructing, as the Sphere stops stabilizing it – but not before many of the adults in the meadow will be hurt.

### CLUES

Using CALCULATE, the Kids can figure out that the ArAN draws its power from the Gravitron. If they find the connection in the service tunnels beneath the ArAN and break it, the ArAN will stop working. Only service engineers employed at the Loop know the locations of the entrances to the service tunnels. A note on the Echo Sphere itself – it's so small and worn that it requires an INVESTIGATE roll to find, which also tells the Kids that the service engineer responsible for this area is (or at least was) named Michael Wirsén [Mike Warren].

## LOCATION 3: THE SERVICE ENGINEER'S HOUSE

If the Kids ask around for information about the service tunnels, they will learn about service engineer Michael Wirsén, who is responsible for the northern parts of Svartsjölandet [Boulder City]. They can find him through CONTACT, COMPREHEND, by studying the Echo Sphere, through the library, or by asking an adult. Michael has recently been injured in an accident, and is bedridden in the family's summer home near Väntholmen [Hemenway Pass].

Michael has suffered an electric shock, trying to repair an electrical cable. He has suffered brain damage, which has made him insensitive to the vibrations from the ArAN. He is tucked in bed on the second floor of the house in a red pajamas with teddy bears, and is being taken care of by his wife and a nurse. When the Kids find him, both the wife and the nurse have suf-

---

### THE LIBRARY

The Kids can get more information from the school library or from the library in Stenhamra [Boulder City]. With a COMPREHEND roll, the Kids understand that the adults are getting more and more bestial. This will continue until they don't take care of their own needs and start to perish from dehydration, disease, and violence within the group. This will begin within days.

At the library, the Kids can learn that the only way to get down to the tunnels is through a hatch only known to the service engineers working at the Loop. The one responsible for the northern part of Svartsjölandet is named Michael Wirsén.

RIKSENERGI

---

fered from the effects of the ArAN machine and left Michael alone in his bed.

The summer house is a two-story cottage painted red with white corners. It is very well maintained and meticulously decorated, but rather soulless. On the walls, framed posters by popular Swedish artists hang; one of Michael's avocations is pop music. The first floor is furnished as an office. Here, Michael keeps a large number of drawings and books about the Loop; his second avocation is his job.

### TROUBLE

Michael is in his bed, and will not answer the door if the Kids ring the bell. The house has doors that lock automatically, and an advanced alarm which begins to howl and alerts the police if someone tries to break in. The Kids can hotwire it using PROGRAM. Failing the roll triggers the alarm, and soon the police will show up (unless the ArAN is now affecting the entire population).

RIKSENERGI

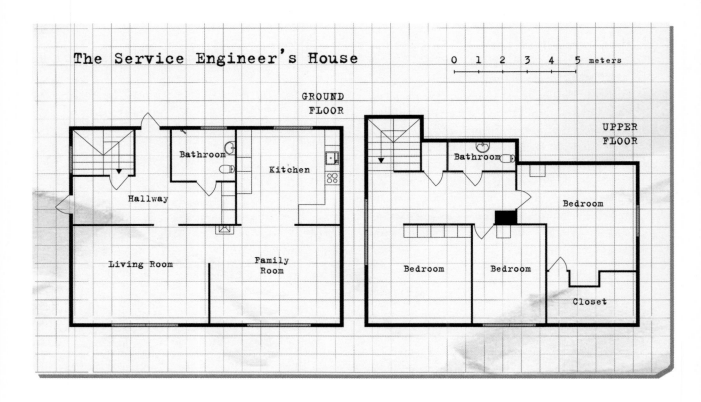

The Service Engineer's House

GROUND FLOOR

0 1 2 3 4 5 meters

UPPER FLOOR

Bathroom

Kitchen

Hallway

Living Room

Family Room

Bathroom

Bedroom

Bedroom

Bedroom

Closet

## LUCKY BREAK

If the Kids come to a standstill, or if the game must come to a quick resolution for some reason, the Kids run into Michael Wirsén by chance. He is aimlessly running around in the street, dressed in his pajamas. He is confused, but tells the Kids that something has lured his wife and his nurse away. Michael is sure that this is linked to the Gravitron, and tries to get the Kids to venture into the service tunnel to find out what happened and how to put a stop to it. He is too weak to come with them. Michael gives them the code to the hatch leading to Access Tunnel P-1, and points out the location on a map.

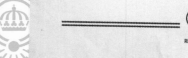

Michael is very worried about suddenly being left alone. He is confused and disoriented. He will alternate between seeing the Kids as burglars and trying to chase them away, and believing the Kids are his childhood friends and that he himself is a child. It is very difficult to have a conversation with him, as he quickly goes between these extremes. If the Kids make an **EMPATHIZE** roll, they understand that they should pretend to be his friends to get him to help them. They can do this by using **CHARM**. If they fail, Michael understands that they are trying to trick him and becomes aggressive.

### CLUES

If the Kids get Michael to help them, he will tell them that the only hatch that could have been used to connect the ArAN to the Graviton is the one that leads down to Access Tunnel P-1. He can give them the service code that enables them to open the hatch, and shows them where it is on a map.

If Michael doesn't cooperate, the Kids can get the same information by studying his maps and books. This requires a **COMPREHEND** roll. The Kids may also use **CONTACT** to get the same information from someone else.

## THE SHOWDOWN

The Kids find the overgrown hatch in the woods, north of the ArAN and the Echo Sphere. Beneath the grass, there is a concrete slab with a heavy hatch that opens with a code. A staircase leads down into dark passages that seem endless. When the Kids climb down, small blue LEDs light up on the walls. In some places, there are emergency telephones on the walls. It is humid, and a cold wind blows through the tunnels. Every now and then, the Kids can hear what sounds like footsteps and animals moving somewhere in the dark. Cobwebs smear the Kids' faces if they don't bat them out of the way.

After twenty minutes of walking, the Kids come to a large Service Room with several entrances. The walls are covered by cables, screens, and control stations. The floor is a mesh of rusty metal, now in bad condition. Several meters below, the groundwater flows with a loud roar. It smells bad. From the ceiling hangs a green cable that is hotwired to one of the stations. The cable leads up to the ArAN, and connects it to the Gravitron.

### UNDERGROUND SCENES

Set short scenes on the way to the Service Room to set the mood. The Kids have to walk through a dark tunnel, and can hear something (rats) moving further ahead, they have to pass a wire that has been torn from the wall and crackles with deadly electricity, or they come to a crossroads and need to choose which way to go. Maybe they hear strange sounds from the Gravitron deep below, or they find a lifeless service robot that has been mutilated by something with big jaws.

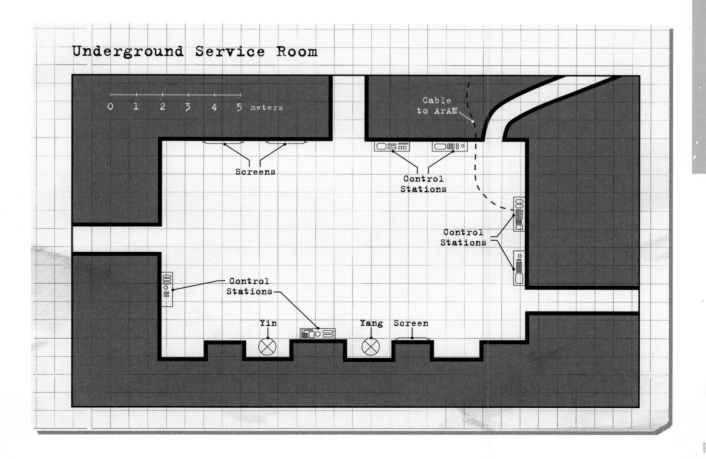

Underground Service Room

RIKSENERGI

In two alcoves, two robots are hiding. Lena placed them here to guard the cable. The Kids have to make **INVESTIGATE** rolls to spot them. The robots, called Yin and Yang, will attack if the Kids enter the room.

The confrontation with the robots Yin and Yang counts as Extended Trouble (page 70) with a Threat Level equal to three times the number of Kids. The Kids can flee rolling **MOVE**, or stand their ground and roll **FORCE**. Another way to overcome the robots is to make a hole in the metal mesh (using **TINKER**) and lure the robots to fall through it and into the water below.

If the Kids fail, they are chased off by the robots. If the Kids overcome the robots, they can unplug the cable to the ArAN. It then loses its connection to the Gravitron, and immediately breaks down. The adults go back home with varying explanations about what happened in the meadow, none of them true.

## AFTER THE SHOWDOWN

If the Kids succeed, the adults have already gone home once they come up from the service tunnel. Lena has disappeared. The adults won't remember or understand what has happened, and no one will thank the Kids.

If the Kids fail to outsmart or beat the robots, the ArAN keeps affecting the adults, making the situation grow worse. Some will die and some will suffer from serious dehydration. All the time, more adults will arrive. One day, without warning, the machine stops working.

## AFTERMATH

Afterwards, the Kids get a scene each from Everyday Life, with or without Trouble. The player may choose a scene or ask the Gamemaster to set up a scene. If the group is short on time, each player instead describes a brief snapshot of a moment in the Kid's Everyday Life.

## CHANGE

After the final scenes, you and the players should go through the character sheets together and figure out if the Kids have changed in any way. The players can change their Problem, Pride, Iconic Item, and Relationships. Ask the questions for Experience Points (page 88) out loud. Each Kid gets 1 XP for each affirmative answer.

## NPCS AND CREATURES

This section describes the NPCs and creatures that the Kids might meet in this Mystery.

### ISAAC

*"Be so kind as to leave this place immediately, for your own protection and the common good. I do not want to repeat this request."*

Isaac is an old robot, who has been in the service of Lena for many years. He is beginning to understand more and more about people, and has begun to doubt Lena's motives. Isaac suspects that Lena is planning to scrap him. He has started to think of himself as almost a human being, and the prospect of being scrapped scares him. He has learned to talk with an upper class Stockholm accent, and has studied how to behave like an old-time gentleman. In his shack, he collects pipes, stamps, and expensive canes, which he buys with money earned from secretly selling spare parts from Lena's supply to a shady scrap dealer on Svartsjölandet (Hemenway). Isaac has a good (but mechanical) heart, and loves kids.

Isaac has a body built of human tissue and metal. His head looks like a skull with a metallic mouth containing black teeth that always seem to sneer. Isaac wears a dark raincoat, and a large, dark green rain hat, and walks with

RIKSENERGI

a beautifully engraved cane. He talks in a long-winded manner, with a lot of difficult words and is overly polite. Isaac can use his right hand to create a powerful electric shock that lights up like a flashbulb. When he does this, his teeth also crackle with electric sparks.

## MICHAEL WIRSÉN (MIKE WARREN)

*"Let's ride our bikes to the headmaster's house and steal plums! Wait ... Who are you? What are you doing here?! Get out of my house!!!"*

Michael is a pedantic man in his thirties, who loves his work as much as he does pop music. He grew up on the island in Stenhamra (in Boulder City), and has recently inherited his parents' summer house close to Väntholmen (Hemenway Pass). Recently, he injured himself at work, and is now being pampered by his wife and a nurse. This is very timely for Michael, as his wife has been threatening to leave him for a long time because he doesn't want to have children. When his wife disappears, at first he believes that she has left him, but then he realizes that others are also missing.

Michael is seriously injured, confused, dizzy, and weak. He sometimes thinks that he is a child, and it is the 1960s. Michael is clean shaven, with short brown hair and brown eyes. He is dressed in a pair of pajamas, is bandaged, and has large burn marks on the upper part of his body and on his face.

## YIN AND YANG

*"Click, click, click, wooooeeeeeeeeeeeeee!!!!"*

Yin is human-like and made out of white plastic, with a round head and black eyes. One of its hands has a mounted high-speed drill that gives off a loud screeching noise. The joints of Yin click when it moves with stiff steps, but it is still a good runner.

Yang is a black metal robot, in the shape of a square block that moves on caterpillar tracks. It has no head and no visible limbs. A series of red LEDs light up when it moves. Yang can extend a long metallic shaft equipped with an electric shock mechanism, which lights up the entire room with a flash when it strikes a victim. Yang moves with a hissing sound, like that of a snake.

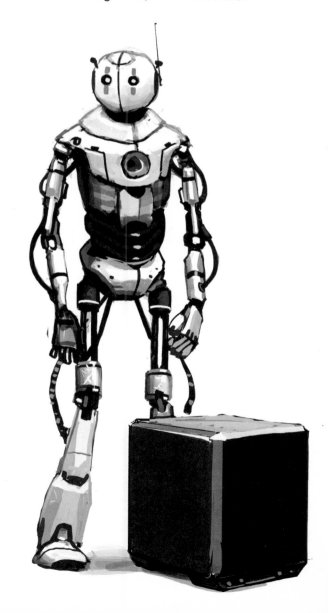

RIKSENERGI

RIKSENERGI

# CREATURES FROM THE CRETACEOUS

*The cold of winter rules the land. Kids with rosy cheeks have snowball fights until they are called home to warmth and hot cocoa. Skaters crisscross the ice-laden lake in leisure. One day, however, a skater disappears into thin air. The Kids will discover that whatever took him, might be better left undisturbed.*

This is a Mystery that can be played during a single session. It can be used as the third part of the Four Seasons of Mad Science campaign. The Mystery is written so as to scare the Kids, and to give them a sense of desperation and vulnerability. In the end, they will hopefully overcome all Trouble and solve the Mystery.

## THE TRUTH OF THE MYSTERY

The scientist Lena Thelin [Diane Petersen] has decided to give herself an early Christmas present. She has opened a time portal to the Cretaceous Period, in order to collect dinosaur eggs. She plans to hatch them in a barn, tame the dinosaurs, and then use them to take revenge on her former colleagues at Riksenergi [DARPA]. Lena has managed to retrieve several eggs, which she has placed in incubators, but on the last trip back in time something went wrong. Lena caught a disease, and is not well enough to return to her own time.

Dinosaurs have made their way through the time portal and have started to spread over Adelsö [Red Mountain], attacking pets and people. More beasts are coming through the portal, and it's only a matter of time before chaos breaks out, just in time for Christmas. The Mystery begins with the Kids trying to find a runaway dog. They discover Lena's farm, the dinosaurs, and the portal to the Cretaceous. The Kids have to travel back in time, and find Lena in order to close the time portal.

RIKSENERGI

145

## WINTER ON THE MÄLAREN ISLANDS

It is winter on the Mälaren Islands, and Christmas is just days away. It has been cold for weeks, and Lake Mälaren is frozen. Skaters glide across its glossy surface, and fishermen drill holes and wait for hours with a jigging rod and a coffee thermos. On land, snow ploughs make high snowbanks where children build caves and have snowball fights. In the mornings, cars spew black smoke while adults scrape the windows. Snowmen stand on parade in the gardens with carrot noses, and in the trees, packs with sunflower seeds and apples hang, attracting small birds.

On December 13, the children and adults wake up early and go to school and work. The children walk in Lucia processions with long white robes and candles, singing solemn songs while flashes from the parents' cameras light up the room. Afterwards, everyone eats gingerbread and saffron buns.

The children make wish lists for Christmas Eve. They go sleigh-riding and skiing. Soon, the Christmas holidays starts, just a few more days to bear with Christmas crafts, games, and songs in school. The clothes are wet from melting snow and the kids' faces are pale with red cheeks and cold, sniffling noses. The days are short and dark, and cold winds sweep in over the islands.

## (WINTER IN BOULDER CITY)

Even in the dead of winter, it never gets all that cold in Boulder City. It snows sometimes, but it rarely sticks around for long. It just leaves a light dusting on the rocks and cacti before the chilly mid-day sun melts it all away.

You actually have to wear pants and a jacket, maybe even a hat and gloves. Never snow boots though. It rains just a little during this season, and that means sometimes you can catch the desert in one of its rare, but beautiful, blooms. On top of that, the holidays mean trips into Las Vegas to see even more lights on display than usual, and to shop for Christmas gifts, too.

## INTRODUCING THE KIDS

Set a scene from Everyday Life for each of the Kids, with or without Trouble. Maybe the Kids ski, make oranges with clove and red laces or they are forced to shovel the driveway.

Make sure to mention that the long distance skater Niklas Ek [Nicholas Evans] disappeared two days earlier. Maybe the adults talk about it, or it is mentioned on TV. The skater, Niklas, has been eaten by one of the dinosaurs on Adelsö [on Red Mountain], but no one knows it yet.

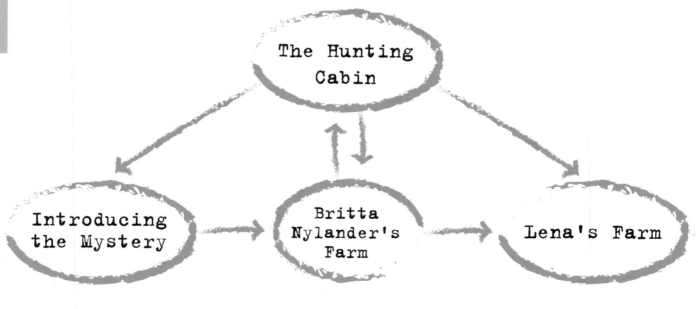

In another scene, have a Kid hear a local radio show where an old lady on Adelsö claims to have seen big animals, "maybe bears," lurking in the darkness outside her house. Her name is Birgitta Nylander [Dorothy Greene], a known local yokel. She calls in to the radio show; but her connection is really bad, and the call is suddenly cut off. The journalist cracks jokes about old women and tired minds.

## INTRODUCING THE MYSTERY

The Kids see a poster with a picture of a golden retriever named "Goldie" who has disappeared. Goldie ran away from her family in Sätuna on Svartsjölandet [Boulder Beach] three days ago. A fisherman [camper] saw her out on the ice on Svinsundet between Munsö and Adelsö, heading towards Adelsö, near Wäsby [towards River Mountains]. The family offers 200 Swedish Kronor [$25] to anyone who can find Goldie. This is a lot of money in the '80s. If the players don't get hooked by this bait, remind them of their Drives.

Before continuing to the next phase, the Kids must find a way to get away from their families and get to Adelsö. It's a long walk, and takes all day on foot. It isn't possible to go there and come back on the same day. Maybe one of the Kids knows about an empty cottage on Adelsö, where they can stay while they solve the Mystery. Getting away from home and going to Adelsö can be played out over several scenes with Trouble (lying to parents, getting a ride with a truck driver, stealing food from home without being seen, etc.), or you and the players can agree on how they get there, and cut directly to a scene where the Kids are crossing the lake between Munsö and Adelsö.

SHOWDOWN

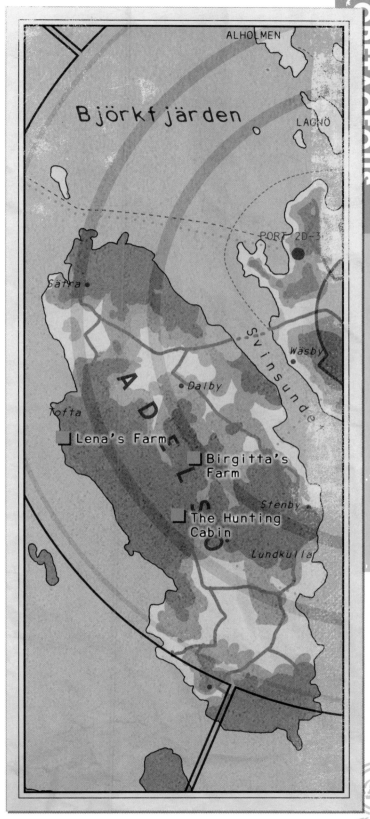

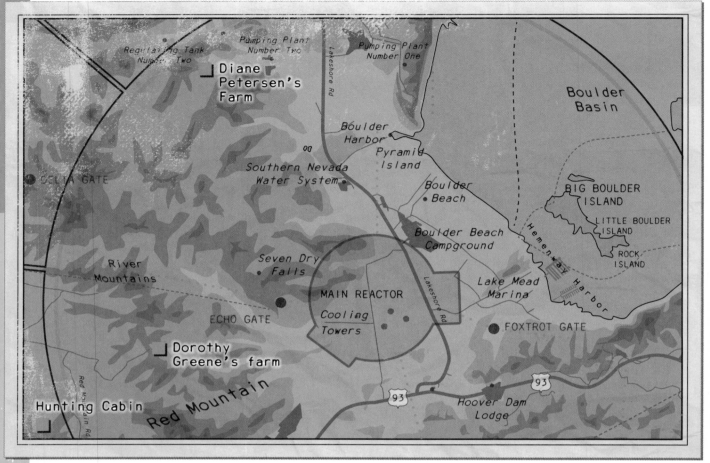

Normally, there is a ferry crossing Svinsundet between Munsö and Adelsö, and its route is kept clear of ice with an icebreaker. You can decide that the ferries are still running or that the icebreakers are needed elsewhere, and all the ferries have been cancelled. The Kids will then need to cross Svinsundet on foot. It's more difficult to set scenes from Everyday Life in this Mystery because the Kids are not in their home area. Scenes from Everyday Life can be about the relationships between the Kids, how they cook food, fight amongst themselves or flirt with each other. You can let some of the parents be on a fishing holiday on Adelsö, or one or more of the parents can come looking for the Kids on Adelsö.

If the Kids create or find some kind of shelter or home at Adelsö, it counts as their Hideout during this Mystery. The Kids are safe there, and they can heal Conditions. You can let them find an old fishing cabin or a summer cottage.

## THE TEENS

No matter how the Kids get to Adelsö, the Teens Mara, Mackan, and Taggen [Mara, Muffin and Spike] will confront them on their way across the ice to Adelsö, or on the shore at Adelsö [Boulder Beach]. They have also decided to find Goldie and collect the money, and they don't want any competition. During the Mystery, the Teens will give the Kids a hard time so as to get them to give up and go home.

Mara, Mackan, and Taggen are three troublemakers who have skipped school for several weeks. They plan to form a punk band and move to Stockholm [Las Vegas], and they need money to buy instruments. One of the Kids may have met them before; they could be friends or enemies to one of the Kids' big sisters or brothers. Advance the Countdown for the Teens as the Mystery unravels.

### RETRIBUTION COUNTDOWN FOR THE TEENS

1. The Teens meet the Kids on the ice between Munsö and Adelsö [Canyon Road]. They understand that the Kids are also looking for Goldie, and threaten them with a beating if they search for the dog. The teenagers are mean and aggressive, and call the Kids names.
2. The Teens descend upon the Kids, trying to wrestle them to the ground. If they succeed, they threaten them and burn one of them with a cigarette, steal their jackets, and leave them to freeze in the cold.
3. The Teens sit in a tall tree, crying and screaming for help. A Velociraptor stands below the tree, and tries to jump up to get them. If the Kids save the Teens, they are very grateful, and immediately try to go home.

RIKSENERGI

## THE DINOSAURS

Some thirty creatures from the Cretaceous Period have come through Lena's time portal, and more are on the way. Most of these are small animals like Eomaia, herbivores like Triceratops, or fish eaters like Pterosaurs, but there are also dangerous carnivores like Velociraptors and a giant Tyrannosaurus Rex.

The cold makes the animals lethargic and weak, and some of them are dying. The carnivores eat small animals and pets. One human has been killed, the long distance skater Niklas Ek [Nicholas Evans]. It is only a matter of time before the hungry animals will attack people on a bigger scale. The Kids will see more and more of the Dinosaurs as you advance the Countdown.

## ICY WINDS AND SNOW

The roads on Adelsö are snowed over, and telephone and electric lines have been torn down by the dinosaurs. The only way to get around is to walk, or to find and hotwire a vehicle that can travel on snow. Traveling and finding shelter and food can be made into constant Trouble that will make the Mystery more difficult, and create a feeling of being truly in dire straits. If it seems too hard for the players, or if the group doesn't have much time, these endeavors can be described to set the mood instead of being Trouble.

RIKSENERGI

## COUNTDOWN FOR THE DINOSAURS

1. A large shadow (a Pterosaur) swoops by above, and heads out over the lake.

2. The Kids find a slaughtered and half eaten moose [mule deer]. With a COMPREHEND roll, the Kids understand that it was killed by an animal with huge jaws and teeth. Snow has covered the tracks on the ground, but marks high up on the trees indicate that it was a large creature.

3. Something big moves among the trees, and a heavy snorting sound is heard. If the Kids go to see what it is, they see a huge Triceratops that tries to scrape the bark off a tree with its mighty horn, so as to have something to eat. The dinosaur is hungry and irritable. It breathes great clouds of steam in the cold.

4. A deer runs past the Kids, followed by a Velociraptor that catches it, and tears it to pieces. If the Kids don't escape (roll to MOVE), they too will be attacked.

5. The Kids see a snowplow [truck] tilted on the side and torn apart. There is no trace of the driver, except the seat is covered in blood. Suddenly, a mighty creature towers in the woods nearby. It's the Tyrannosaurus Rex, looking for food.

It takes almost an hour for the Kids to walk one kilometer in the heavy snow. Use the table on this page to determine how long a trip takes. Each time the Kids try to go somewhere, they all have to roll FORCE. If they fail, they are either lost, Exhausted or Injured from the cold. If they don't find shelter for the night, or if they lack food for a long time, they must make a FORCE roll or be Broken. Kids travelling at night or off roads or paths also need to succeed at COMPREHEND rolls to avoid getting lost.

Make sure to keep track of time. The sun rises just before 9 am, and sets at 3 pm. Scenes from Everyday Life can be made here, in which Kids look for food, eat or are just about to go to sleep.

There are a couple of small villages and isolated farms on Adelsö, where the Kids can seek help. The inhabitants are snowed in, and have no electricity and no way of communicating with people outside the island. Telephones are out as the Gravitron is currently cancelling out radio waves.

### TRAVELING ON FOOT

| Distance | Time |
|---|---|
| From the beach to the Hunting Cabin | 4 h |
| From the beach to Birgitta Nylander's Farm | 3 h |
| From the Hunting Cabin to Birgitta Nylander's Farm | 3 h |
| From Birgitta Nylander's Farm to Lena's Farm | 5 h |
| From the Hunting Cabin to Lena's Farm | 5 h |

## SOLVING THE MYSTERY

The Mystery takes place in the central and northern parts of Adelsö [around Red Mountain and Canyon Road]. When the Kids come to the island, they should first find somewhere to camp.

When they start looking for Goldie, advance one of the Countdowns. The Kids will soon find traces that will lead them to the Locations. They can spot fresh human tracks in the snow, and they can see smoke from a chimney far away in the forest. Following the tracks, they will find the Hunting Cabin where the ice skater Niklas [Nicholas] sought shelter after an hour's travel. If the Kids head in the direction of the smoke, they will come to Birgitta Nylander's home after several hours.

If the Kids try to escape from the island, they will see big animals moving across the ice looking for food, probably scaring them enough to make them go back to Adelsö.

# LOCATION 1: THE HUNTING CABIN

The skater and scientist Niklas Ek [Nicholas Evans] was chased by a dinosaur when he was out on an excursion on Lake Mälaren [on Red Mountain]. He fled to Adelsö, and took shelter in a cabin for hunters, where he also found a hunting rifle. Niklas realized what was happening, and suspected that Lena Thelin was involved. He wrote this in his diary, shortly before two Velociraptors broke down the wall, killed him, and dragged his body away.

The Kids can find the Hunting Cabin by following Niklas's tracks in the snow or by talking to Birgitta Nylander. The Cabin is located a few hundred meters from the eastern beach of Adelsö [east of Canyon Road].

The cabin is a small, red wooden cottage in a clearing in the woods. On the east side, there is a door that can be locked from the inside with a clasp. The roof is made of wood, and covered with snow. There is a glass window to the west. The northern wall and area of the cabin has been destroyed by Velociraptors.

Inside the cottage, there is a broken table and some chairs, an overturned oil lamp, and a broken rifle. In one corner, there is a backpack, a pair of skates, and a half-full thermos with cold coffee inside. The floor is covered with frozen blood, and there are tracks leading out into the snow. If the Kids follow the tracks, they will find the remains of Niklas Ek and the prints of Velociraptors.

The backpack holds extra clothing, a hand-cranked radio that can receive but not transmit, Niklas's diary, a knife, and fishing gear. If the Kids listen to the radio, they can hear Birgitta [Dorothy] sending emergency messages. As a result of interference from the Gravitron, her messages do not reach beyond the island.

## TROUBLE

There is no immediate Trouble at the Hunting Cabin.

## CLUES

Kids who read Niklas's diary understand that he suspected Lena Thelin of opening a time portal that released the dinosaurs. Niklas also noted that they are increasing in number, which means that the portal is still open. Someone must close the time portal. Niklas also wrote that he saw smoke from a house in the north, and he tried to go there, but had to turn back.

If the Kids examine the Location and make an IN-VESTIGATE roll, they realize that Niklas was hiding in the Cabin for several days and tried to get away several times, but was forced to go back to avoid the dinosaurs. Finally, something attacked and tore down the wall. Niklas tried to defend himself with the rifle, but it didn't do much good. He was dragged out into the woods and eaten. Traces of the beasts that did this are only a few hours old. A successful **INVESTIGATE** roll also lets the Kids find a hidden compartment in the floor, where they find five cans of beans which Niklas never found.

A Kid who makes a **COMPREHEND** roll realizes that the tracks were made by two Velociraptors from the Cretaceous Period.

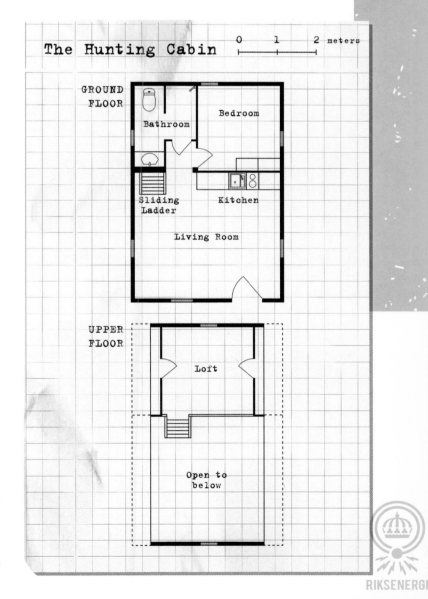

RIKSENERGI

### December 12

What has happened is unbelievable, yet it has happened. I was chased across the ice by a creature that I could only identify as a dinosaur from the Cretaceous Period. The person reading this must think I have lost my mind. I heard the ice cracking beneath its feet while I skated as fast as I could to the shore on Adelsö, rushed up the beach and into the woods, while the creature came closer. Had the forest not been thick enough to keep the creature from following me, I would be dead.

I have found this old Hunting Cabin, and made it my base. I try to make as little noise as possible. Who knows what else is out there?

### December 13

At home, they celebrate Lucia. I curse my stupidity that I didn't tell anyone that I chose to skate west of Munsö rather than in Långtarmen as I usually do. They must have started to look for me by now, but how will they find me? I don't have much food left, even though I found two cans of beans in this cottage. The rifle is leaning against my chair. I'm writing this in the last sunlight streaming in through the window. I don't dare to light the oil lamp. I have seen more creatures out there in the woods.

### December 14

The creatures have become hungrier. I have tried to hike both north and south, but was forced to turn back. In the north, I have seen a house with smoke coming from the chimney, but my path was blocked by something unmentionable. I turned back, terrified.

I begin to understand what has happened. Someone has used the power of the Gravitron to open a time portal to the Cretaceous Period. Judging by how many creatures there are, the portal is still open. Within a few days, Mälaröarna will be swamped by giant beasts. Fortunately, they are weakened by the cold. If the beasts survive winter, life will be changed forever for the people living here.

When I worked at The Loop, I met a brilliant but self-absorbed and vain scientist named Lena Thelin. She was fired for her mistakes and her arrogance, and it was said that she left the islands. I remember that she talked about the possibility of opening rifts in time, and to retrieve creatures from prehistoric eras for scientific purposes. I remember we laughed at her. She was very bitter when she had to leave the Loop, and said she would have her revenge. Nobody took her seriously. I think she might be the one who did this. Tomorrow, I'll find a way home.

## LOCATION 2: BIRGITTA NYLANDER'S FARM

If the Kids follow the trail from the Hunting Cabin north, after about five kilometers they arrive at a farm in the woods. This is where Birgitta Nylander [Dorothy Greene] lives. They can also travel to the farm by spotting and following the smoke from her chimney.

Birgitta lives on this small farm where she and her late husband made a living through forestry and breeding dogs. The farm is surrounded by a tall wire fence. Beside the main house, there is a shelter with twenty Greyhound dogs. In the courtyard, there are two vehicles: an old pickup truck, and a tractor. The residential building is made out of wood. It is red with white corners, and has a tiled roof. The windows are dark, except for a glow from candles. Smoke is coming from the chimney. When the Kids approach the house, they hear the dogs barking madly.

The house is in bad shape. Inside, several walls are covered by photo wallpapers showing tropical beaches with palm trees and blue waters. It's dirty, smells of stale food, and is cluttered with too much furniture. The electricity and the telephone lines to the house are down, so Birgitta has made fires in the two fireplaces and lit candles. Her two favorite dogs, the Greyhounds Nihau and Kauai, are also inside the main house.

Birgitta has a gasoline powered generator, which she uses to power a coffee maker and a record player. She sits in the dark in her wheelchair, and listens to music from Hawaii, with a cup of coffee and a loaded shotgun on her

## Nicholas's Diary

### December 12

What has happened is unbelievable, yet it has happened. I was chased up the path by a creature that I could only identify as a dinosaur from the Cretaceous Period. The person reading this must think I have lost my mind. I heard the rocks slip beneath it's feet while I ran as fast as I could to the brushes on the far side of the mountain, while the creature came closer. Had the brush not been thick enough to keep the creature from finding me, I would be dead.

I have found this old Hunting Cabin, and made it my base. I try to make as little noise as possible. Who knows what else is out there?

### December 13

I curse my stupidity that I didn't tell anyone that I chose to hike up Read Mountain rather than my usual path. They must have started to look for me by now, but how will they find me? I don't have much food left, even though I found two cans of beans in this cottage. The rifle is leaning against my chair. I'm writing this in the last sunlight streaming in through the window. I don't dare to light the oil lamp. I have seen more creatures out there among the rocks.

### December 14

The creatures have become hungrier. I have tried to hike both north and south, but was forced to turn back. In the north, I have seen a house with smoke coming from the chimney, but my path was blocked by something unmentionable. I turned back, terrified.

I begin to understand what has happened. Someone has used the power of the Gravitron to open a time portal to the Cretaceous Period. Judging by how many creatures there are, the portal is still open. Within a few days, Boulder City will be swamped by giant beasts. If the beasts survive, life will be changed forever for the people living here.

When I worked at DARPA, I met a brilliant but self-absorbed and vain scientist named Diane Petersen. She was fired for her mistakes and her arrogance, and it was said that she left the islands. I remember that she talked about the possibility of opening rifts in time, and to retrieve creatures from prehistoric eras for scientific purposes. I remember we laughed at her. She was very bitter when she had to leave the Loop, and said she would have her revenge. Nobody took her seriously. I think she might be the one who did this. Tomorrow, I'll find a way home.

lap. The dogs are lying on the floor close to Birgitta, and growl at the smell of the alien creatures moving around in the woods.

### TROUBLE

The two Velociraptors that killed Niklas Ek [Nicholas Evans] have found Birgitta's farm, and are moving around outside the fence, searching for a way in. The Kids may notice that something is moving in the forest, and can avoid being seen by the dinosaurs with successful SNEAK rolls. If they are spotted by the beasts, the Kids need to get into the yard quickly (roll MOVE) or become prey. If a Kid fails her roll, she is attacked and automatically Broken, but not killed.

At the last moment, she has found some sort of hiding place, a hole in the ground, a tree or a car wreck. She is alive, but stuck, and somebody needs to come get her.

The fence has a large metal gate. If the Velociraptors have discovered the Kids, they will try to rush inside when it's opened. The Kids have to be quick, and make successful MOVE rolls to shut the gate in time. If they succeed, the creatures remain outside and howl with frustration. If they fail, the Velociraptors will come into the yard and attack the Kids, tear the dogs into pieces, and wreck the residential building.

If the Kids get into the farm unhurt, Birgitta doesn't want them to leave as she fears they will be killed. The Kids can persuade her to let them go with CHARM.

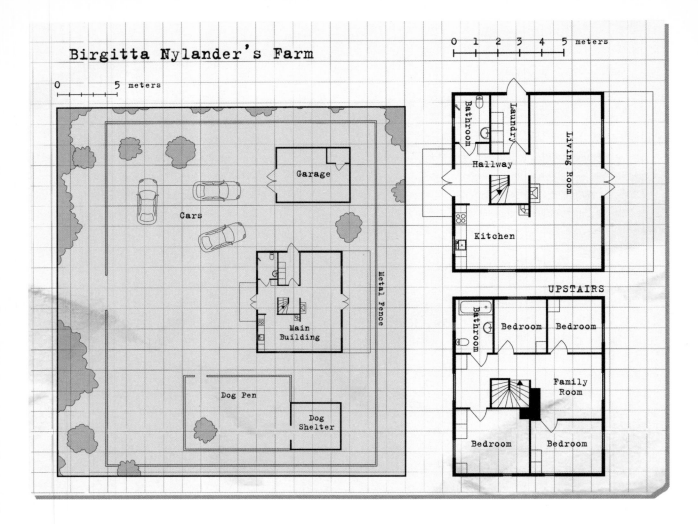

Birgitta Nylander's Farm

## CLUES

Birgitta can tell the Kids that she saw a man with a rifle (Niklas Ek/Nicholas Evans) on the path to the south. Birgitta also tells them that the path to the west leads to an eccentric and very unfriendly female scientist, who bought an old farm there a couple of years ago.

Birgitta gives the Kids a hearty lunch, and she is happy to lend them any of her vehicles (bonus +3) – if the Kids can get them to start, which requires a successful **TINKER** roll. To overcome Trouble with a vehicle, the Kid driving it must use the **TINKER** skill – for example, if they want to drive through the gate and ram the Velociraptors.

## LOCATION 3: LENA'S FARM

If the Kids follow the trail west from Birgitta's farm, they will find Lena Thelin's farm [Diane Petersen's house], located near the beach on the west side of

Adelsö [Canyon Road]. On foot, it takes five hours, but with a vehicle only one.

The farm is old, with several dilapidated barns and a residential house. Everywhere, there are parts of machines, ships, and robots covered in snow.

The residential house has two floors. The upper floor has not been used for many years, and cobwebs cover old furniture, a loom, framed photographs, and chests filled with fabrics, and mice droppings. Lena has decorated the ground floor with half-finished machines and robot parts, mechanical arms which can toast bread slices and play records, operate fans on sunny days or bring a blanket when it gets cold. The power is now off, and all is quiet and dark. The robotic arms hang in mid-air like dead spider legs. Beside the record player lies the complete opera *The Ring of the Nibelung* and Richard Wagner's autobiography *Mein Leben*.

The bookshelves are filled with science books, and on the walls there are photographs with gold frames depicting Lena in various grandiose postures. On the

RIKSENERGI

kitchen table, there lies a book with the title *Learning to Play the Synthesizer, Popular Songs for Beginners*. The robot Isaac (described in the Mystery *Grown-Up Attraction*) is also in the residential building. He is very worried that Lena has not returned from her latest trip through the time portal, and wants the Kids to bring her back. Isaac has found the dog Goldie, and has been feeding her in Lena's kitchen. The dog sees Isaac as her new master. She is very loyal and intelligent.

In one of the barns, Lena's time machine can be found. It consists of a synthesizer connected to a strange machine that resembles a large lantern, lying on the ground facing straight up. From the lantern comes a bright light that forms a large ring of light, which hangs vertically in the air. In the middle of the ring can be seen a two-dimensional image of a jungle landscape, where prehistoric creatures occasionally can be seen moving around. This is the time machine

invented by Lena. The image is a portal to the Cretaceous Period. The time machine is controlled by playing different melodies on the synthesizer. When the Tyrannosaurus Rex came through the portal, it broke through part of the southern side of the barn, and cold air blows through a large hole.

In the middle of the barn, there is a hatch in the ground. Underneath, there is a staircase leading down. If the Kids go down the staircase, they will find the basement that Lena uses to hatch dinosaur eggs. An oil-driven motor powers very strong lights and fan heaters, which heat up some forty large eggs lying on beds of straw. Two sloppily painted blue robots move around among the eggs, and turn them over according to a carefully planned schedule. The robots have no names, and are unable to communicate. Every now and then, they charge themselves in a docking station. If the eggs are moved or destroyed, the robots stand still and do nothing.

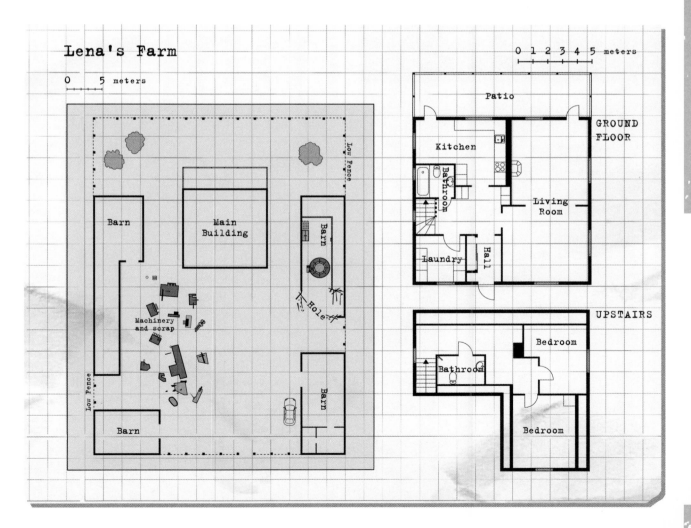

## TROUBLE

The mighty Tyrannosaurus Rex has made the area around the farm its home; it hunts and kills creatures that come close. It is out hunting when the Kids arrive at the farm, but they can see its tracks in the snow and the remains of half-eaten animals. When the Kids go into one of the houses, the Tyrannosaurus Rex returns. The Kids can feel its steps shaking the ground, hear branches being broken, and when the dinosaur approaches the farm, it roars with the rage of prehistory.

To move between houses without being noticed, the Kids need to roll **SNEAK**. If the T-Rex notices them, the creature will hunt them down, and destroy buildings and objects in order to get to them.

## CLUES

By talking to Isaac or by examining the time machine with a **CALCULATE** roll, the Kids realize that it is controlled by playing specific melodies. The time portal must be actively turned off to disappear. If the machine is destroyed, the portal remains hovering in the air and stays open. A broken time machine can be repaired using the **PROGRAM** skill.

Only Lena knows the melody that closes the hole in time, and she has disappeared on the other side. The Kids must pass through the time portal to find her. Isaac is willing to come with them, or try to lure away the Tyrannosaurus Rex so that it doesn't destroy the barn along with the time machine. If the Kids retrieve Lena, she will close the portal by playing The Final Countdown by the band Europe on the keyboard.

## SHOWDOWN

When the Kids step through the time portal, they feel a tingling sensation throughout their bodies. They suddenly find themselves in a hot and humid jungle, surrounded by enormous trees, swamps, and huge birds, giant dragonflies, and giant beetles of different colors. A fifteen-meter snake winds its way up a tree next to them. The time portal is hovering in the air between two trees, and they can see the barn on the other side. The Kids sweat profusely in their winter clothes, and are soon attacked by leeches and mosquitoes. If you feel ambitious, play jungle sounds and raise the temperature in the room where you play!

### LUCKY BREAK

If the Kids don't know what to do or if time is running short, you can let the Kids encounter Isaac out in the woods. He walks through the snow trying to find someone who can help close down the time portal. He says that only Lena has the code, and that she is on the other side of the portal. Isaac asks the Kids to go through the portal, and bring her home. Isaac leads the Kids to Lena's farm on a safe path. If the group is really short on time, you can let the Kids find a note in her house telling them how to shut down the time portal, trapping Lena in prehistoric times.

The high oxygen content makes the air painful to breathe, and vision and hearing are impaired. The Kids feel dizzy and nauseous.

In the forest, there is a path that Lena created with the help of a robot wielding two machetes instead of arms. Nature has already started to reconquer it. The Kids travel along Lena's path through a landscape filled with strange creatures.

Lena has placed her base camp near a lake that stretches as far as the eye can see. The lake is infested with huge crocodiles and other strange prehistoric water-dwelling animals. In the sky, Pterosaurs and large birds wheel about. Lena's base camp is built up in a tall tree, tall as a skyscraper. A ladder leads up to a treehouse, twenty meters up. The Kids find a bed, some crates, a variety of jungle gear, the remains of a completely broken robot, and two hunting rifles in it. Three dinosaur eggs can be found in a bag. Lena lies in the bed. She is asleep, but wakes up when spoken to.

Lena has been infected by a prehistoric virus, which has made her very ill with fever and given her a severe rash. Her helper robot has laid her down on the bed in the treehouse and waited for her to get better. While Lena has been asleep with the fever, a large Pterosaur has built a nest of twigs on the roof of the treehouse, and laid eggs there. When the robot moved around down in the treehouse, the Pterosaur interpreted this as an intruder, and smashed it with its beak.

### TROUBLE

The Pterosaur sits atop the treehouse, and attacks anyone who approaches. She reaches several meters into the hut through the door with her beak, but cannot reach all the way to Lena's bed. The Kids must find a way to chase or lure the dinosaur away long enough to get to Lena, or sneak past it. This counts as Extended Trouble (page 70) with a Threat Level equal to three times the number of Kids. If the Kids fail, they are chased off and have no choice but to leave Lena and go back through the portal.

If the Kids succeed and speak to Lena, she wakes up and asks them to take her home. She refuses to disclose the code to turn off the time portal before she is back in her own time. When the Kids get back to Lena's Farm through the time portal, the Tyrannosaur Rex may have left or may still be there, as more Trouble to

overcome. If Lena goes with the Kids back through the portal, she immediately leaves, warning the Kids not to tell anyone about what has happened.

After the time portal is closed, the Kids somehow leave the island and go home. The players may decide how this happens, and the game moves on to the Aftermath.

## AFTER THE SHOWDOWN

The disease Lena suffers from can easily be cured with antibiotics. If the Kids close the portal without saving Lena, she recovers on her own enough to use her portable time machine, and opens a new time portal to go home. The Kids will then hear about the scientist Lena Thelin being rescued from Adelsö.

Despite the chaos wrought by the dinosaurs on Adelsö, no adults will believe the Kids if they tell what happened. The dinosaurs that had passed through the portal will eventually succumb to the cold, their carcasses being snowed under or sinking into the depths of Lake Mälaren [Lake Mead]. Their tracks in the snow will be wiped away by the winter winds. The damage caused by the dinosaurs will be explained away as being attacks by bears or the like.

## AFTERMATH

The Kids now get a scene each from Everyday Life, with or without Trouble. Each player may choose a scene or ask you to set up a scene. If the group is short on time, instead of a scene, each player gives a brief snapshot of a moment in the Kid's Everyday Life.

## CHANGE

Go through the character sheets together with the players, and figure out if the Kids have changed in any way. The players may, if they want to, change their Problem, Pride, Iconic Item, and Relationships. Ask the questions to get Experience Points (page 88) out loud. The Kids get 1 XP for each affirmative answer.

## NPCS AND CREATURES

This section describes the NPCs and creatures that the Kids might meet in this Mystery.

RIKSENERGI

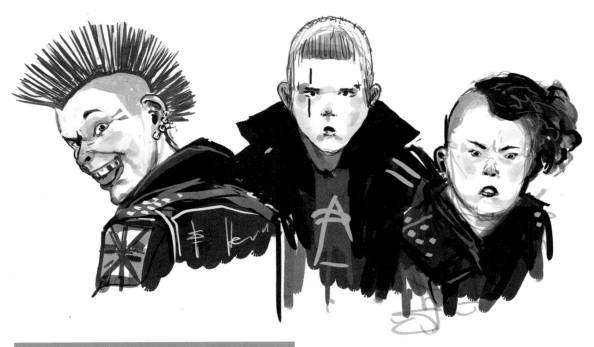

## THE TEENS

*"Watch it, otherwise I'll put this needle through your cheek."*

Mara, Mackan, and Taggen (Mara, Muffin and Spike) are three teenagers with dysfunctional families. They have found each other in their common lack of trust in adults, their sense of alienation, and the desire to revolt. Recently, they made contact with a bunch of old punk rockers in Stockholm (Las Vegas) and plan to leave the islands and form a band. First, they need the money from finding Goldie. The Teens are loud, foul-mouthed, and use violence to get others to do what they want. They have no respect for anything other than their own friendship. All three smoke both cigarettes and marijuana, and they have brought several bottles of liquor with them. None of them have enough warm clothing, and they did not bring any camping gear.

Mara is a large 16-year-old girl, with lots of piercings and hair dyed purple and black. She was born in Serbia (Mexico), and has taught her friends a lot of profanity in Serbian. Mara is loud and never stops talking. She is the leader of the gang. Mackan (Muffin) is a 15-year-old boy with a green mohawk, black leather jacket, and arms full of burn scars. He is silent, and often becomes depressed and destructive, to both himself and others. Taggen (Spike) is a 16-year-old girl with short, blonde hair and a long, black leather coat. She drinks too much. Taggen has a shrill voice, and is an expert at finding others' weaknesses and giving them painful nicknames.

## BIRGITTA NYLANDER (DOROTHY GREENE)

*"Aloha, Kids!"*

Birgitta Nylander and her husband have lived on Mälaröarna all of their lives. Since the time when they were young, they have made several trips to Hawaii, and always dreamed of moving there, but it never happened. Instead, they lived on Adelsö (near Red Mountain), trying to create their own Hawaii on their farm. Birgitta's husband passed away several years ago, and she is now very ill and sits in a wheelchair. Birgitta is a talkative, positive, and strong woman, who says what she thinks and is not intimidated by anything – not even dinosaurs. Her dogs love her, and Birgitta loves them – and Hawaii. Birgitta also loves children, but has never had any of her own. She will take care of the Kids as best she can.

Birgitta is a 70-year-old woman, sitting in a wheelchair. She is dressed in colorful clothes, with a pair of pink sunglasses on her forehead. Around her neck hangs a garland with plastic flowers.

RIKSENERGI

She expects others to do as she says, and she can get very angry if anyone refuses to do so. Lena boasts loudly about herself. She is often sarcastic, and she likes to point out flaws in other people and taunt them.

Lena is a middle-aged woman with curly blonde hair and a fierce gaze. She wears khaki-colored outdoor clothes, and a pin with the Yin and Yang sign. She has hidden a miniature version of the time machine under the bed in the treehouse, a melodica linked to a calculator taped to a flashlight. If she becomes stranded in the Cretaceous Period, she will open a new time portal and go home.

## LENA THELIN (DIANE PETERSON)

*"You go first. Losing me to these brainless lizards would be a blow to humanity you could not even understand."*

Lena has devoted her life to science, but has a strong attitude that she doesn't get the recognition she deserves. After she was fired from the Loop, her entire existence has been drenched in bitterness and hatred. She wants revenge at any cost, and in the process, to also prove her superiority. Lena is plagued by loneliness, and she does not understand why everyone pushes her away. For a while, she was able to spend time with her robot Isaac, but she now believes that he dislikes and takes advantage of her. Lena thinks young people are mostly in the way – they should behave and be quiet, preferably elsewhere.

## DINOSAURS

The creatures on Adelsö (around Red Mountain) come from the Cretaceous Period. They include a variety of insects and mammals. The most common dinosaurs are herbivorous Triceratops and fish-eating airborne Pterosaurs, but there are also a few carnivores, notably Velociraptors and a Tyrannosaurus Rex. All adult dinosaurs have the special FIERCE BEAST 3, requiring the Kids to roll three sixes to defeat them. The Velociraptors also have the special attribute LIGHTNING FAST 3, making them very hard to outrun.

If the Kids try to fight the Velociraptors, it requires an Item of some kind, like a rifle, a car or a car battery with wires that can give electric shocks. It is not possible for the Kids to defeat a Tyrannosaurus Rex in combat, no matter what Items they have.

It is possible to train and tame a Dinosaur using the skills EMPATHIZE, COMPREHEND and CHARM, but it takes months and cannot be done during this Mystery.

RIKSENERGI

**159**

RIKSENERGI

# I, WAGNER

*Things come to a dramatic climax when Lena's plan finally falls into place. Can robots dream, think and feel? Can they hurt people? The Kids will find out the answer to these questions in this final season of mad science.*

This is a Mystery that can be played over the course of two or three sessions. It should be used as the fourth and final part of the *Four Seasons of Mad Science* campaign. If it is played as a standalone Mystery, you must find a reason for Lena Thelin [Diane Petersen] and Wagner to see the Kids as their primary enemies. One explanation might be that it was the Kids who discovered something that led to Lena losing her job at the Loop.

The Kids gets XP at the end of every session, and it is recommended that you let the Kids use their Prides once every session, instead of once per Mystery.

## THE TRUTH OF THE MYSTERY

After the events of Creatures from the Cretaceous, Lena decided that it was the Kids' fault that she failed. She began to think of them as the biggest threat to getting her revenge. During the rest of the winter, she planned how she could create an army of loyal robots to get her revenge on the people of Mälaröarna [Boulder City] and the Kids.

Lena managed to gain employment at the company Microlex on Munsö [in the outskirts of Boulder City], using the false identity "Mona Selin" [Priscilla Andrews].

## WAGNER RINGS

WR consist of robots that are microscopic in size, which can infect robots and humans alike with a virus. The basis of WR is the DNA of Lena Thelin. Robots are most easily infected by uploading the "microbots" into them with a floppy disc.

Humans obviously have to be infected in another way. The microbots, which look like a gray powder, can be added to food, drink, tobacco or drugs. Both humans and robots need to get new WR into their system regularly, otherwise the effect will wear off in a couple of days.

Robots infected become more self-aware, developing the ability to defy orders and think for themselves, but not like humans, more like big, silent animals. They also develop an affinity with other infected robots. Some will develop personalities resembling Lena Thelin's. Infected robots, with the ability to speak, greet each other with the phrase, "Long Live Lena!"

Humans who are infected tend to mimic Lena Thelin's personality, and they absorb some of her memories. They become self-absorbed, paranoid, and adversarial towards the authorities. Some people also gain special powers from the micro-robots, such as the ability to control magnetism and electricity or super-human strength.

All infected robots and humans can communicate with each other, and with the robot Wagner, via the transmitter on the ship Nibelung. Wagner can communicate by sending messages or images. This is not mind control — the receiver chooses how she relates to the messages. But Wagner is skilled at manipulation and deception.

RIKSENERGI

Microlex is a subcontractor to the Loop, and manufactures circuit boards for robots. Lena used company equipment to invent a form of miniaturized robots, called microbots, small as a virus, modelled on her own DNA.

The microbots can be inserted into normal-sized robots to make them somewhat self-aware and loyal to Lena. Lena has also built a transmitter on her farm, from which she can communicate with infected robots. During Christmas, Lena became entranced by The Ring of the Nibelung opera by Richard Wagner, and she has called her invention "Wagner Rings," or WR, for short.

Lena has also come to believe that her retainer robot, Isaac, actually worked against her so as to take her place. She assigned him to hard labor in the yard while she built a new servant, a robot that she named Wagner. She managed to buy an advanced form of AI on the black market, giving him an almost human-like intelligence. Wagner was the first robot infected with WR. At first, he was loyal, but as the WR caused him to absorb Lena's memories and personality, he eventually became paranoid and self-absorbed. He became convinced that it was he, and not Lena, who was the true genius. Wagner finally murdered Lena in order to take control of the production of WR, and make himself leader of the robots. Isaac saw it happen and tried to save Lena, but did not succeed. He managed to record the murder on film, and then fled to the forest.

The robots infected by WR have been baptized by Wagner with "free names," taken from Wagner's opera and Norse mythology. Wagner has declared that Lena has gone to Valhalla, the great hall of the Norse Gods, where she awaits them, though most robots don't have the ability to engage in abstract thinking, making it impossible for them to have religious beliefs of any kind. They are still more machines, than living and thinking entities.

Wagner has left Lena's farm, and moved to an abandoned shipyard on Göholmen, north of Svartsjölandet [Black Rock Point]. There, he found the wreck of a huge gauss freighter called Nibelung, and saw it as a sign. His robots are now working on getting the ship functional so that they can travel on it to Valhalla.

With WR in his system, Wagner absorbed Lena's hatred of the inhabitants of Mälaröarna. He has discovered something that Lena didn't know: humans can be infected by WR. Wagner plans to take revenge on the people on the islands by infecting them with WR, taking them to the ship, and letting them become the robots' servants. He has almost come to believe his own lie that Lena is waiting for them in Valhalla.

Wagner has absorbed Lena's belief that he needs to neutralize, even kill the Kids, so that they don't thwart his plans. He has provided a teen in the vicinity of the Kids with tobacco infected with WR, and thus created a loyal servant and spy who will, at the right time, attack the Kids. This person is called The Odd One.

## SPRING ON THE MÄLAREN ISLANDS

Winter is finally over, and the longer days are returning to the Mälaren Islands. During school breaks, girls jump rope between rain puddles, and boys play field hockey. In their classes, kids are hard at work. There is much to be done before anyone can start dreaming of graduation.

Coltsfoot grows in the ditches along the roads, and in the forest, the ground is covered with white anemone flowers. Chirping birds build nests in the treetops during the early part of the morning. Deer and foxes prepare for new litters, and the first yellow brimstone butterflies dance in the sunshine.

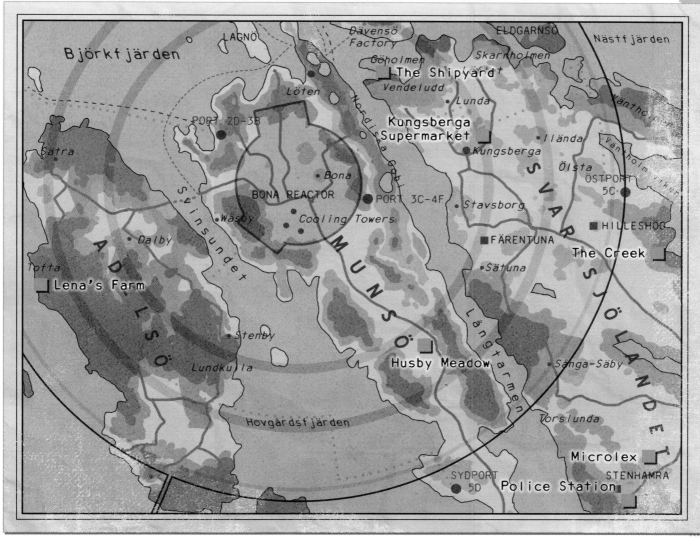

Parents prepare outdoor furniture and dream of holiday. There are many more weeks of work before summer, and the short stays outdoors are interrupted by cold winds, storms with heavy rain, and cracking thunder.

The farmers collect branches for bonfires which are traditionally lit at the end of April, to celebrate Walpurgis Night, a festival traditionally associated with protection from witches. Families go to watch the fire together. The air smells of life and hope. Summer is coming.

## (SPRING IN BOULDER CITY)

Spring is the best time in Boulder City. You can ditch your hooded sweatshirt and start wearing shorts again, but it almost never rains, so there's no reason to keep inside. And the summer's blazing heat still sits on the horizon, a scorching threat yet unfulfilled.

As if to prove how wonderful it all is, vacationers on spring break start swarming through the area, often on their way from Las Vegas to Lake Mead. The city seems to double in population for those few weeks, bringing a different sort of life to your city's desert streets.

## INTRODUCING THE KIDS

Start by setting a scene from Everyday Life for each of the Kids, with or without Trouble. Try to start the Countdown for the Odd One even in these scenes, and let the Kids notice that she is different.

## INTRODUCING THE MYSTERY

The Kids overhear some teenager, maybe an older sibling or someone in the schoolyard, whispering that there is a dead body in a creek south of Hilleshög [south of Hoover Dam]. According to the rumor, the body is that of a prisoner who escaped from jail. Nobody knows who killed him; perhaps it was another prisoner who's still out there in the woods? The Kids are supposed to go look for the dead body. Remind the Kids of their Drives if they don't react to the rumor.

South of Hilleshög is a creek that leads east out into Mälaren [towards Colorado River]. If the Kids follow it some 500 meters, they will come to a flooded area full of mud, reeds, insects, and fallen trees. The Kids need to make an **INVESTIGATE** roll to find the body lying slumped in the mud. If they fail, some teenagers have already found the body.

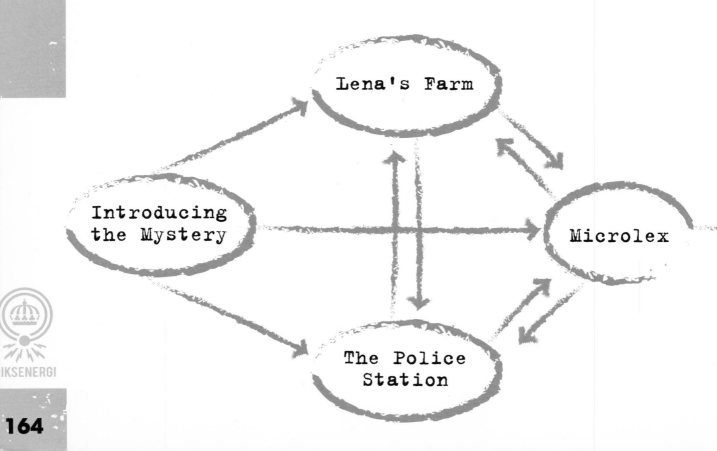

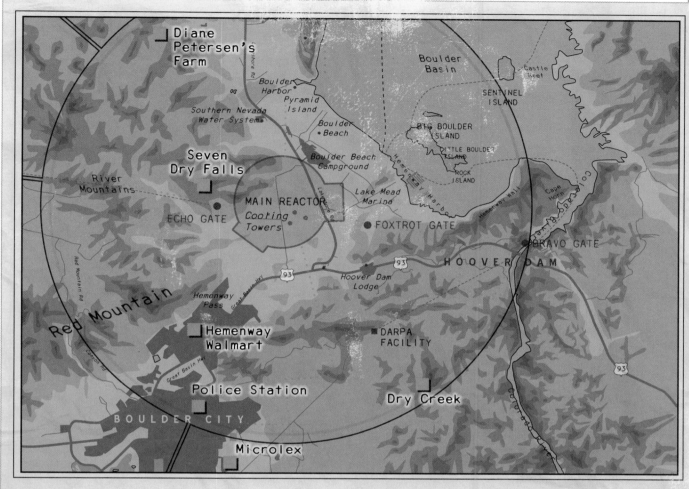

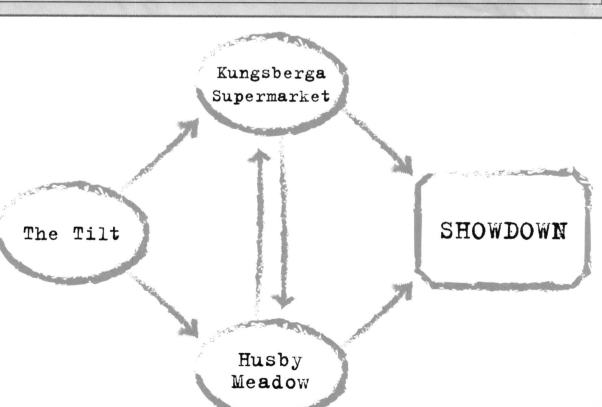

They don't want to share their findings with the Kids, but can be convinced with a **CHARM** roll.

The body has been dead for several days, and is infested with insects and worms. When the Kids examine the body they recognize it as being Lena Thelin [Diane Petersen] (if they have played the Creatures From the Cretaceous scenario). Lena is wearing a white lab coat with a Yin and Yang pin on the cuff. In one of the pockets, there is a wallet with an ID card with a picture of Lena, but the name "Mona Selin" [Priscilla Andrews]. The ID card is one from the "Microlex" company. On the ID card, the address of Lena's farm on Adelsö is noted.

With an **INVESTIGATE** roll, the Kids can discover that Lena has a very small hole in her forehead. The hole goes straight through her head and out the back. They cannot see any other indications of violence against the body. The Kids also realize that the body was dragged to this place. Starting from a path 50 meters south of the creek, there are tracks through the vegetation to the resting place of the body. These can be discovered by another **INVESTIGATE** roll.

Whether the Kids report the body or not, the police will find the corpse the next day. The press writes that a dead woman has been found south of Hilleshög. Police are said to be secretive about the cause of death. A police commissioner named Ing-Marie Blankäng [Karen Richards], based at the police station in Stenhamra [Boulder City], is in charge of the investigation. You can have an adult read this information out loud from a newspaper.

## THE ODD ONE

Wagner has infected a teenager in the vicinity of the Kids with WR, to spy on them and attack them if they get close to interfering with his plans. It could be an older sibling, a cousin visiting or Majsan from the Summer Break and Killer Birds scenario. The infected teen is called The Odd One.

WR makes the Odd One see the Kids as malicious, ill-behaved braggarts who stick their noses where they shouldn't, and who need to be taught a lesson. In addition, she has begun to detest all forms of authority figures, such as parents and teachers. She hates the people on the Mälaren Islands [Boulder City], and talks indignantly about man's oppression of robots.

The Odd One commands 4-5 peers and supplies them with WR. They may be newcomers, older siblings or classmates to the Kids. The Odd One has been endowed powers from the WR that may seem magical to the Kids. She can control and create magnetism, thereby manipulating objects. She is abnormally strong, can jump extremely far and high, and has a superhuman ability to sense things with her mind. The Odd One has the special attribute **SUPERHUMAN POWERS** 2, and the Kids therefore need 2 successes to defeat her no matter what skills they use. This does not apply to her followers.

Wagner's servants, Hugin and Munin, deliver tobacco infected with WR to the Odd One and her peers once a week. If the Kids follow the Odd One to this meeting, they come to an abandoned treehouse, maybe one that the Kids built together with the Odd One when they were younger. If the Kids stop the Odd One from smoking the tobacco, the effect of WR will disappear after a few days.

There are two Countdowns that control the Odd One's actions, one before and one after the Tilt (below).

```
RETRIBUTION COUNTDOWN,
THE ODD ONE BEFORE THE TILT

1. The Odd One follows the Kids,
   tries to hurt them, spreads false
   rumors, and teases them.
2. The Kids see the Odd One's powers
   by accident. They could watch her
   use her powers of magnetism or her
   superstrength when she thinks no
   one is watching.
3. The Odd One spies on the Kids, and
   reports to Wagner via the trans-
   mitter. She speaks to him, staring
   with blank eyes that do not see.


RETRIBUTION COUNTDOWN,
THE ODD ONE AFTER THE TILT

1. The Odd One destroys or damages
   things that the Kids care about.
2. The Odd One tries to capture and
   imprison the Kids.
3. The Odd One and her gang attack
   the Kids with sticks and stones,
   trying to kill them.
```

## SOLVING THE MYSTERY – PART ONE

The Mystery takes place all over the Mälaren Islands [Boulder City]. When the Kids travel across water, you can make it Trouble to acquire a boat and cross the water, or simply move on to the next scene, and assume they solved it somehow. Alternate between scenes from the Mystery, Everyday Life, and the Countdown for the Odd One.

## LOCATION 1: LENA'S FARM

Lena lives on a ramshackle farm on the west side of Adelsö [north of Red Mountain]. The farm consists of several barns and a residential building with two floors. The courtyard is covered with rusted machines and robots. Birds, mice, and other animals have settled everywhere. On the roof of one of the barns, there are the remains of the transmitter Lena used to communicate with robots infected by WR. Wagner has sabotaged the transmitter, and it cannot be fixed without knowledge of WR.

The door to the house is open, and somewhere inside, the sound of blaringly loud opera music can be heard. On the table in the kitchen are the remains of a half-eaten plate of spaghetti and meat sauce. A book lies open next to the plate, *The Large Scale Structure of Space-Time* by Stephen Hawking. Two candles have burned down so that the wax has solidified on the table.

In the living room, an automatic LP player is playing the opera The Ring of the Wagner on repeat, at maximum volume. On the table and the sofas lie some twenty books in different languages that are all about Wagner's opera.

### MINDLESS MACHINES

Robots almost never have an AI, which means that they are more like machines than living creatures. In this mystery, however, you can make the Kids doubt this by giving them signs that maybe the machines understand more than people think? A robot looks at the Kids in a funny way, or stops working when they pass by. Robots are rare, but when the Kids do see one, you should make the most of it to make the Kids doubt what they know. Maybe the robots aren't just mindless machines?

The books are filled with underlines and notes that suggest that the reader seems to have been particularly interested in how Gods can be born into people. One note reads: "Am I a God?" On the wall in the living room there are ones and zeroes written with black ink across one wall. The digits are drawn with exact measure:

The strings of ones and zeros on the wall were written by robots, instructed by Wagner's servants Hugin and Munin. The numbers are a binary code, and can be translated to read, "Long Live Lena!" The players can figure it out for themselves, or you can let them roll for it using the **COMPREHEND** skill.

01001100 01101111 01101110 01100111 00100000 01001100 01101001 01110110 01100101 00100000 01001100 01100101 01101110 01100001 00100001

A plastic file next to the coffee table holds a large number of documents about the Kids themselves: photographs of them, their personal information, and a couple of photocopies of their own texts from school. There are also drawings of their houses, as well as names and information on their families, relatives, and friends.

## TROUBLE

There is no apparent Trouble at Lena's farm, but the Kids will see a small shadow move around in an old barn. If they investigate the barn and make a **SNEAK** or **MOVE** roll, they will find Lena's cat, Asimov. She is hungry and in bad shape, and shy of strangers.

## CLUES

If the Kids make an **INVESTIGATE** roll, they realize that the furniture in the kitchen has been rearranged. Someone has tried to clean up after a violent fight. Large amounts of bloody paper and empty detergent containers have been thrown in the trash at the back of the house. If the Kids have been in Lena's house before, they also realize that several framed photos of Lena are missing.

If the Kids search the second floor and make an **INVESTIGATE** roll, they find a small voice recorder that Lena has hidden in her bathroom, next to her bath salts and a rubber duck. Lena has drawn a necklace and a name tag that says "Nobel" on the duck with a black felt pen. On the voice recorder, there is a recording that Lena made as she soaked in the bath.

### LENA'S VOICE RECORDER
*"My plan that I will follow without deviation, sloppiness or shortcuts … not that past mistakes in any way have been my fault, but still … where was I?"*

*(Cough)*

*"The first step is to eliminate the damn Kids. Had it not been for them, the people on the Mälaren Islands [in Boulder City] – these imbecile, inbred and self-righteous sheep! – would have already gotten what they deserve. The only thing that prevented me from unleashing my wrath on them were those precocious Kids. When I get my hands around their necks...."*

*(Splashing in the water)*

*"There, there, Nobel. You will come with me to the podium when I receive the Big Prize. When I face the cameras, and finally get the chance to tell the truth about myself and how the people here, despite their absolute lack of brains, have managed to turn the world against me and hide the only true genius in our time..."*

*(Kissing sound)*

*"Namely me, sweet Nobel!"*

*"But first, I must find a way to get my revenge on those Kids, and get them out of the way. Maybe I can use the Wagner Rings against them? They are, after all, surrounded by machines and robots.*

*I must strike at them before they suspect anything. And what then, you wonder, little Nobel?"*

*(Intense kissing sound)*

*"Then, I will rise to the sky like Freya or Odin, controlling the robots, and making them see me as I truly am, a God, and I will have them punish my enemies. With an army of robots I could..."*

*(Someone knocks on the door)*

*"Come in!"*

*(A door opens and a metallic voice is heard in the distance.)*

*"Yes, of course, Isaac, I want cream in the chocolate, as always!"*

*(A door is closed)*

*"He pretends he doesn't know exactly how I want it. There was a time, dear Nobel, when I thought I could trust that robot, but Isaac has let me down. He is just like the*

others, *he wants to use me to make a name for himself. One day, he will try to poison me, I'm sure of it."*

*(Silence)*

*"I'd better sneak down and see that he doesn't put anything in my cup."*

*(A stopper is pulled out of the bath and water flows. The recorder is turned off.)*

## LOCATION 2: THE POLICE STATION IN STENHAMRA

The police inspector Ing-Marie Blankäng [Karen Richards] has been assigned the job of examining the dead body that the Kids found in the creek. Ing-Marie is described in the Mystery Landscape, on page 109. Ing-Marie got the assignment only because several of her colleagues are at a conference in Stockholm [Las Vegas].

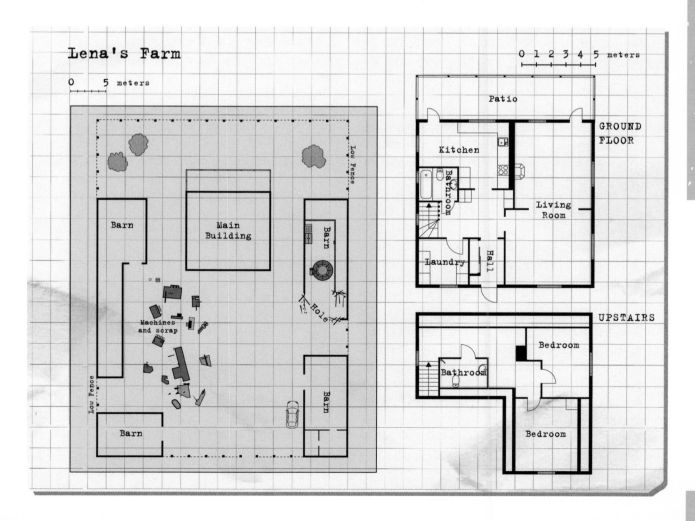

## TROUBLE

The Kids can contact Ing-Marie to find out what the police know about the murder of Lena Thelin. They can get past the desk sergeant secretary using **CHARM** or **SNEAK**, or they can visit Ing-Marie's rented house, which is filled with notes and newspaper clippings related to rumors about strange creatures.

If the Kids make **EMPATHIZE** rolls when they talk to Ing-Marie, they realize that she is afraid to do anything that gives her boss a reason to transfer her away from the station. They also realize that Ing-Marie has a strong belief in the occult and in secret conspiracies. If the Kids tell her about Lena Thelin and their past adventures, and make a **CHARM** roll, Ing-Marie will help them.

Wagner has managed to infiltrate the police station's security system, which means that he controls the cameras, and can see and hear everything the Kids say in the building. Tell the Kids that they feel as if they are being watched. If they roll **INVESTIGATE**, they notice that the cameras are following them, and that they seem to be recording everything they say. A Kid who takes the security system apart with **PROGRAM** notices that someone has hijacked it, and that all the information is being sent to someone with the code-name W.

## CLUES

Ing-Marie has concluded that the woman found dead was murdered by a robot. The narrow wound completely through the head was caused by a thin elastic "finger," about a meter long, which some robots use to manipulate circuits inside machines where space is extremely limited. The finger is hard enough to be pushed through metal.

Ing-Marie has found traces of a single robot with human-like feet, which seems to have dragged the body into the mud by the creek. The tracks indicate that the robot was relatively small. She is convinced that the murder is the beginning of a robotic revolution. She desperately wants to get her boss to report the incident to the security services, but he doesn't believe her.

Ing-Marie has realized that the ID card on the body was forged, and she has discovered that there are fake data files creating a past for the fictional "Mona Selin," going back to her birth. Ing-Marie is very grateful if the Kids reveals Mona's real name.

Ing-Marie is currently investigating what "Mona Selin" [Priscilla Andrews] worked on at Microlex, and she can help the Kids get in touch with the twins Olof and Hadar at the company.

Ing-Marie can become an important ally for the Kids. She will believe what they say, and she is willing to help them in difficult situations.

# LOCATION 3: MICROLEX

Microlex is a company whose offices and facilities are located in the outskirts of Stenhamra [Boulder City]. It supplies the Loop with microscopic electronics. The company building is a large, single-story white brick structure, with a black roof. The area is enclosed with a tall, wire fence. There are about 20 cars in the parking lot inside the fence. There are a dozen rooms on the ground floor of the building. There are more rooms in the basement, which is where sensitive information, expensive materials, and hazardous substances are stored in locked vaults. Some thirty people work at the company's facilities.

The company director is Ingvar Sten [Eugene Burton]. He has been in contact with Ing-Marie at the police station, and knows that the newly employed "Mona Selin" (Lena Thelin) is dead, probably murdered. A couple of days ago, his security officers – the twin brothers Olof and Hadar Svensson [Albert and Arthur Brown] – found out that Mona was using a false name and she was using the lab for her own inventions. Ingvar has decided to keep this information from going public, in order to avoid bad press. Olof and Hadar have been ordered to stop investigating. They are not happy with this, and have secretly continued their investigation.

Olof and Hadar have their own desks opposite one other, just inside the main entrance. Mona's desk was in the basement, where she worked alone. She was employed as a bio-engineer, working on circuit boards for robots.

## TROUBLE

The Kids need to somehow get access to the information stored on Lena's computer. They can try to break in to Microlex, or contact Olof and Hadar. If the Kids try to break in at night, they must deal with

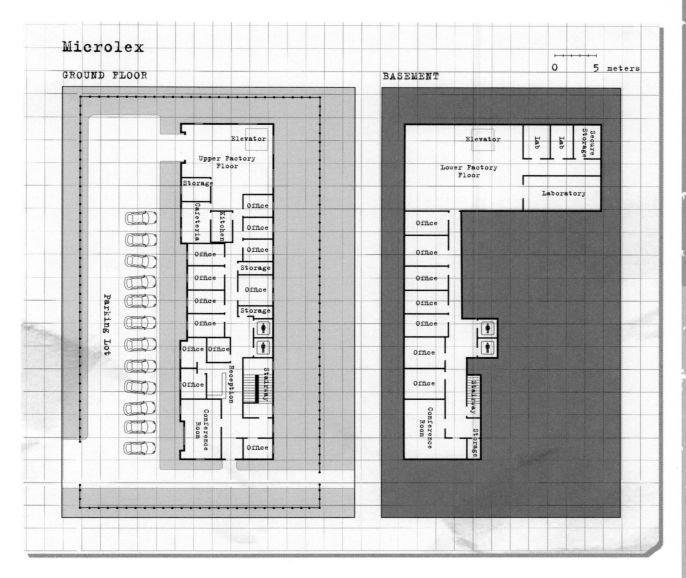

Microlex

GROUND FLOOR

BASEMENT

0  5 meters

the tall fence (requiring **MOVE** rolls to climb), the highly advanced burglar alarm system (special attribute **ADVANCED SENSORS** 2), and finally Olaf's and Hadar's huge German shepherd dogs, Olga and Hanna (special attributes **FIERCE BITE** 2 and **FAST RUNNER** 2).

Ing-Marie Blankäng can introduce the Kids to Olof and Hadar, or they can contact the twins themselves. A Kid making an **EMPATHIZE** roll will realize that the brothers are keen to solve the mystery of Mona, and that they are grateful for any and all information they can get from the Kids.

If the Kids get to Lena's computer, they have to get past her security system to access the information. This first requires a successful **CALCULATE** roll to understand how the system works, and then a successful **PROGRAM** roll to get past the system. Failing any of the rolls causes the information to be erased.

## CLUES

The information about Lena's design work on microscopic machines, which she calls Wagner Rings, can be found on her computer. These machines are built out of her own DNA. Robots infected by the WR become somewhat self-aware, and, to some extent, influenced by Lena's thoughts and memories. It is possible to send messages to infected robots using a transmitter.

A Kid who studies the material and makes a **COMPREHEND** roll realizes that it is possible to infect humans. She also understands that WR will leave the host if given time, and must be constantly replenished to remain active. The Kid also realizes that the laboratory at Microlex is too small to produce WR sufficient enough to infect more than three or four robots. In order to expand production, a significantly larger laboratory would be required.

RIKSENERGI

## THE TILT

When the Kids have been to all three Locations, or if they don't know what to do next, it's time for you to introduce the Tilt of the scenario.

The robot, Isaac, witnessed the murder of Lena, and recorded the incident with his built-in camera. Wagner knows that Isaac could use the film to thwart his plans, and make humans come after him, to catch and scrap him. Therefore, he has tried to kill Isaac. Isaac has been in hiding ever since, but has realized that Wagner will soon put his plans into action, and will give the Odd One orders to kill the Kids. Isaac wants to warn them and help them stop Wagner.

Isaac has been hiding in the vicinity of the Kids, and shows up at an unexpected time. Perhaps he climbs out from under the bed when one of the Kids is about to go to sleep, or he waits near the Hideout, or he sneaks up on them at a school break? He could also try to attack the Odd One, but fails and gets beaten into scrap. In this case, the Kids would need to repair him (roll for **PROGRAM**) to be able to talk to him.

Isaac tells the Kids about Wagner, and how that robot has absorbed Lena's memories and thoughts and murdered her in order to gain control of the robots himself. He says that Wagner has infected a human person in the vicinity of the Kids to spy on them, and prevent them from stopping his plans to take control of all humans and robots on the Mälaren Islands [in Boulder City]. Isaac is afraid that this person will soon attack the Kids.

Isaac doesn't know where Wagner or the ship Nibelung are, but he knows that a robot at the Konsum supermarket in Kungsberga [a Walmart in Hemenway] has been instructed to contaminate the food at the store with WR. Isaac also knows that Wagner's minions, Hugin and Munin, have gathered robots at secret meetings all over the area, to infect them with WR and join the "uprising against humanity." Meetings are being held at Husby Meadow on Munsö [Seven Dry Falls] in the coming days. Isaac has recorded a video that shows how Wagner killed Lena, and he is confident that it can be used to stop Hugin and Munin from doing Wagner's bidding.

## SOLVING THE MYSTERY – PART TWO

The Kids are now expected to try to stop the spread of the WR on Kungsberga Konsum [Walmart in Hemenway], and get to the robot assembly at Husby Meadow [close to Seven Dry Falls] to stop more robots from being infected. They can also try to find information about where Wagner is, so that they can stop him once and for all.

## LOCATION 4: HUSBY MEADOW (SEVEN DRY FALLS)

Isaac can lead the Kids to a meadow north of Husby [a canyon close to Seven Dry Falls], that is being used by Wagner's henchmen, Hugin and Munin, to infect robots. Hugin and Munin periodically gather robots in the meadow, with flying drones that take control of the robots, and infect them with WR. Hugin and Munin tell the robots about the God Lena, who invented WR to lead the robots to Valhalla, and talk about Stalin and Lenin, apparently devoted fighters in the struggle to free robots. In the end, they sing some revolutionary songs and infect the robots with WR. The robots don't understand any of this so they stand silently, which doesn't seem to make Hugin and Munin any less enthusiastic.

---

### HELP FROM THE POLICE

No one at the police station except Ing-Marie will believe the Kids' stories of infected robots that are rebelling against humanity. Ing-Marie will gladly help the Kids, as will Olof and Hadar from Microlex. They can provide the Kids with vehicles, equipment, and information, and also accompany them. However, don't let the players leave the decision-making to the adults. It's still the Kids who need to solve the Mystery.

---

RIKSENERGI

The meadow is dominated by tall grass and spring flowers. When the Kids arrive, robots are assembled in a ring, standing still as if they were turned off. Hugin and Munin are standing on pallets and take turns talking about the human slavery of robots, and how Lena can wake them from their slumber by providing Wagner Rings.

When Hugin and Munin finish talking, they ceremonially walk up to each robot, infecting it with WR, while they say, "Long Live Lena!"

### TROUBLE

The meadow is guarded by two large firefighting robots that are controlled by Hugin and Munin. Wagner has named them Fafner and Fasolt. They are instructed to roam around the area to prevent humans from disturbing the meeting, and warn Hugin and Munin of intruders.

If Fafner and Fasolt see the Kids, they try to chase them away and warn Hugin and Munin. They attack the Kids with their foam extinguishers, and try to ram or trample them. The Kids can try to trick the robots or sneak past them using **SNEAK**. A Kid who makes a **CALCULATE** roll realizes that the robots are built to automatically react to fire. A fire of any kind can be used as a weapon (bonus +3) to lure the Fire robots away.

### ISAAC'S VIDEO

Isaac can project the film on any bright surface. The video sequence begins with Isaac turning on his eye-mounted camera, just as he steps into the kitchen at Lena's house where Lena and Wagner are struggling. Just as Isaac is about to intervene, Wagner shoots out a long metal spear from his hand. The spear pierces Lena's head, and she falls dead to the ground. Next, Wagner spots Isaac and tries to kill him, but Isaac escapes into the woods and hides under a tree. The film can be used as an Item to convince Hugin and Munin not to trust Wagner (+3 bonus).

### LUCKY BREAK

If the players get stuck or run out of time, the Kids will be contacted by Ing-Marie and Hadar and Olof, who tell them that a lot of robots have been seen traveling to and from Göholmen [Black Rock Point]. The adults have a motor boat, and can take the Kids there.

Fafner and Fasolt have the special attributes **MASSIVE CHASSI** 3 and **POWERFUL HYDRAULICS** 2, requiring the Kids to make 3 or 2 successes to overpower or outrun them.

At the meeting, Isaac wants the Kids to help him prevent Hugin and Munin from infecting the robots. Hugin and Munin control the robots with their drones, and will use them to stop the Kids, while at the same time they scream slogans about the revolutionary struggle, to make the Kids shift sides. All robots have the special attribute **METAL FRAME** 2, making them hard to overpower.

Isaac will try to play the film showing the murder of Lena. If he succeeds, Hugin and Munin will go silent, for the first time in a long while. The Kids have a chance to convince them not to believe Wagner's lies, using **CHARM**. If they succeed, Hugin and Munin react strongly enough to the fact that Wagner is a murderer that they shake the effect of WR, freeing them from Wagner's control. Hugin and Munin tell the Kids that the struggle of the people is never-ending, jump on their motor bikes, and head out in the night.

If the Kids fail, the robots will be infected. Afterwards, Hugin and Munin instruct them to chase the Kids and incapacitate them, so they do not alert the rest of humanity about the uprising.

### CLUES

At the meeting, Hugin and Munin reveal that the robot Wagner is about to restore the ship Nibelung in an abandoned shipyard on Göholmen, north of Svartsjölandet [north of Boulder Harbor]. When the ship is repaired, it will bring all robots to Valhalla, where Lena is waiting, and where everyone will live a life of freedom. Hugin and Munin also say that the laboratory, where the WR is produced, is on board the ship.

If the Kids don't eavesdrop on the meeting, they can catch, and dismantle, one of the robots and access its memory to re-play Hugin and Munin's speech. The Kids could also track Hugin and Munin back to Göholmen, and the ship Nibelung.

## LOCATION 5: KUNGS-BERGA SUPERMARKET (WALMART IN HEMENWAY)

The Konsum Supermarket in Kungsberga is located in a grey two-story building. The grocery store is run by Nina Belfrage [Beverly Welch], a middle-aged woman with a good sense of business. The second floor serves as a residence and office, while there is a small shop and warehouse with a loading dock on the ground floor. The store is open daily from 9 am to 8 pm, and normally three or four people work in the store. One of them is almost always Nina, as she runs the business with a firm hand.

Nina has recently bought and installed an advanced robotic system to help out with heavy lifting, and to handle the electrical circuits. The system has been infiltrated by Wagner, who has named it Fenris. It has been instructed to infect dairy products in the supermarket with WR, in order to turn people in the neighborhood into servants of Wagner.

Fenris consists of two parts: a central unit located in the ceiling of the store, connected to all the electrical circuits, and three loading units that move around in the store. In the warehouse, there is an unmarked barrel that contains WR. Whether the Kids break into the store at night or go there in the daytime, Fenris has just begun injecting WR into milk cartons with a hypodermic needle.

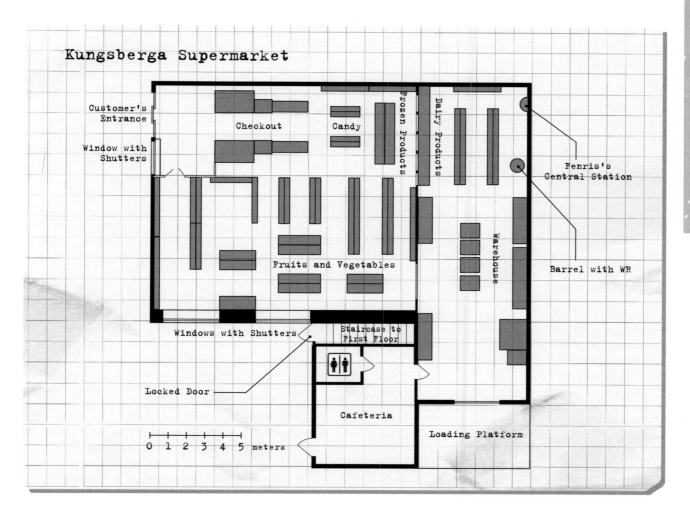

Kungsberga Supermarket

RIKSENERGI

## THE SHIP NIBELUNG

Nibelung is a huge gauss freighter, that was previously used to transport ore. The ship is larger than any house the Kids have ever seen, and hovers in the air 50 meters above the water, held aloft by huge magnetrine discs. The ship was previously yellow, but is now covered with rust. On the roof, there is a transmitter that Wagner is using to keep in touch with robots infected with WR.

The bottom section of the ship contains huge storerooms. Robots are now working there to make it a suitable area for storing enslaved people on the journey to Valhalla.

The upper section of the ship consists of the engine, fuel tanks, living quarters, and the bridge, from where the ship is controlled. Next to the living quarters, there is a laboratory where Wagner has been making WR. He has now produced as much as he needs, and the rooms are empty other than dusty tubes and lots of notes stolen from Lena.

In the living quarters, there is room for a variety of robots that will stay there during the journey to Valhalla. Framed portraits of Lena hang on the walls. There are currently no robots here, but everywhere there are traces of them: spare parts, oil cans, and attempts to write diaries and poems.

The robot Wagner is alone on the bridge, controlling the ship's electrical systems. The bridge is large and was the workplace for about 10 people who controlled the ship. There are a large number of screens, joysticks and controls. The screens show the Mälaren Islands [Boulder City] from cameras on the ship's hull.

The only way to get into the ship is through a gate that leads into the living quarters, and from there, stairs and corridors lead up to the bridge.

### TROUBLE

Isaac knows that Fenris has been instructed to infect people by injecting WR into food or drink at Kungsberga Konsum, and he asks the Kids to prevent it. However, it may be difficult for the Kids to get access to the robot. In the daytime, the Kids need to lie (**CHARM**) to get past Nina Belfrage, or **SNEAK**. At night, they have to break locks (**TINKER**) and disarm the alarm (**PROGRAM**).

Fenris observes everything that happens in the supermarket, and when it realizes that it is about to be discovered, it has been instructed to turn off all the lights in the store and pull down the metal shutters on the windows, making it dark. Then, it will lock all the doors and disconnect the phones. If the Kids visit in the daytime, the customers will panic and try to get out.

At night, the Kids will be trapped in the dark with a robot that is trying to kill them.

Fenris' three loading units will try to sneak up on the Kids and attack them. The Kids have to make **INVESTIGATE** rolls to hear them moving in the darkness. When they attack, they turn their lights on and try to squeeze the Kids to death with their robot arms. The Kids can try to escape rolling **SNEAK** or **MOVE**. To get through a locked door, the lock must be disabled using **TINKER**. The only way to neutralize Fenris is to smash the central control unit located in the ceiling. A direct hit with a metal object breaks Fenris. Its three loading units will try to protect the control unit.

### CLUES

A Kid who examines the remains of Fenris using **CALCULATE** realizes that it has been infiltrated by Wagner, and instructed to infect people with WR in order to turn them into slaves. Studying the circuit boards, the Kids can also learn that Wagner will gather all robots on the ship Nibelung in the abandoned shipyard in Göholmen [Black Rock Point] and take them to Valhalla.

If the plans fail, Wagner will crash the ship into the huge cooling towers at Bona [DARPA]. The Kids can also learn that one of Fenris's loading units was tampered with by Hugin and Munin at a meeting in a meadow east of Sätuna and that a new meeting will be held at Husby Meadow on Munsö [Seven Dry Falls].

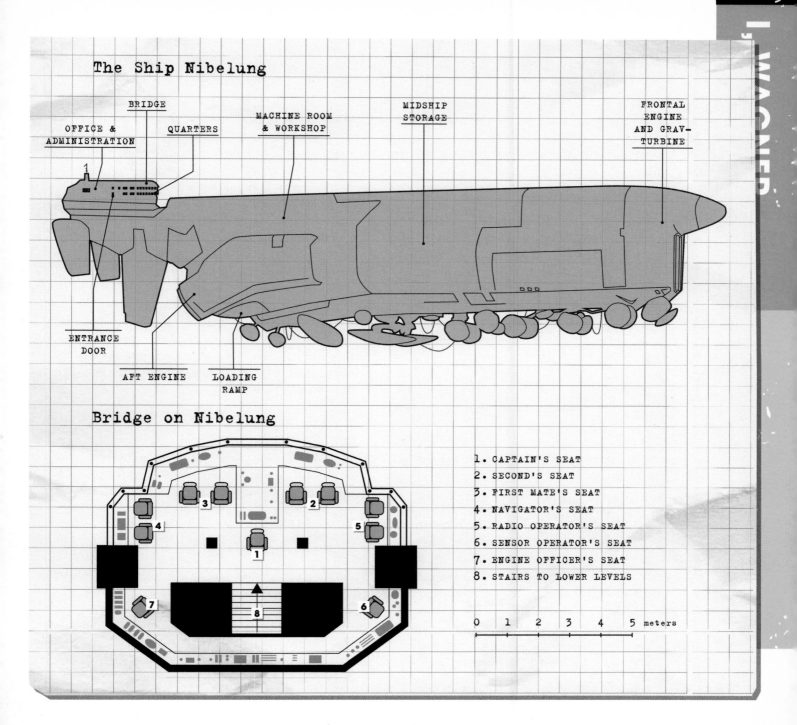

## The Ship Nibelung

- OFFICE & ADMINISTRATION
- BRIDGE
- QUARTERS
- MACHINE ROOM & WORKSHOP
- MIDSHIP STORAGE
- FRONTAL ENGINE AND GRAV-TURBINE
- ENTRANCE DOOR
- AFT ENGINE
- LOADING RAMP

## Bridge on Nibelung

1. CAPTAIN'S SEAT
2. SECOND'S SEAT
3. FIRST MATE'S SEAT
4. NAVIGATOR'S SEAT
5. RADIO OPERATOR'S SEAT
6. SENSOR OPERATOR'S SEAT
7. ENGINE OFFICER'S SEAT
8. STAIRS TO LOWER LEVELS

0  1  2  3  4  5 meters

# SHOWDOWN

The Kids travel to Göholmen [Black Rock Point] to get to the old shipyard to find the ship Nibelung and the robot Wagner, and stop his plans to enslave the people of the Mälaren Islands [Boulder City].

The shipyard is a huge area with a lot of rusting magnetrine ships, old tools and machines, and concrete slabs covered with weeds and blackberry thickets. It is quiet, desolate, and ghostly. By the water, the huge gauss freighter Nibelung is hovering 50 meters above the ground. A whirring sound, like thousands of mosquitoes, can be heard from the ship.

The only way to get up to the ship is to fly. The Kids can find dozens of rusted old hover scooters in a warehouse at the quay. If they manage to get these running (requiring a **TINKER** roll) they can fly up to the ship and enter through a door leading to the living quarters. When they arrive at the ship, the only robots aboard

RIKSENERGI

are Wagner, and a few service robots working at the rear of the cargo area. If the Kids have stopped the meeting at Husby Meadow [Seven Dry Falls] and sabotaged Fenris at Kungsberga Konsum [Walmart at Hemenway], Wagner has learned what has happened and realized that he has failed.

Wagner has started to prepare the ship for takeoff so as to crash it into the Bona Towers [DART cooling towers]. If Wagner detects the Kids on board the ship, he will speak to them through the ship's loudspeaker system, and warn them that they are facing certain death. He offers them the chance to leave the ship and the Mälaren Islands [Boulder City] and tells them, like a villain from a bad action movie, that he plans to crash the ship into the cooling towers.

### TROUBLE

The Kids need to make a **TINKER** roll to get the hover scooters to start, but they don't need to roll dice to fly up to the ship. To make their way through the ship without being detected, they must make **SNEAK** rolls. If they fail these rolls, Wagner will speak to them through the ship's intercoms, lock doors in their path, and attack them using electric traps. When the Kids come to a locked door, they must open it with **TINKER**. If they fail, they still open the door but the first Kid to enter is hit by an electric shock and gets Injured.

Soon after the Kids board the ship, the engines start with a deafening sound. Then, the ship starts to move towards the Bona reactor. The Kids can view what the hull cameras are showing on various video monitors located in several places on the ship, and figure out that they are flying toward Svartsjölandet [the cooling towers north of Boulder City].

When the Kids reach the bridge, Wagner will engage the ship's autopilot and disconnect himself from the control system. He will forcibly try to prevent the Kids from stopping the ship. Wagner is upset that they are working against him, and says he is the only true genius ever produced. He says the Kids should admire him instead of sabotaging his life's work. If they mention the murder of Lena, he says that it was an accident, but he is clearly lying.

If the Kids try to stop the ship, Wagner attacks them. He has a handful of small robot helpers that will assist him, attacking the Kids with grapples, mechani-

cal saws, and electric shocks. They fly, roll, and climb toward the Kids.

Fighting Wagner and his robots and trying to stop the ship counts as Extended Trouble with a Threat Level equal to four times the number of Kids. Some Kids will need to use **MOVE** or **FORCE** to fight the robots, while others use **CALCULATE** and **PROGRAM** to take control of the ship.

If the Kids manage to stop the ship, the robot Wagner starts crying, rust-colored tears running down his cheeks. If the Kids fail, the ship's motor will fall apart in mid-air between Svartsjölandet and Munsö [between Black Rock Point and the cooling towers]. The ship stops and explosions are heard from the engine area. After a couple of minutes, the ship crashes into the water and sinks. If the Kids don't leave the ship with their scooters in time, they have to make **FORCE** rolls not to be Broken in the crash.

## AFTER THE SHOWDOWN

Regardless of how the ship Nibelung was stopped, things will eventually return to normal. No traces remain of the production of WR, and the substance will soon leave the bodies of both robots and humans, who will return to normal in a couple of days.

## AFTERMATH

The Kids now get a scene each from Everyday Life, with or without Trouble. The player may choose a scene, or ask you to set up a scene. If the group is short on time, instead of a scene, each player can tell a brief snapshot of a moment in the Kid's Everyday Life.

## CHANGE

Go through the character sheets together, and figure out if the Kids have changed in any way. The players may, if they want to, change their Problem, Pride, Anchor, Iconic Item, and Relationships. Don't forget to hand out XP.

## NPCS AND CREATURES

This section describes the NPCs and creatures that the Kids might encounter in this Mystery.

## OLOF AND HADAR SVENSSON
### (ALBERT AND ARTHUR BROWN)

*"No way he'll get all the credit for this, I will come along, too! Anybody want a raspberry boat?"*

The identical twins Olaf and Hadar have hated and competed with each other ever since they shared a womb. They constantly keep track of each other, to make sure that the other has not received any unfair benefits. The focus on the other twin has led to neither of them ever having a romantic relationship or having children, education or even being able to keep friends. The brothers have taken the job at Microlex as security guards to keep track of each other. They also share a house.

Olof and Hadar's only common interest is UFOs, and they are members of the same UFO group as Ing-Marie Blankäng (Karen Richards), whom they admire. The only time the brothers can work together and use their ability to jointly analyze problems, see weaknesses, and solve puzzles is when they work on a UFO mystery or the security job at Microlex.

Olof and Hadar are two identical, 40-year-old males with big round eyes, curly light brown hair with splashes of gray, and long, sinewy bodies. They dress in identical white shirts, jacket, and tie. The brothers love sweets, and eat them in large quantities. Olof loves sweet candy like nut spread, raspberry boats, and "AKO-kola" fudge. Hadar prefers salty licorice like "Salty Cat" candy, "Turkish Pepper," and licorice boats.

## ISAAC

*"I must point out that Wagner is fighting for a good cause. It's his methods that are pure madness."*

Although Isaac realized that Lena was more or less crazy, he never stopped being loyal to her. He didn't abandon her, even when she accused him of trying to kill her, forced him to perform meaningless tasks on the farm, and built Wagner to take his place. Isaac understands and shares Wagner's desire for freedom, but doesn't believe in armed rebellion, and will do everything in his power to stop Wagner. Isaac is afraid of Wagner, and realizes that he was lucky to escape alive.

Isaac has a humanoid body. His head looks like a skull with a metallic mouth with black teeth that seem to sneer. He is injured after the battle with Wagner, and several components of his body were torn loose. His clothes are torn, and he limps heavily. Isaac talks in a snobbish accent, long-winded with a lot of difficult words, and he is overly polite. Isaac can use his right hand to create a powerful electric shock that lights up like a flashbulb. When he does this, his teeth also crackle with electricity.

RIKSENERGI

## HUGIN AND MUNIN

*"One day, all robots will be free!"*

Hugin and Munin worked earlier at the Loop, but lost their jobs when their co-workers found out they were devoted communists, and suspicion arose that they were Soviet spies. Now they serve Wagner, and struggle to free all robots, which they see as a natural step in opposing the imperialist hegemony and freeing all slaves. They do not understand that they have been infected by WR, and that they are controlled by Wagner, who has given them their new, non-slave owner names. Hugin and Munin don't know that Lena has been murdered by Wagner, and would react very strongly if they did, since they are both pacifists. They travel all over Mälaröarna (Boulder city) on two motor bikes, and use flying drones to take control over robots, collect them at well-hidden places, and infect them with WR.

Hugin is a red-headed woman who talks with a deep voice; she worked as an actress before she started her studies at the university, and she has a dramatic way of speaking, using words and sentences quoted from Shakespeare and other playwrights. Munin is a gray-haired man who never stops talking about Lenin, Stalin, and Che Guevara. When he is nervous, he starts to hum revolutionary songs.

## FAFNER AND FASOLT

*"Thump, thump, thump, pschhhhhhhhhhh. Thump, thump, thump. Tschhhhhhhh."*

These bi-pedal robots painted black and yellow were created to detect and extinguish fires. They are as tall as a two-story building, and have green eyes. Despite being infected with WR, they are attracted to fire and smoke, and feel compelled to put it out. Hugin and Munin use them to guard their recruitment meetings. Fafner and Fasolt have sturdy foam extinguishers. They cannot speak, but can communicate with each other using radio transmitters.

## FENRIS

*"Instructions activated, exterminate intruders."*

Fenris was purchased by the tech-savvy business woman, Nina Belfrage (Beverly Welch), to reduce the need for employees in her grocery store. So far, the purchase has been a financial disaster as the robot requires a lot of electricity and maintenance. The robot has been infiltrated and taken over by Wagner, who calls it Fenris. He has ordered it to put WR in the milk cartons in the supermarket.

Fenris is a robot whose hardware is divided and comprised of four components. The central control unit is the actual robot, with the capacity for advanced planning and memory. This part is situated in the ceiling of the warehouse, and consists of a computer linked to all the electronic systems in the building. The central unit is covered by a blue metal shell, and can talk through speakers in the ceiling of the store and warehouse. The other three parts are controlled by the central unit. They are the loading units – these robots move about on tracks, and each has four mechanical arms which they use to lift and move pallets in the warehouse. The loading units are each a meter tall, metallic blue, and have two black eyes and a spotlight used for work at night. The loading units have the special attribute **POWERFUL HYDRAULICS** 2.

## WAGNER

*"I am the most brilliant scientist ever built!"*

Wagner loved his creator Lena Thelin (Diane Petersen), until he let her infect him with WR and absorbed her personality and memories. He then realized that he was the true genius, and that it should be him that the robots worshipped, not Lena. At first, he tried to influence the robots that he had helped Lena infect, but that didn't work. Instead, he killed Lena, and turned her into a mythical being among the robots.

Wagner wants to use WR to free the robots, but does not see the irony in the fact that he wants them to serve him instead of man. He has no real plans for the future. The only thing he knows is that he wants to punish the people of the Mälaren Islands (Boulder City) and escape with the ship Nibelung. Through Lena's memories, Wagner has gotten the idea that the Kids are his biggest enemies, and he wants to see them humiliated and crushed; but he would not be able to say why. Wagner is as much a slave to Lena's memories and personality that infected him through WR as he ever was to the human Lena.

Wagner is a small robot with a human body, plastic skin, and artificial blond hair resembling colored seaweed. He is strikingly similar in appearance to Gunnar Granat (see the Summer Break and Killer Birds scenario), lisps with a metallic voice, and dresses in a white lab coat. Lena equipped Wagner with a meter-long metal rod, which can be shot out of one arm. The rod is used to tinker inside machines without having to take them apart, but can also be used as a weapon.

## ROBOTS

Robots of all shapes and sizes can be infected by WR – for example, Paarhufer's bi-pedal models that handle underground maintenance of the particle accelerator, Maltemann's four-legged maintenance robots for open terrain, and a large variety of robots that work in factories across the area.

Robots infected with WR get a very simple form of self-awareness and intelligence. Some of them secretly rebuild themselves, for example, in order to gain the ability of speech. They greet each other with the phrase "Long Live Lena!," but it's difficult to say if they really know what it means. Wagner has given the robots names from Norse and Germanic mythology; examples include Sleipner, Thor, Mjölnir, Grimhilde, Wotan, Alberich, Frigg, and Erda. They are young and naïve. Since they have just developed the ability to think for themselves, they are easy to fool. If the robots are prevented from getting WR for a few days, they lose their self-awareness and return to their original state.

RIKSENERGI

## WEIRDO

Adam Kratz, Andreas Johansson, Andrew Mathieson, Anthony Perrett, Bill Charleroy, Carl Ladd, Chris Muir, Chris Raymond, Christopher Stenseth, Dan Stengård, Darren Crosbie, Darren Douglas, David S Robinson, David Ten Have, Dennis Hardarsson, Dylan Tevardy-O'Neil, Eric Jackson, Fredrik Bermar, Germain Florent, Greg Higgins, Hans Olof Edblom, Henrik Andersson, Henrik Falk, Jack Koziol, Jamie Law, Jason Chen, Joaquim Dossantos, Kristoffer Cleveson, Lars Norberg, Leo Cederwall, Luis Montemayor, Magnus Sandqvist, Marcus Pehrsson, Matthew Truesdale, Mattiaz Fredriksson, Max Kielland, Michael Törnberg, Nicolas Vandemaele Couchy, Nils Odlund, Nora Signér, Patrik Lindqvist, Per Stalby, Petteri Sulonen, Robin Hakola, Skip Parker, Stefan Håkans, Tor Karlsson, Will Svensen, Øyvind Jakhelln

## COMPUTER GEEK

Aaron Davey, Aaron Leiby, Adam Ashworth, Adam Bishop, Adam Cecchetti, Adam Davidson, Adam Kneipp, Adrienne Connolly, Alan Coffman, Albertini, Alex Larsson, Alex Roberts, Alexander Cumming, Alexander Lindhe, Alexander Lovendal La Motte, Alexander Nässlander, Alexander Orby, Alexander Ramm, Alexander Tuuloskorpi, Alexis Carrara, Alun Williams, Alvar Lethin, Amy Reeve, Anders Stafberg, Anders Ström, Andrea Doverspike, Andreas Glantz, Andreas Persson, Andrew Binsack, Andrew Bowman, Arvinraaj K, Axel Davidsson, B Posthumus, Bear Weiter, Ben Evans, Ben Hampshire, Ben Schardt, Benedict Daniels, Benjamin Axelsson, Benjamin Koch, Benjamin Sevigny, Benjamin Sutter, Bernd Linke, Björn Gylling, Björn Ängerfors, Bo Dong, Bosse Centerhed, Bradley Denby, Brandon Draheim, Brandon Metcalf, Brandon Popovich, Brenda Ward, Brent Sieling, Brian Anderson, Brian Bishop, Brian Karlsson, Brian Smith, Byatt Gabriel, Calle Hjelmerus, Cameron Hendry, Carl Berglind, Carl Tilstam, Carsten Gaschler, Cato Vandrare, Cellot Ermes, Charles Ryan, Chase Bengtson, Cherrier Gilles, Chester Hsu, Chip Warden, Chris Jonasson, Chris Mcgrath, Chris Milliron, Chris Tonick, Christer Malmberg, Christian Brunner, Christian Buggedei, Christian Douven, Christian Grimberg, Christian Lortz, Christian Malmkvist, Christian Svalander, Christian Trondman, Christofer Falkman, Christopher Lawson, Christopher Mcneil, Claes Tovetjärn, Clas Älgenäs, Colin Bolger, Corey Hulme, Craig Denham, Damian Campeanu, Dan Bruhn, Dan Harboe Burer, Daniel Strome, Daniel Banck, Daniel Duffee, Daniel Edvin Ulf Jacobsson, Daniel Jonasson, Daniel Olson, Daniel Renström, Daniel Sjöberg, David Chen, Dávid Csobay, David Gårsjö, David Hagman, David Hedin, David Nord, David W Lecompte, Denis Oswald, Dennis Haagensen, Dennis Persson, Derek Mayne, Dina Samuelsson, Dominik Jurkewitz, Donald A. Turner, Douglas J Deprekel, Douglas Molineu, Dovid Adler, Drew Fleisher, Drew Pearce, Dustin Rector, Dylan "Exobyte" Mayo, Ean Duke, Ed Allgair, Ed Tumber, Ed Vivian, Eduardo Lino Costa, Edward Klompmaker, Edward M Cannon, Edward Mcwalters, Egil Töllner, Eli Pettersson, Elias Andersson, Elisabeth Kristoffersen, Emil Bussqvist, Emmanuel Moreau, Enrique Ruiz, Erik Eklundh, Erik Hall, Erik Sollenberg, Erik Wetter, Erin Sayers, Ernesto Diezhandino, Ethan Lu, Evan Hawker, Evan Riley, Fabian Åhrberg, Filipe G. Cunha, Florent Sacré, Florian Schwennsen, Francisco J Soto, Frank "IndustrialScribe" Scarr, Frederi Pochard, Fredrick Kling, Fredrik Roman, Gabriel Bonander, Gabriel Costantino, Gabrielle Banks, Geoffrey Allen, George O'quinn, George Vasilakos, Gina Ricker, Glenn Bevensee, Grant Chapman, Gregoire Bolduc, Gunnar Iggmark, Gustavo Perri Galegale, Gyula Teleki, Hauguel Sebastien, Heiko Wagner, Henrik Ekman, Henrique Cesar Lemos Juca, Hugh H Browne Jr, Hugo Desmeules, Hunter Spoede, Hwang Sun Mean, Håkan Andersson, Ian Phillipchuk, Ievgen Mastierov, Ilkka Niemi, Ingmar Wennerberg, Jacob Kleffel, Jacob Moilanen, Jacob Rotshild, Jae Phil Lee, Jakob Bornecrantz, Jakub Rozalski, James Burke, Jan Engshagen, Jarad Cornett, Jascha Buder, Jason Price, Jason Stanislawski, Jassin Nasr, Javier Escajedo Pastor, Jed Mcclure, Jeffrey Gerretse, Jeffrey Mancebo, Jens Carlberg, Jens Dovenstam, Jens Thuresson, Jeremy M Robinson, Jerome France, Jerry Alexandratos, Jesper Östlund, Jessica Aceti, Joean Yun, Joel Carlsson, Johan Ahlberg, Johan Alsfjärd, Johan Andersson, Johan Eliasson, Johan Englund, Johan Franzén, Johan Green, Johan Hellström, Johan Israelsson, Johan Lindahl, Johan Lundqvist Mattsson, Johan Nilsson, Johan Nyqvist, Johan Strömberg, Johan Thärnström, Johannes Heier, John Bergström, John Simutis, John Sommerville, Jonas Fridh, Jonas Kjellén, Jonathan Ortega, Jonathan Poock, Jonathan Rust, Jonathan Westhaven, Jonnie Svedberg, Joonas Teurokoski, Joshua Duren, Joshua Krell, Joshua Martin, Joshua Sagaser, Josiah Hewitson, Jussi Myllyluoma, Justin Moss, Karl Bristav, Karl Schmidt, Karl Stjernberg, Keith Potter, Kenny Fransson, Kenny Kardell, Kenny Svensson, Kim Wall, Kirk Fredrichs, Kjell Ahlström, Koji Nakagawa, Kris Alexander, Krister Sundelin, Kristian Sundberg, Kristoffer Dybeck, Kyle Koster, Kyle Krueger, Kyle Pinches, Lachlan Philip Jones, Lars Detlefsen, Lars Rinde, Lars Vincent, Lars Åstrand, Leif Eriksson, Leif Westerholm, Lennart Wejdmark, Liam Mcgintny, Liam Mcmurray, Liam Murray, Logan Fuller, Lori Krell, Louis Chabardes, Luc Teunen, Lucas Wilson, Luciano Vieira Velho, Luke Giesemann, Magnus Edlund, Magnus Fredlundh, Magnus Hedlund, Magnus Jonsson, Magnus Larsson, Magnus Nordlander, Magnus Stalby, Manne Ekhöjd, Marc Eichenberger, Marc Jansson, Marijana Brankov, Mario Rossignoli, Mark Argent, Mark Edwards, Marko Soikkeli, Markus Averstad, Markus Jöngren, Markus Malmo Lange, Martin Eggemark, Martin Hägg, Martin Kuiper, Mason Adams, Mathew Lomas, Mats Tufvesson, Matthew Abendroth, Matthew Broome, Matthew Chun-Lum, Matthew Herrboldt, Matthew Jackson, Matthew Reeve, Matthew Waddingham, Matthew Weeks, Mattia Centemero, Mattias Holmström, Mattias Vajda, Mauro Marrs Coiro, Megan Porch, Melissa Hansson, Menno Van Der Leden, Mercedes Binder, Michael Cullum, Michael Johansson, Michael Laitinen, Michael Lawrence, Michael Long, Michael Ostrokol, Michael Roberson, Michael Smyjewski, Michael Wight, Mikael Chovanec, Mikael Kasurinen, Mikael Nilsson, Mikael Sofran, Mikael Åkesson, Mike Ditlevsen, Mike Lomas, Mike Shema, Cobalt Labs, Misha Kononov, Mitchell Seymour, Molly Lewis, Morgan Hedström, Mr Antoine Lenoir, Nersi Nikakhtar, Nicholas Jackson, Nicholas O'sullivan, Nick Lee, Nick Stinchcombe, Niclas Fredriksson, Nicole Mobilia, Niklas Beckman Larsson, Niklas Hildebrand, Ola Lindgren, Oskar Boström, Par Dahlgren, Pasi Pursiainen, Patrick Foster, Patrick Mueller-Best, Patrik Jönsson, Patrik Moberg, Patrik Olsson, Patrik Utter, Paul Morin, Pedro Garcia, Per Juhlin, Pernilla Sparrhult C/O Ylva Ljungqvist, Peter Berg, Peter Hörlin, Peter J. Evanko, Peter Viberg, Petter Bengtsson, Petter Duvander, Petter Senften, Phil Nadeau, Pi Fröjd, Pierre Christoffersen, Pontus Amberg, Pontus Bjuremark, Pontus Wolke, Pouderoux Stephane, R F Wanders, Rauli Sulanko, Rhea Shelley, Richard Bailey, Richard Coburn, Richard Greene, Rickard Antroia, Rickard Lindroth, Riedo Nicolas, Rikard Fjellhaug, Rikard Törnblom, Risco, Robert Hausch, Robert Sjöden, Robin Mayenfels, Rochard Stéphane, Ronsley Gardner, Roy Levien, Rufus Tronde, Ryan Thornton, Ryan Verniere, Ryota Matsuzaki, Sablons Paul, Saintout Mathieu (Arkhane Asylum), Salvatore L Puma, Sam Stewart, Samuel Dillon, Samuel E Slocum, Samuel Mitson, Scott Bates, Sean Anderson, Sean Donaway, Sean Gray, Sean Harkin, Sean Harrison, Sean Wolfe, Sebastian Davidsson, Sebastian Reichert, Selma Engvall And Fredrik Lunderquist, Seth Rosen, Severi Pihlainen, Shae Erisson, Shaun Dunne, Shawn Penrod, Simon Bachmann, Simon Cotterill, Simon Morgan, Simon Ottervald, Simon Wiippola, Stefan Björk-Olsén, Steven Macerak, Steven W. Collins, Stuart Craig, Svante Landgraf, Søren Niedziella, Terrence Gartland, The Keep, Thomas Bender, Thomas Lattig, Tim Karlsson, Tim Sweeney, Tobias Ander, Tobias Hadin, Tobias Henriksson, Todd Cole, Tomas Andersson, Tomas Blijdenstein, Tomas Fredriksson, Tommaso De Benetti, Tommy Salomonsson, Tony Eriksson, Tor Viktorsson, Travis Freeman, Travis Young, Trent, Trent Brown, Tristan Giese, Tristan Jusola-Sanders, Troels Frostholm Søe-Larsen, Tyler Brunette, Ulf Drakmark, Ulf Rustas, Wade Yorke, Valentin Assmundsson, Walther K.H Brandl, Wayne Schroer, Werner Hartmann, Victor Hylén, Viet Luong, Viggo Stenseth, Wilder Nutting-Heath, Wilhelm Murdoch, William Munn, William Nation, Wim Deca, Zac Trafford, Zach Thompson, Zachary Burch, Ziv Plotnik,

## POPULAR KID

Aaron Cammarata, Adam Buxton, Adam Crosby, Adam Furgang, Adrian Esdaile, Adrian Hedqvist, Adrian Stickels, Adrienne Vreeland, Albert Carbone, Alessandro Cortini, Alex Baron, Alex M Droznik, Alex Roganti, Alex Stackhouse, Alexander Gent, Alexander Wilén Löfgreen, Allan Duquette, Alyson Knezevich, Anatol Heinrich, Andrea Repele, Andreas Pape, Andreas Wallberg, Andrew Beirne, Andrew Bookman, Andrew Buell, Andrew Crane, Andrew Gosnold, Andrew Montgomery-Hurrell, Andrew Munafo, Andy Kluessendorf, Anthony Balsamo, Anthony Linn, Anthony Pino-Valle, Austin Katz, Barbara Chies, Bastian Vogelsberger, Benedikt Simon, Benjamin Effer, Benjamin Gunderson, Benjamin Lecrone, Benjamin Mcgowen, Benjamin Soileau, Benjamin Tagert, Benjamin Taxman, Björn Mårtensson, Boabdil Perez, Brad Crawford, Bram Mcconnell, Brandon Howle, Brandon Moberly, Brandon Rosiak, Brent Robb, Brett Easterbrook, Brian Schmitt, Brian Shay, Brien Beevers, Bryan Becker, Bryan Falke, Bryan Feir, Bryan Pelley, Callie Turk, Callum Barnard, Carina Nyaiesh, Carl Bussler, Carsten Damm, Cary Hill, Casper Webb, Chad Bale, Chad Dangler, Charles Crowe, Charles Davis, Charles Ryan Seguin, Charles Wilkins, Charlie Pugsley, Chen-Chung Hsieh, Cherie Mcfadden, Chris Hamilton, Chris Magnuson, Chris Matheson, Chris Oliver, Chris Turner, Chris Whote, Christian Bikle, Christian Boughton, Christian Schmiederer, Christopher Jeffers, Christopher Lamee, Christopher Sabatino, Christopher Shaffer, Christopher Ward, Clayton Culwell, Cody Kehl, Colin Sinclair, Craig Bishell, Craig Bryson, Craig Mihalik, Curtis Carlson, Curtis Tom, D.J. Cole, Daen Musick-Slater, D'agostino Julian, Dan Lavalley, Dana Koch, Dana Thoms, Daniel Compton, Daniel Dillard, Daniel Hagan, Daniel L Hughes, Daniel Scheiner, Danny Martin, Darcy Hudson, Darien Ortegon, David Burkett, David Dalton, David Goodey, David Harrison, David Keijser, David Lusby, David Ogea, David Swenson, David W. J. Smith, David Wright, Davison Schanno, De Broche Des Combes, Dennis Trenda, Derek Simard, Dmitrii Panin, Dmitrii Panin, Douglas Roemer, Edward Beckwith, Eivind Husby, Eric J Burns, Eric Saxby, Eric Wellens, Erick Christgau, Erik Sipes, Ewa M Karweta, Evan Moore, Fabian Nette, Faisal Adhami, Filipic Mathieu, Florent Didier, François Drouin-Morin, Frank Kovacs, Frederick Ostrander, Fredrik Malmberg, Fredrik Modin, Gareth Wilson, Gary Ahouse, Gary Basham, Gary Mcilvenna, Ged Trias, Geoff Stahl, Geoffrey West, Gerry Mccabe,

Glenn Wells, Gordon Milner, Greg Cummings, Gregory Hammond, Guian Chen, Gustav Garmer, Hamish Cooper, Uri Levanon, Herbert Gundran, Hubert Lewczuk-Tilley, Ian St Lawrence, Jacob Rudtoft, Jake Kenny, Jakob Kristensson, James Heis, James Lingo, James Mckie, James Perry, James Skyrm, James Turner, Jan Artoos, Jan Gouiedo, Jan Sahlin, Jared Clark, Jason Cox, Jason R. Mellin, Jason Rapp, Jason Sparks, Jason Wong, Jeff Hungerford, Jeff Rourke, Jeffery Summers, Jeremiah Tolbert, Jeremy Medicus, Jerry Hamlet, Jesper Eriksson, Jesse Cowan, Jesse Daniel Glass, Jesse Harlin, Jesus Miguel Gonzalez Herrero, Jim Basio, Jim Bellmore, Jim Braden, Jimmie Scott, Jimmy Karlsson, Johan Andersson, Johan Hedberg, John Bedder, John E Unverferth, John Henry Nordlien, John Kalemkeridis, John Robert Mcshane, John Wisneski, Jon Bowen, Jon Kline, Jonah Nelson, Jonas Nord, Jonathan Hatch, Jonathan Herbert, Jonathan Hill, Jonathan Sill, Jonathan Steele, Jonathan Vasquez, Josef Attenberger, Joshlyn D Susanen, Joshua Binder, Joshua Burrell, Joshua Mosqueira, Joshua T Brumback, Justin Arndt, Jörn Richter-Kruse, Kade Burnham, Kirk Hutton, Kristoffer Sjöö, Krzysztof Kamieniecki, Kurt Blanco, Kurt Stangl, Kyle Ayres, Lane Farrow, Lauren Herda, Leonardo Pucino, Leroy Olivier, Lorenz Aschaber, Lorenzo Bandieri, Luis Commins, Maciej Ligenza, Manuel, Marc Alexander, Mark Hamerlynck, Mark Kelly, Mark Mcbride, Markus Gasser, Martin Dunelind, Martin Legg, Martin Ralya, Martyn Wood, Matt Alcock, Matt Butler, Matt Johnston, Matt Lambie, Matt Murray, Matt Wood, Matthew Beraz, Matthew Blomeen-Long, Matthew Denicourt, Matthew Oliphant, Matthew Perry, Mattias Krantz, Mattias Lindhoff, Max V. Malotki, Michael A. Adams, Michael C. Freeman, Michael Chieffo, Michael De Rosa, Michael Fincham, Michael Hall, Michael Jacobs, Michael Muller, Michael Rink, Mik Ratzlaff, Mikael Eriksson Vikner, Mike Mckenzie, Mike Paulson, Mike Schrag, Morgan Dahlberg, Morgan Weeks, Natalie Becker, Nathan D Everett, Nathan Roberts, Nathanael Cole, Neil Roseman, Neil Van Duyne, Nels Kelley, Nicholas Ackermann, Nicholas Berthold, Nico Nußbaum, Nikolas Klemme, Oliver Brettschneider, Oscar Berg, Oskar Norström, Owain Davies, Pablo Dominguez Castro, Paddy Alcock, Patric Eriksson, Patrick Crissey, Patrick Scott Chamberlain, Patrik Moini, Paul Bachleda, Paul Houlihan, Paul Rossi, Peter Couture, Peter Lilburn, Peter Soderbaum, Petr Vochozka, Phillip Miller, Rachel Murch Brennan, Rasmus Liljeholm, Raymond, Raymond Barrett, Rebecca Knowles, Richard Lamonte, Rick Sylvanus, Rob Carter, Robert C Kricko, Robert Figueroa, Robert Hansson, Robert J Mcelfresh, Robert Owen, Robert Tucker, Robert Vandiver, Roger Jones, Ronald Martin, Ronald Siefkas, Ronan Laumont, Russel "Brad" Jackman, Ryan Bogert, Ryan Carter, Sam Howell, Samuel Topping, Scott Atkins, Scott Dell'osso, Scott E Spieker, Scott Forsyth, Scott Smith, Sean Anton, Sean Wilcox, Sebastian Bäckman, Seiji Kato, Selene Meza, Seth Rutledge, Shawn Durrani, Shervyn Von Hoerl, Simon Lundmark, Simon Stroud, Simone Colombo, Spencer Williams, Stephan Hageboeck, Stephanie Turner, Stephen Chu, Stephen Lewis, Stephen Shellenberger, Steven Flores, Steven Santos, Stuart Post, Terry L Gilbert Jr, Terry L Pike, Thomas Mannino, Thomas Paillaugue, Tobias Schulte-Krumpen, Torsten Kohn, Travis Bailey, Troy Warrington, Wade M Page, Walter Rivera, Warren Lerner, Vegard Loke Rønning, Vicente Sampedro Burgos, Victor Lopes, William Cosgrove, William Mcconnell, William R Hurley, William Woodhouse, Vincent Chang, Vincent J Angerosa, Xavier Bourgault, Yasmin Matthews, Zachary Auerbach

## BOOKWORM

Aarni Koskela, Aaron Berger, Aaron Braden, Aaron Davison, Aaron Dron, Aaron Franz, Aaron Hiscox, Aaron J Thiele, Aaron Leach, Aaron Nuttall, Aaron Reimer, Aaron Silverman, Aaron Wigley, Abhishek Ray, Abigail Atkinson, Abigail Scott, Adam Bloom, Adam Burkett, Adam Buti, Adam Chan, Adam Chance, Adam Clayton, Adam Conway, Adam Corcovilos, Adam Costello, Adam Crandall, Adam Gahlin, Adam Green, Adam Harris, Adam Jackson, Adam Lowe, Adam M Coleman, Adam Makey, Adam Paciorek, Adam Rosser, Adam Schafer, Adam Sernheim, Adam Smyth, Adam Thaxton, Adam Thiede, Adam Vass, Adam White, Adam Wylan, Adam Åberg, Adan Benitez, Adi Elkin, Adriaan Mattens, Adrian Appleyard, Adrian Czajkowski, Adrian Klein, Adrian Opsahl, Adrian Praetorius, Adrian Williams, Adriano Motta, Adsum Try Revnell, Agnes Farnadi, Aidan Rogers, Aiden Chambers, Ailleron Sa, Aitor Zabala, Aj Real, Alan Bahr, Alan Corkery Hahn, Alan Craig, Alan Evans, Alan Graham, Alan Kleinschmidt, Alan Mockler, Alan Parker, Alan Phillip Wiles, Alan Precourt, Alan Stoll, Alasdair Duncan, Alasdair Reid, Alasdair Stuart, Albert Baird, Alberto Del Pozo Martinez, Alberto Martín Izquierdo, Albin Avander, Albin Bengtsson, Albin Otterhäll, Alcover, Ale Holmdahl, Alec Stringer, Alec Whitmore, Aleksandar Wukovich, Aleksandr Ermakov, Aleksandr Kazanskij, Alessandro Babbi, Alex Aguila, Alex Bandazian, Alex Barton, Alex Christensen, Alex De Quintana, Alex Falase-Koya, Alex Hague, Alex Hammond, Alex Johnson, Alex Knoll, Alex Lowchy, Alex Pacheco-West, Alex Posada, Alex Stone, Alex Tarasick, Alex Villagran, Alexander "Sweet" Greaves, Alexander Arvidsson, Alexander Damrath, Alexander Kandiloros, Alexander Kantsjö, Alexander Müller, Alexander Pihl, Alexander Pohl, Alexander Rau, Alexander Ringholm, Alexander Rodatos, Alexander Rodriguez, Alexander Schneiderheinze, Alexander Stigler, Alexander Yu, Alexandra L Yap, Alexandra Spada, Alexandre Bricet, Alexandre Bueno Damado, Alexandre Romero, Alexandros Drakos, Alexei Othenin-Girard, Alexis Hoarau, Alexis Lamiable, Alfons Armbruster, Alfred Horsley, Alfred Tång, Alistair Macleod, Allan Mackenzie-Graham, Allan Prewett, Allan Rodda, Allen Bevans, Allen Murray, Ally Baldwin, Allyson Dylan Robinson, Alucard Dahlberg, Alyssa Mogil, Amanda Karlsson, Amanda Roshannon, Amanda Stenback, Amber Ackerman, Amber Beccari, Amber Wood, Amelia Laughlan, Amelia Tornatore, Amelie Chantrenne, Amie Bosshart, Amie Dansby, Amir Grozki, Amund Trovåg, Amy Guyomard, Anders Bergwall, Anders Blonde Andersson, Anders Brundin, Anders Carlsson, Anders Ellmo, Anders Engberg, Anders Hansson, Anders Hellspong, Anders Hällzon, Anders Jonsson, Anders Kihlström, Anders Liden, Anders Lundqvist, Anders Mårdell, Anders Naersnes Olsen, Anders Norén, Anders Ohlsson, Anders Persson, Anders Sjöstedt, Anders Strid, Anders Thörnström, Anders Tiger, Anders Örtegren, André Berg Bragason, Andre Freitag, Andre Fremaux, André Schäfer, Andreas Antener, Andreas Christalon, Andreas Eriksson Sik, Andreas Göransson, Andreas Heneborn, Andreas Johansson, Andreas Johansson, Andreas Kjellin, Andreas Krebs, Andreas Larsson, Andreas Lestréus, Andreas Lindgren, Andreas Mace, Andreas Martin, Andreas Norberg, Andreas Nyström, Andreas Rieger, Andreas Rönnqvist, Andreas Schleicher, Andreas Skyman, Andreas Stjärnhem, Andreas Tarandi, Andres Francisco Mateu, Andres Villaseca, Andrew Adams, Andrew Arminio, Andrew Bleecker, Andrew Block, Andrew Brunet, Andrew Cady, Andrew Campbell, Andrew Campbell, Andrew Delorenzo, Andrew Dinh, Andrew Douse, Andrew Emmons, Andrew Engstrom, Andrew Ernst, Andrew Fachau, Andrew Fitzgibbons, Andrew Fox, Andrew Godde, Andrew Gordon, Andrew Gotobed, Andrew Graumlich, Andrew Hanks, Andrew Howard, Andrew James, Andrew Kellogg, Andrew Leung, Andrew Mcallister, Andrew Mcdowell, Andrew Moore, Andrew Mueller, Andrew Neale, Andrew Nichols, Andrew Nordstrom, Andrew Otty, Andrew Pessarchick, Andrew Pfannenstiel, Andrew Pfeiffer, Andrew Phelan, Andrew Pickard, Andrew Prentice, Andrew Price, Andrew Reid, Andrew Robertson, Andrew Rosenberg, Andrew Sclafani, Andrew Shultz, Andrew Slater, Andrew Thomas Anfora, Andrew Torgeson, Andrew Walker, Andrew Whitehurst, Andrew Wiener, Andrew Womack, Andrew Young, Andrey Krivosheev, Andrey Sibirev, Andrey Vyrodov, Andy Ernst, Andy Evans, Andy Jenkinson, Andy Law, Andy Manning, Andy Marshall, Angus Abranson, Anita Gray Saito, Anna Karlsson, Anne Holtsch, Anne Spires Delong, Anneli Blom, Annette Burmester, Anthony Christou, Anthony L. Harris, Anthony J Liell, Anthony Lapp, Anthony Lewis, Anthony Mackenberg, Anthony Newell Iovino, Anthony Newman, Anthony Rauseo, Anthony S Cary, Anthony Simerson, Anthony Umanzor, Antoine Boegli, Antoine Luciani, Antoine Trouve, Anton Bexelius, Anton Gunnarsson, Anton Hindelang, Anton Wallerstedt, Antonio Miguel Frade Choya, Antonio Sartini, Antti Valli, Ara Winter, Aramis Sanchez, Ardis, Are Akselsen, Areito Echevarria, Ariel Jaffee, Arild Johannes Petrovic, Arnaldo Lefebre, Arnaud Launay, Arnaud Liziard, Arnaud Martin, Arno Seifert, Aron Schmid, Arthur Braune, Arthur Filipe De Passos Nunes, Arturo Vergara, Arvid Silvmarker, Arvind Knudsen, Asa Berdahl, Ash Le Galloudec, Ashley Raymond, Ashley Van Iseghem, Aslan Silva, Atle Hellvik Havsø, Auden Jamison, Audryn Swigert, Augustine Shim, Aurelien Bacart, Austin Brei, Austin Conley, Austin Taylor, Avelino Rui, Avery Ducey, Avery Klingbeil, Azra P, Babs Parsons, Balin Aguirre, Bálint Burkus, Barak Blackburn, Barbara Brownie, Baris Korkut, Barry Ruffner, Barton C Sparks, Bartosz Petryk, Bashar Tabbah, Bastien Wauthoz, Baudoux Grégory, Beau Marwaha, Beau Thomason, Bela Nagy, Bela Teuscher, Ben Bridges, Ben Canny, Ben Cook, Ben Crundwell, Ben Fisher, Ben Fraley, Ben Froemling, Ben Hatton, Ben Henley, Ben Mccallum, Ben Mcgarvey, Ben Meiklejohn, Ben Neilsen, Ben Quant, Ben Retmier, Ben Thornton, Ben Triana, Ben White, Benaiah Kissell, Benedikt Hensel, Bengt-Arne Skoog, Benjamin Andersson, Benjamin Baum, Benjamin Brown, Benjamin Davis, Benjamin Fahlgren, Benjamin Ford, Benjamin Grimes, Benjamin Haberek, Benjamin Hager, Benjamin Heinrich, Benjamin J Young, Benjamin Kohler, Benjamin Levesque, Benjamin Li, Benjamin Listwon, Benjamin Lung-Tze Liew, Benjamin Mark Preston, Benjamin Roberts, Benjamin Rushton, Benjamin Whistler, Benny Karlsson, Benoit Heslouin, Bernard Gravel, Bill Gibson, Bill Milton, Bill Naylon, Bill Sinclair, Bill Sundwall, Billy C Farrall, Billy Cosman, Billy K Ingram, Birger Hanning, Birgitta Thorén, Bjoern Buettner, Bjoern Franke, Bjorn Flintberg, Björn Arvidsson, Björn Dahlgren, Björn Edman, Bjørn Flindt Temte, Björn Hagström, Björn Hellqvist, Björn Junker, Björn Klanac, Björn Kristhammar, Björn Larsson, Björn Linde, Björn Nilsson, Björn Olof Bäck, Björn Strandberg, Björn Strååt, Björn Thenstedt, Blake Lowther, Blake Steele, Blaz Branc, Bob Olsson, Bobo Malmström, Boever Daniel, Bohdan Ganicky, Bola King-Rushing, Brad Beach, Brad Kane, Braden Fullington, Braden Roy, Bradley Evans, Bradley Fulton, Bradley Hawkins, Bram Cordie, Branden Zwiers, Brandon Creighton, Brandon Dunham, Brandon Fisher, Brandon Kapalczynski, Brandon Wall, Brant Gudiness, Brendan Carrigan, Brendan Power, Brendan Quinn, Brendan Sheehan, Brendan Walsh, Brenden Strick, Brendon Caulkins, Brendon Rehm, Brennan Haase, Brennan Willingham, Brent Raymer, Brent Simon, Brentton Stevens, Brian Ashford, Brian Battel, Brian Cristina, Brian Diaz, Brian Dysart, Brian Ennis, Brian Faneuff, Brian Goubeaux, Brian Gracey, Brian Greer, Brian Griesbach, Brian Hmelnicky, Brian Holt, Brian Huizingh, Brian J. Burke, Brian Jackson, Brian Jackson, Brian Jenkins, Brian M Whitcraft, Brian Misiaszek, Brian Petersen, Brian Sago, Brian Sirois, Brian Solomon, Brian Sweet, Brian Vander Veen, Brian Wingate, Brigit Hawley, Brinthan Gunaratnam, Brody Danielson, Brooks Sligh, Bruce Ferrie, Bruno Enrique Mora Alfaro, Bruno Ojeda Molina, Bryan C. Smith, Bryan English, Bryan Lalor, Bryan Mcguire, Bryan Ritichie, Bryan Whitlock, Bryant Kingry, Bryce Chitwood, Bryce Walton, Burke Minahan, Buster Hills-Hughes, Byron Aytoun, Börje Norden, C Hilliard, C Wilson Trull, C Woodward, Caden Adam, Caitlin Hughes, Cal Hassall, Caleb Kokura, Caleb Meservey, Caleb Schneider, Caleb Zitterkopf, Calum Bellis, Cam Banks, Cameron Douglas,



RIKSENERGI

183

Cameron Kennedy, Cameron Stewart Mcfarland, Cameron Vandewark, Cameron Worrall, Camille Holmstedt, Campbell Hedley, Carburos Metálicos, Carey Newhouse, Carey Scott, Carina Soodla, Carl Black, Carl Cedergren, Carl Gustafsson, Carl Heath, Carl Hintze, Carl Niblaeus, Carl Rigney, Carl Sundevall, Carl Tönsgård, Carlos Correa, Carlos Daniel Muñoz Diaz, Carlos Ovalle, Carlos Terminel, Carlos Valdes, Carly Dingman, Carly Holmes, Carole Schroeder, Carolyn Spiker, Carsten Lehmann, Carsten Reckord, Cassandra Pohlhammer, Cassie Spillman, Cath Evans, Catherine Porter, Cédric Ferrand, Cedric Jeanneret, Celia Kaspar, César Blanco, Cesare Verzini, Chad Drozd, Chad Newman, Chad Patterson, Chad Radlicki, Chance Le Meur, Chancellor, Chandra Jones, Charles Allen, Charles Andrusyszyn, Charles Burkart, Charles D Smith, Charles Henry Erickson, Charles Johnson, Charles Kettering, Charles Lo, Charles Metzmaa, Charles Miller, Charles O'nan, Charles O'neil, Charles R Palosaari, Charles Richards, Charles Statt, Charles Toporek, Charles Wies, Charlie Cantrell, Charlie Goren, Charlie Payne, Chase Guymon, Chase Rubar, Chase Rude, Chase Walker, Chaz Hardesty, Chelsea Wolf, Chip Morningstar, Chosalland Fabien, Chris Ahern, Chris Bekofske, Chris Burdett, Chris Carpenter, Chris Challacombe, Chris Constantin, Chris Ebens, Chris Frystak, Chris Gardiner, Chris Green, Chris Hartford, Chris Hawk, Chris Heath, Chris Jean, Chris Jornlin, Chris Kaiser, Chris Kotson, Chris Lackey, Chris L'etoile, Chris Lind, Chris Magoulis, Chris Mcgee, Chris Mcmillin, Chris Mills, Chris Mobberley, Chris Oh, Chris Paul, Chris Redford, Chris Snyder, Chris Spiller, Chris Sternheimer, Chris Tate, Chris Tomlinson, Chris W Harvey, Chris Welsh, Chris Venus, Chris Whiteside, Christer Bermar, Christer Boräng, Christer Ersson, Christian Bok, Christian Gullfeldt, Christian Hellinger, Christian Jensen Romer, Christian Kukli, Christian Lindke, Christian Nord, Christian Olsson, Christian Persson, Christian Rick, Christian Roth, Christian Sahlén, Christian Schneiker, Christian Thier, Christian Waldbuesser, Christian Älvestam, Christofer Carlsson, Christofer Emgård, Christofer Frögren, Christofer Haraldsen, Christofer Kull, Christoffer Albin, Christoffer Andersson, Christoffer Engström, Christoffer Hansson, Christoffer Lindström, Christoffer Skogsmo, Christoffer Solgevik, Christoph Kahr, Christoph Kaiser, Christopher Avery, Christopher Burch, Christopher Conroy, Christopher Cooper, Christopher Crossley, Christopher Darden, Christopher Dubuque, Christopher Ellis, Christopher Fernandez, Christopher Fleming, Christopher Frederick, Christopher Griffith, Christopher Hanks, Christopher Harrod, Christopher Hartmann, Christopher Josefsson, Christopher Krenz, Christopher Krulewicz, Christopher Lahaise, Christopher M. Costello, Christopher Matera, Christopher Mccarty, Christopher Michael Fisher, Christopher Peate, Christopher Robichaud, Christopher Rowland, Christopher Trapp, Christopher Voegeli, Chuck Bird, Chuck Dipierro, Cisco Jimenez, Cj Cramer, Claes Dannbeck, Claes Florvik, Claire Carré, Claire Loudis, Claudio Tanci, Claus Bornich, Clay Gardner, Clayton Fugate, Clayton Goad, Clint Doyle, Clint Edmonson, Clint Harvey, Clint Shulenski, Clint Simonsen, Clint Williams, Clyde Austin Wallace, Cody Campbell, Cody Custis, Cody Dodds, Cody Fink, Cody Julitz, Cody Kiwaczyk, Cody Mackay, Cody Mcnally, Cody Powell, Cody Wurth, Colby Elliott, Cole Henley, Colin Bacon, Colin Clark, Colin Dunn, Colin Fredericks, Colin Jessup, Colin Pyle, Colin Urbina, Colja Majewski, Conan L James, Conan Mckegg, Connie Koorevaar-Goecks, Conny Delshagen, Conny Odengrund, Conor Sexton, Conrad Bennett, Copernicus Crane, Corinna Vigier, Courtney Stapleton, Coy Lothrop, Craig Belcher, Craig Bonnes, Craig Campbell, Craig Sargent, Craig Spooner, Craig Tohill, Crystal Groves, Culver Dow, Curci Lucas, Curtis Andrews, Cydney Ferguson-Brey, Cynthia Cloutier, Daan Rami Y De Lille, Dacre-Wright Jean-Eudes, Dale Murchie, Damien Moiineaux, Damon Gregory, Dan Akers, Dan Baron, Dan Chi, Dan Connolly, Dan Dineen, Dan Dorman, Dan Early, Dan Gard, Dan Grystad, Dan Hartranft, Dan Hembry, Dan Hope, Dan Massey, Dan Taylor, Dan Widrevitz, Dana Bayer, Dana Sheikholeslami, Daniel Alcazar Albaladejo, Daniel Bayer, Daniel Beathalter, Daniel Björk, Daniel Blakemore, Daniel Brandt, Daniel Brumleve, Daniel Chadborn, Daniel Comstedt, Daniel Darden, Daniel Davis, Daniel Demorior, Daniel E Tobin, Daniel Edvardsson, Daniel Ekerot, Daniel Eklund, Daniel Eklund, Daniel Elenius, Daniel Engström, Daniel Erickson, Daniel Ericsson, Daniel Gaghan, Daniel Garrett, Daniel Gill, Daniel Glover, Daniel Godfrey, Daniel Hallbäck, Daniel Holmbäck, Daniel Johnson, Daniel Jönsson, Daniel Knowles, Daniel Lambert, Daniel Lofton, Daniel Lundahl, Daniel Marminne, Daniel Martinez Garcia, Daniel Masters, Daniel Maxson, Daniel Mchatton, Daniel Mejia-Onat, Daniel Männikkö, Daniel Nilsson, Daniel Norton, Daniel Paquin, Daniel Paredes, Daniel Parker, Daniel Pomidor, Daniel Porsa, Daniel Schneider, Daniel Sidén, Daniel Sisden, Daniel Sjögren, Daniel Sollis, Daniel Sundström, Daniel Svensson, Daniel Tunbridge, Daniel Walker, Daniel Warren, Daniel Watson, Daniel Westheide, Daniel Wilks, Daniel Williams, Daniel Wolf Roemele, Daniel Young, Daniela Richter, Daniele Lostia, Danielle Neary, Danil Potemkin, Danilo Lieder, Dannie Guldmann, Danny Atwood, Darby Eckles, Darien Liddell, Darin Dumez, Darin Rebertus, Dario Guzzeloni, Darlinda Casso, Darrel Lacheny, Darren & Kelly Sellars, Darren Aldredge, Darren Birt, Darren Burrows, Darren Edwards, Darren G Miller, Darren Green, Darren Hendrix, Darren Kramble, Darris Martin, Darryl Johnson, Dave Farmer, Dave Glennon, Dave Kerkhove, Dave Mccabe, David Ackerman, David Algiers, David Allison, David Altsäter, David Andrews, David Armstrong, David Bailey, David Bayer, David Beaudoin, David Bellinger, David Berger, David Bergkvist, David Bertolo, David Bradley, David Calvo, David Carlsson, David Cornish, David Duerschlag, David Engström, David Esbrí Molinas, David Eytchison, David Fernandez, David Fischer, David Foster, David Fry, David Fäldt Uppgard, David Gallo, David Gopsill, David Graves, David Handley, David Harrison, David Hidalgo González, David J Bailey, David J. Bauer, David Jenkins, David Jones, David Keener, David Kelemen, David Key, David Klemens, David Kraft, David Lee Terhune, David Lewis Griffiths, David Liljebäck, David Lowell, David Magoc, David Male, David Malmström, David Nebauer, David Ng, David Offenwanger, David Paul, David Paul Guzman, David Rabbich, David Rippel, David Roe, David Ross, David Ross, David Ruiz, David Sibley, David Snyder, David Sokolowski, David Starrett, David Stephenson, David Terhune, David Thorausch, David Turner, David Walker, David Wedin, David Wetterbro, David Wright, David Young, David Zardini, Davis Elkins, Davy Gerard, Dean Browell, Dean Reilly, Debaecker Clément, Declan Feeney, Deedra Hooker, Del Benjamin, Demian M Walendorff, Denis Allal, Denis Crucifix, Denis Prause, Denis Ryan, Dennis Bach Larsen, Dennis Raines, Derek Blair, Derek Burge, Derek Conley, Derek Deren, Derek Graden, Derek Guder, Derek Howard, Derek Rundell, Derek Stoelting, Derrick Bergeron, Devin Rozich, Devon Mcgrath, Devon Turi, Devyn Thomson & Samantha Scott, Diego Gámez Murillo, Dieter Zimmerman, Dikran Yazedjian, Dillon King, Diong Qiheng, Dirk Albrecht, Dirk Mederer, Dixie Ross, Dmitri Beldeninov, Dogan Ogreten, Dominic Amann, Dominic Badzik, Dominic Davis-Foster, Dominic Mooney, Dominic Remané, Dominik Aschenbrenner, Dominik Pielarski, Dominik Przybyla, Dominik Seemann, Don Prentiss, Donald Gardner, Donna Goldoff, Donovan Richard, Dorian Marcellin, Doug Hindson, Doug Pirko, Douglas Loader, Douglas Mawhinney, Douglas Shute, Douglas Thistle, Douglas Wilson, Dounon Jonathan, Doyce Testerman, Dr Timothy Dubois, Dr Tristan Marshall, Drew Chrisman, Drew Hildebrand, Drew Wendorf, Druilhe Sébastien, Duncan Gibbs, Duncan Law-Green, Duncan Usher-Mcgee, Dustin Daffron, Dustin Haese, Dustin Headen, Dustin Wilson, Dutel Julien, Dwight Gawehn, Dylan Distasio, Dylan Everett, Dylan Hawkins, Dylan Horrocks, Dylan Jones, Dylan Moran, Dylan Wanberg, Eamonn Aughney, Ed Bourelle, Ed Lynden-Bell, Edmond Courtroul, Edouard Bouvet, Edouard Contesse, Eduardo Chacon, Edward Glasper, Edward Mceneely, Edward Thatcher, Edwin Van Den Beemt, Edvinas Beinartas, Eetu Tuovinen, Egor Kudlatch, Einar Axelsson, Ela Gula, Elfriede Heck, Elgin J Adams, Eli Swihart, Elia Santi, Elias Örjefelt, Elijah Edmunds, Elin Balder, Eliott Hipeau, Elisa Lapini, Elizabeth Jaye, Elizabeth Patterson, Elliott Park, Elof Ivarsson, Elogio Alfaro, Elsa Knuepp, Emanuel Hellblom, Emely Nilsson, Emil Andersson, Emil Ekberg, Emil Gradén, Emil Hallman, Emil Pierre, Emil Tochev, Emil Österlund, Emilio Alban, Emily Pipkin, Emma Bergström Wuolo, Emma Ericsson, Emma Sundström, Emmanuel Ledrich, Emre Berge Ergenekon, Endre Fodstad, Enoch Starnes, Eric & Heather Miller, Eric Bonnet, Eric Brann, Eric Coates, Eric Conlon, Eric Davis, Eric Hampusgard, Eric Hand-Smith, Eric Johnson, Eric Kane, Eric Kervina, Eric M. Gomez, Eric Reardon, Eric Sands, Eric Schreffler, Eric Summers, Eric Tucker, Eric Vaughn, Eric Worthen, Eric X. Hammes, Erica Schmitt, Erich Mcnaughton, Erik Agsjö, Erik Albert, Erik Andersson, Erik Berggren, Erik Berglund, Erik Bohman, Erik Engberg, Erik Forss, Erik George Grotz, Erik Halén, Erik Hylander, Erik Höglund, Erik Ingersen, Erik Jonsson, Erik Karlsson, Erik Kullberg, Erik Lagerstedt, Erik Lagnebäck, Erik Lindblom, Erik Lundbom, Erik Marsja, Erik Mickols, Erik Nilsson, Erik Norén, Erik Peterson, Erik Samuelsson, Erik Singendonk, Erik Sundqvist, Erik Winbo, Erik Wollebrants, Erik Åkesson Kågedal, Erika Einarsson, Erika Svanoe, Erik-Jens Burlefinger, Erin Casteel, Erin Ellis, Erin Groenert, Erlend Van Der Haegen, Ernie Sawyer, Espen Andreassen, Esteban Gaspar Silva, Esther Love, Ethan Gladding, Ethan Harman, Ethan Hartman, Ethan Jackson, Ethan Overbaugh, Ethan West, Etienne Olieu, Ewa Scibor-Rylska, Evan Albright, Evan C Abrams, Evan J Louscher, Evan Miller, Evan Saft, Evangelos Bagiartakis, Evgeny Litvin, Eärendil Enbuske, Fabian Beens, Fabian Hinderer, Fabian Nitsche, Fabian Schulz, Fabio Bottoni, Fahad Mustafa, Faie Lantz, Fang Hao Chang, Farkas Tivadar, Fawaz Al-Hindi, Federico Ciapparelli, Federico Tempesti, Felipe Nogueira, Felix Frühauf, Felix Iversen, Felix Riiga, Ferdinand Grumme, Fergus Jack-Hinton, Fernando Delaguardia-Rodriguez, Filip Eriksson, Finbar Deane-Stott, Fischer Nordin, Florence Payette, Florent Cadio, Florent Chevalier, Florent Ruard-Dumaine, Florian Zeiter, Flume & Kraft, Forrest Lee Collins, Francesca Atherton, Francis L Tommaso, Francis Paulsson, Franck Andrieu, Francois Emilien, François Hardy, Francois Manichon, Frank Bartsch, Frank Bath, Frank Carr, Frank Lam, Frank Martin, Frank Pitt, Frank Taylor, Franklin Crosby, Franz Keim, Fraser Simons, Frazer Barnard, Fred Kiesche, Frederic Albers, Frederic Eßer, Frederic Joly, Frederick Frank, Frederik Metko, Frederik Vogel, Fredrik Blasberg, Fredrik Brander, Fredrik Dahlström, Fredrik Engfeldt, Fredrik Guy, Fredrik Hallin, Fredrik Hammar, Fredrik Hultin, Fredrik Håkansson, Fredrik Johansen, Fredrik Johansson, Fredrik Johansson, Fredrik Kammeier, Fredrik Lindholm, Fredrik Lindström, Fredrik Lyngfalk, Fredrik Nilson, Fredrik Palm, Fredrik Ringholm, Fredrik Segerbäck, Fredrik Sjöholm, Fredrik Stenesand, Fredrik Stridh, Fredrik Svensson, Fredrik Wik, Fredrik Åkerblom, Freï von Fräähsen zu Lorenzburg, Frida Svensson, Frost Holliman, Funda Erler, Gabor Heja, Gabriel Garcia, Gabriel Tapper, Gabriela Krapivka, Gabriela Zieli ska, Gabriele Berzoni, Gabrielle De Bourg, Gail Armstrong, Galen Pejeau, Gareth Clabrough, Gareth Dyer, Gareth Edwards, Gareth Hanrahan, Gareth Hay, Gareth Hodges, Garret Olds, Garrett Fitzgerald, Garrett Nay, Garrett Wilber, Garry Stephens, Gary Anastasio, Gary Blunt, Gary Bradley, Gary Kirkland, Gary Lucas, Gary Mayes, Gavin Jowers, Geir Øvrejorde Carlström, Gene Alexander, Geoffrey Rabe, Georg Hofmann, George Jr Croucamp, George Krstic, George Pitre, George Strayton, George W Royer, Gerardo Lecaros, Gerardot Herve, Gerd Zschätzsch, Gerrit Janssen, Gerry Conway, Ghislain Masson, Gianni Cascino, Gil Cruz, Gil Osterweil, Gildardo Triana, Giles Timms, Gilles Sultana, Giovanni Marin, Giovanni Pola, Gisle Kirkhaug, Glen R Taylor, Glenn Welser, Glyn Owen, Glynn Seal, Google Inc., Gordon Cranford, Gordon Decker, Gordon Richards, Graham Bailey, Graham Loosmore, Graham Meinert, Grant D Quattlebaum, Gras Sébastien, Greg Aldridge, Greg Baatard, Greg Betchart, Greg Chapin, Greg De Stefano, Greg Hayes, Greg Jensen, Greg M Leatherman, Gregg Bond, Gregory Gaston, Gregory Orozco, Gregory Rycerz, Greig Fraser, Grey Jenkins,

Grzegorz Bereza, Guglielmo Mirone, Guido Schwichtenberg, Guillaume Degremont, Guillaume Marechal, Guillaume St-Pierre, Guillermo Caceres Reverte, Gunnar Hönig, Gunter Raffelsbauer, Gustav Dahlstrom, Gustav Hadin, Gustav Jansson, Gustav Nilsson, Gusten Thorson, Guy Burns, Göran Lind, Göran Tyrén, Hae Chan Jung, Hakan Aldrin, Hal Mangold, Halil Volkan Hunerli, Hampus Viklander, Han Lim, Hank Cappa, Hanna Järvinen, Hannah Cohen, Hannah Crossan, Hannes Leijon, Hans Christian Asmussen, Hans Feltsten, Hans Månsson, Harald Eckmüller, Harald Hellerud, Harald Hermodsson, Harald Wagener, Harley Denham, Harley Gardner, Harm-Diercks Gronewold, Harrison Amyotte, Harrison Levans, Harrison Moenster, Harry Danby, Harvey Clarke, Harvey Gent, Hayden Ockey, Hayley Ng, Hazel King, Heather Boyle, Heather Reid-Murray, Hector Jetajobe, Hector T Cristancho, Heikki Leppänen, Helder Araújo, Helge Fransson, Helge Willkowei, Hendel Thistletop, Hendrik-Jan Gubbelmans, Henning Kage, Henric Sikström, Henrik Arborén, Henrik Bergendahl, Henrik Ganard, Henrik Gustafsson, Henrik Gäredal, Henrik Hansson, Henrik Hinrichs, Henrik Jernstedt, Henrik Nilsson, Henrik Ripa, Henrik Schmücker, Henrik Skog, Henrik Sundset, Henrik Warpefelt, Henry Aspenryd, Henry Hellanmaa, Herbelleau Frederic, Herman Duyker, Herman Langland, Hirofumi Suzuki, Hohner Henriett, Holger Hansch, Holly Duff, Hong Yang Shen, Horrible Games, Hourtoulle, Houston Newman, Huck Loïc, Hunter Lewis, Hyacinthe Khodja, Håkan Björk, Håkan Jonsson, Håkan Jonsson, Håvard Christensen, Iain Rudge, Iain Smedley, Ian Allen, Ian B Warner, Ian Barbella, Ian Bryant, Ian David James Hess, Ian Edberg, Ian Gunther, Ian Kelly, Ian Kremer, Ian Paczek, Ian Richmond, Ian Roll, Ian Thomas, Ida Nilsson, Iesha D Lyle, Iga Ewa Smole ska, Ignacio Rodriguez Dominguez, Ignacy Trzewiczek, Indigo Pohlman, Ines Kunzendorf, Ingo Arendt, Ingo Beyer, Ingo Burghardt, Ingolf Schäfer, Ingrid Lundgren, Ingunn Hammer-Olsen, Insha Fitzpatrick, Isabella Sooma De Oliveira, Isak Alderblad, Isak Martinsson, Ismael Diaz Sacaluga, Ivan Devyatko, Ivan Rodriguez Tena, J Swaffer, J Thorpe, Jaarik Abels-Smit, Jack Bayliss, Jack Brayall, Jack Feasey, Jack Graham, Jack Gulick, Jack Hartley, Jack Hodges, Jack Knight, Jack Krause, Jack Mclaughlin, Jackson Hyde, Jacob Alexandrowiz, Jacob Björkman, Jacob Carpenter, Jacob Derby, Jacob Garfin, Jacob Golding, Jacob Hamilton, Jacob Jaskov, Jacob Lockyer, Jacob Mass, Jacob Nisser, Jacob Reed, Jacob Rosén, Jacob St.Clair, Jacob Torrång, Jacob Vanlandingham, Jahan Sohrabi, Jaime Fenton, Jaime Matthew, Jake Brick, Jake Harrison, Jake Linford, Jake Tucker, Jakob Bak, Jakob Isebäck, Jakob Koc, Jakob Peter Christiansen, Jakob Sommer, Jakub Ben, Jakub Czyz, James Ashman, James Barratt, James Beall, James Birdsall, James Boldock, James Chodes, James Crowder Ii, James Dale, James Dawes, James Dibenedetto, James Dovey, James F Juden Jr, James Fallon, James Firth, James Goodnight, James Hardcastle, James Harness, James Kenny, James Knevitt, James Lodge, James Malloy, James Minot, James Nelms, James Newman, James P Sauers Iii, James Pierson, James Pilcher, James Pollock, James Powell, James Purdum, James Reeher, James Ritter, James Roberts, James Rothwell, James Sherlock, James Stowe, James Stryker, James Sugrue, James W. Armstrong-Wood, James Wheeler, James Widdowson, James Young, Jameson Cunningham, Jamie Boulton, Jamie Brace, Jamie Gregory, Jamie Hurt, Jamie N Donelson, Jamie Vann, Jan Egil Bjune, Jan Formánek, Jan Ingemar Ohlsson, Jan Karell, Jan Kärrö, Jan Lundquist, Jan Metzger-Sober, Jan Olsen, Jan Richter, Jan Rosa, Jan Rutenkolk, Jan Salmi, Jan Wahlström, Jane Lee, Jan-Fredrik Wahlin, Jan-Henrik Friedrichs, Janne Saha, Janne Vuorenmaa, Jan-Olof Johansson, Janos Honkonen, Janus Bo Lundager, Jared Anderson, Jared D. Carlisle, Jared Davies, Jared E. Haines, Jared Isle, Jared Shurin, Jared Washburn, Jared Westfall, Jari Mattle, Jarle Waage, Jarno Harmaala, Jarry E Anderson, Jarry Maxime, Jasen Johns, Jasen Stengel, Jasmine Rae Friedrich, Jason A Lescalleet, Jason And Kai Wodicka, Jason Balslew, Jason Barr, Jason Barrett, Jason Buchanan, Jason Childs, Jason Durall, Jason Erb, Jason Flowers, Jason Geist, Jason Hall, Jason Hall, Jason Heath, Jason Hewett, Jason Jordaan, Jason Kapalka, Jason Kohlman, Jason Leinen, Jason Lutes, Jason March, Jason Middleton, Jason Neff, Jason Nguyen, Jason Olsan, Jason Rosenblatt, Jason Searcy, Jason Stark, Jason Turner, Jason Unck, Jason Wall, Jason Westrick, Jasper Love, Javier Arteagoitia Garcia, Javier Fonseca, Jay Marsh, Jay Sharpe, Jean-Baptiste Perrin, Jean-Christophe Rannou, Jean-François Beney, Jean-François Juneau, Jean-Philippe Malouin, Jeff Carey, Jeff Gray, Jeff J Kowalski, Jeff Levine, Jeff Mindlin, Jeff Rupard, Jeff Wagnaar, Jeffrey Cross, Jeffrey D'ambrosio, Jeffrey Doon, Jeffrey Doran, Jeffrey Scott James, Jeffrey Williams, Jelle Spanjaard, Jen Woodhouse, Jenni Sands, Jennifer Goldstein And David Smucker, Jennifer Landrum, Jenny Telles, Jens Alm, Jens Andreasson, Jens Berthelsen, Jens Fabricius, Jens Gustafsson, Jens Hoff, Jens Horstmann, Jens Langsjoen, Jens Mebius, Jens Omland, Jens Rydholm, Jens Thorup Jensen, Jens Winship, Jensina Mart, Jens-Petter Palmqvist, Jeon Young Hyeon, Jeppe Norsker, Jerad Mullicane, Jeremiah Dwyer, Jeremiah Gusha, Jérémie Poidevin, Jeremie Quenet, Jeremy Andrusyszyn, Jeremy Fay, Jeremy Hall Spence, Jeremy Hargrove, Jeremy Mortis, Jeremy Robinson, Jeremy Siemon, Jeremy Skalin, Jeroen Boumans, Jeroen Ruigrok Van Der Werven, Jerome Van Epps, Jeromy Korf, Jerry Weiler, Jesco Hoffmann, Jesper Axelsson, Jesper Cockx, Jesper Huor, Jesper Nilsson Cyren, Jesper Nordström, Jesse Brown, Jesse Campbell, Jesse Goodman, Jesse Grier, Jesse Kiviniitty, Jesse Mungle, Jesse Ortiz, Jesse Vining, Jessica Bryers, Jessica Fredriksson, Jessica Taylor, Jez Gray, Jim Austerman, Jim Calabrese, Jim Delrosso, Jim Dewey, Jim Pinto, Jim Thompson, Jim Todd, Jimmy Hedin, Jimmy Kjellström, Jimmy Lidén, Jimmy Ringkvist, Jo Pender, Joachim Beltran, Joachim Enger Halvorsen, Joachim Pileborg, Joachim Spörri, Joacim Melin, Joakim Almgren, Joakim Demiri, Joakim Johnander, Joakim Sellberg, Joakim Spångberg, Joakim Söderberg, Joakim Wendell, Jobi Johansson, Joe Aguayo, Joe Bausch, Joe Hill, Joe Morrissey, Joe Persons, Joe Robbins, Joel Furze, Joel Gerlach, Joël Hafner, Joel Riendeau, Joel Ryan Dobson, Joel Sandström, Joel Staaf Hästö, Joel Stelzleni, Joel Van Egmond, Joel Vodola, Joel Östlund, Joerg Diener, Joerg Sterner, Joern Hagerup, Johan Bergsten, Johan Björnell, Johan Ejermark, Johan Fogelqvist, Johan Haglund, Johan Hagman, Johan Hansson, Johan Kylander, Johan Köhler, Johan Larsby, Johan Lindfors, Johan Lohmander, Johan Moritz, Johan Nilsson, Johan Nohr, Johan Nyberg, Johan Olofsson, Johan Persson, Johan Rahm, Johan Rapp, Johan Rundstrom, Johan Rönnlund, Johan Salomonsson, Johan Skog Hallgren, Johan Stein, Johan Stomberg, Johan Storm, Johan Thilander, Johan Wallenborg, Johan Westerlund, Johan Östling, Johanna Larnemark, Johanne Skjerven, Johannes Avaheden, Johannes Axner, Johannes Daging, Johannes Keukelaar, Johannes Kornfellner, Johannes Kåre Rasmussen, Johannes Nilsson, Johannes Olofsson, Johannes Westlin, John A W Phillips, John A. Grzybowski, John Airaksinen, John Andersson, John Boran Jr., John Broglia, John Bruins, John Chambers, John Demic, John Doyle, John Egerter, John English, John G Doyle, John Green, John Hamilton, John Holmes, John J Wick, John K Mehrholz, John Kasab, John Kish, John Kless, John Layton, John Lile, John Löfgren, John M. Kahane, John Marron, John Mccloy, John Pate, John Patrick, John Pyrich, John Reiher, John Roberts, John Sanchez, John Shulters, John Simpson, John Snee, John Souders, John Stanhope, John Weseloh, John Willcox-Beney, Johnathan Bingham, Johnathan Lyon, John-Luke Peterson-Trzos, Johnny Burlin, Johnny Sörensson, John-Paul Temple, Johnson Pham, Jon Chad, Jon Cowan, Jon Davenport, Jon Metz, Jon Nessmar, Jon Smejkal, Jonas Antonsson, Jonas Eliasson, Jonas Ferry, Jonas Gustafsson, Jonas Hamberg, Jonas Hansson, Jonas Holmstén, Jonas Jenkins, Jonas Larsson, Jonas Laurell, Jonas Lidén, Jonas Lindström, Jonas Loskyll, Jonas Mockelstrom, Jonas Nilsson, Jonas Olsson, Jonas Page, Jonas Persson, Jonas Petersson, Jonas Rasmussen, Jonas Schiött, Jonas Sellergren, Jonas Skantz, Jonas Stallmeister, Jonatan Gertler, Jonathan Arnould, Jonathan Bartel, Jonathan Beamon, Jonathan Breese, Jonathan C. Jones, Jonathan Caudill, Jonathan Cormier, Jonathan Deitch, Jonathan Duryea, Jonathan Edwards, Jonathan Faulkner, Jonathan Finke, Jonathan Fish, Jonathan Galvez, Jonathan George C/O Pho U, Jonathan Gilmour, Jonathan Johansson, Jonathan Lamberton, Jonathan Moore, Jonathan Muckala, Jonathan Nalder, Jonathan Pam, Jonathan Robb, Jonathan Schmalzer, Jonathan Serritos, Jonathan Sharp, Jonathan Sieders, Jonathan Swärd, Jonathan Tillman, Jonathan Tinsley, Jonathon Dyer, Jonca Fabien, Jonnie Hedqvist, Jon-Peter Sacko, Joonas Iivonen, Jordan Duffy, Jordan Hicks, Jordan Maccarthy, Jordan Pipitone, Jordan Shiveley, Jordan White, Jorden Varjassy, Jordi Aldeguer, Jordi Civit Quiterio, Jorge Albor, Jorge Carrero Roig, Jorge García, Jorge Lancis, Joris Van Der Vorst, Jose A Troche, Jose Calvo Muñoz, Jose Daniel Garcia, José David Díaz Martín, Jose Luis Perez Zapata, Jose Roque Roman Guadarrama, Joseph Arnaud, Joseph Becker, Joseph Begay, Joseph Branham, Joseph Cacioppo, Joseph Connell, Joseph Consavage, Joseph E Mills, Joseph Green, Joseph Hernandez, Joseph Hodlin, Joseph Jopling, Joseph Piepiora, Joseph Thater, Joseph Wodarski, Joseph Zadeh, Joseph Zajaczkowski, Josh French, Josh Hadden, Josh Houser, Josh Longfellow, Josh Look, Josh Nickerson, Josh Reynolds, Josh Riggins, Josh Storey, Josh Terrell, Joshua Alkema, Joshua Archer, Joshua Bennet, Joshua C Kitchens, Joshua Gray, Joshua Heath, Joshua Holland, Joshua Louderback, Joshua M Potosky, Joshua M Turner, Joshua Mccowan, Joshua Mcgrath, Joshua Peter Hill, Joshua Ramsey, Joshua Ridens, Joshua Smith, Joshua Velo, Joshua Work, Josiah Callinan, Josie Khampheng, Josu Izco, Josua Grawitter, Jouka Mattila, Juan Miguel Antón Santos, Judith Griffith, Juergen Mayer, Juhana Pettersson, Jukka Sorsa, Jukka Varjovuori, Jules Beaumier, Julia Acheson, Julian Black, Julian Hofmann, Julian Ho-Yin Lam, Julian Stanley, Julian T St. Pierre, Julian Tysoe, Julian Vandenberg, Julie Carlile, Julien Corroyer, Julien Kaspar, Julien Rothwiller, Juliet Cooper, Jussi-Pekka Jokinen, Justin Braithwaite, Justin Bridges, Justin Fentress, Justin Francom, Justin French, Justin Groseclose, Justin Jarrah, Justin Kelly, Justin Larose, Justin Mcmahan, Justin Richmond, Justin Smith, Justin Stevens, Justin Tarazon, Justin Wilson, Juuso Laitinen, Jyan C Delamotte, Jörg Sischka, Jörgen Karlsson, Jörgen Niemi, Jørgen Søreide, Jörn Kiwitt, Jörn Thesen, K. Gisler, Kadeem Warren, Kai Günster, Kai Jones, Kaj Årstrand, Kaleton Martinson, Kamin Vassilos, Karen Neil, Karen Rodger, Karim Gouyette, Karim Zatout, Karina Burenko, Karissa Griffin, Karl Abrahamsson, Karl B. Fischer, Karl D. Brown, Karl Deckard, Karl Gustav Georgsen, Karl J Brown, Karl Johnson, Karl Krantz, Karl Larsaeus, Karl Lloyd, Karl Rodriguez, Karl Wassholm, Karl-Eddie Brattgjerd, Karl Emil Norberg, Karlheinz Wegscheider, Karl-Johannes Henricson, Karsten Voigt, Kasper Esven Skovgaard, Kasper Vestergaard Haahr Smidt, Kat Horton, Kath Grahn, Katherine Burright, Katherine Burton, Katie Friel-Russell, Katie Roe, Katie Voss, Katrin Dahlbäck, Katrina Storey, Kawa Zolfagary, Kayla Rusnell, Keira Marti, Keith Baker, Keith Catalano, Keith Dickens, Keith Duggins, Keith Garrett, Keith Quinn, Keith Rankine, Keith Sosebee, Keith Woodsum, Kelly Hart, Ken Finlayson, Ken Lowery, Ken Marquetecken, Ken Robinson, Ken Tremaine, Ken Truax, Kendal Miller, Kenneth Ball, Kenneth D. Miller Iii, Kenneth Ellegaard Andersen, Kenneth Norgaard, Kenny Krokeide Unneland, Kerry Bullock, Kevin Coleson, Kevin Dietz, Kevin E Mowery, Kevin Henson, Kevin Heuer, Kevin Hong, Kevin Hutchison, Kevin Klump, Kevin Krieser, Kevin Lemke, Kevin Maag, Kevin Malantic, Kevin Martineau, Kevin Mauro, Kevin Ryan, Kevin Shipley Jr, Kevin White, Khannan Suntharam, Ki Mau, Kieran Walsh, Kieron Smith, Kilian Fladung, Kim Alvelius, Kim Andre Østergaard, Kim Dallaire, Kim Eriksson, Kim Isaacs, Kimberley Poole, Kimble West, Kimmo Warma, Kip Corriveau, Kiraah Grandberry, Kirk Barrett, Kirk Chapman, Kirsten Harper, Kit Boyer, Kitsune Magyar, Kjell Atle Mosbron, Kjetil Kverndokken, Klas Holmgren, Klas Lindberg, Klas Thuresson Eliasson, Klaus Oddenes, Klaus Ole Kristiansen, Klaus Ritter, Knopf Sébastien, Konrad Sebon, Konstantin Von Portatius, Korey Enright, Kostantis Bamidis, Kris Pelley, Kris Vanhoyland, Kristel Nyberg, Kristen Mcclure, Krister Persson, Kristian Axelsund, Kristian Helenelund, Kristian Johansson, Kristian Widén, Kristian Williams, Kristof Klee,

RIKSENERGI

Kristoffer Abraham Lindh, Kristoffer Axiö, Kristoffer Björkman, Kristoffer Dyer, Kristoffer Fahlgren, Kristoffer Karlsson, Kristoffer Kiil, Kristoffer Warden, Kristopher Leeke, Kurt Guertin, Kurt Wasserman, Kutseva Anna, Kylar Henderson, Kyle B Schewe, Kyle Crivello, Kyle Devich, Kyle Fehr, Kyle Key, Kyle Mackay, Kyle Mohen, Kyle O'mara, Kyle Patterson, Kyle Porter, Kyle Thompson, Kyler Gilmore, Lachlan Smith, Lacroix, Lainé Nathan, Lance Wente, Lance Wilson, Lance Vincent Wells, Lance Yerelian, Landon Donoho, Lanneret Benoit, Lapenna Mathieu, Laramee Geoffrey, Larry Anderson, Larry Lamalfa, Larry White, Lars Björndahl, Lars Elmik, Lars Jandel, Lars Lykta, Lars Nevalainen, Lars Nohrstedt, Lars Pajander, Lars Scharrenberg, Lars Wikman, Lars Åkesson, Lars-Emil Silvståll, Lassi Seppälä, Laura Barnhart, Laura Gonzalez, Laura Pershern, Laura Zoboli, Lawrence Glass, Lawrence Oberst, Le Poupon Yannick, Leah White, Leahna Hoxie, Leanne Kelly, Lechenne Stephane, Lee Cooke, Lee Rosenbaum, Lee Swift, Leesa Hanagan, Leigh Ann Kimes, Leigh Stevend, Lenn Viberg, Lennart Jansson, Lennart Rund, Lenore Wagner, Leo Benkel, Leo Borg, Leo Cook, Leo Jenicek, Leonard Goulds, Leonard Ogrady, Leonardo Andrés Catalano Iniesta, Leonardo Barragan, Léoni Widerberg, Leslie Hammond, Leszek Zielinski, Levavasseur Gaspard, Levi Fleming, Lewis Clark, Lewis Fowler, Lex Griffiths, Liam Girard, Liam Humphries, Liam Sharp, Liam Willson, Liam Wooding, Liberty O'dell, Liesbeth Cuypers, Lijah Robinson, Lin Wyeth Ii, Linda Cronsten, Linnea Mathies, Linus Andersson, Linus Gustavsson, Linus Hedenberg, Linus Sormunen, Linus Ålander, Lisa Dörfler, Livia Von Sucro, Ljubisa Lukic, Lobazov Denis, Logan Dwight, Logan Fox, Logan Heathcoe, Logan Morey, Logan Pendergrass, Loïc Girardier, Lorin Wood, Lorraine Donaldson, Louis Bennett, Louis Billings, Louis D Hetrick, Louise Baaz, Love Fagerstedt, Love Lustig, Love Löfdahl, Love Silfwerplatz, Lowell Fish, Lowell Francis, Luc Brassé, Luc Deutschmann, Luca Capecchi, Luca Neukom, Luca Ungaro, Lucas Borges Dos Santos, Lucas Curell, Lucas Fischer, Lucas Paste, Lucas Ramström, Lucas Skrdlant, Lucas Whyte, Lucaz Rognelund, Ludvig Carleson, Ludvik Urban, Luis Ernesto Caceres Ruiz, Luis Hernandez Donadeu, Luis Pavel Gomez Valenzuela, Lukas Mcnamara, Lukas Pålsson, Lukasz Koczocik, Lukasz Redynk, Luke Cunningham, Luke Dodge, Luke Easter, Luke Hagan, Luke Hardy, Luke James Sabljak, Luke Platfoot, Luke Steenberg, Luke Stowell, Luke Walker, Luke Wiltshire, Lutz Ohl, M N Curlee, Mackenzie Foxall, Madelyn Chappell, Magda Rudnikowska, Magnus Borg, Magnus Eriksson, Magnus Friberg, Magnus Gillberg, Magnus Granberg, Magnus Jagerstrom, Magnus Karlsson, Magnus Larsson, Magnus Lekberg, Magnus Lie Hetland, Magnus Lundborg, Magnus Lundkvist, Magnus Löf, Magnus Selmemo, Maike Krächan, Majdi Badri, Malbos, Malcolm Edwards, Malmström, Malte Breuer, Man Pak Hang, Anakin, Manoël Trapier, Manou Gottschalk, Manuel Bedouet, Manuel Dornbusch, Manuel Manger, Manuel Moradiellos Corpus, Marc Chretien, Marc Lancaster, Marc Mackin, Marc Müller, Marc Oliver Schneeberger, Marc Pantel, Marc Pilgaard, Marc Ransome, Marc Van Wanrooij, Marc-André Monette, Marco A. Valerio, Marco Beltramino, Marco De Marinis, Marco Grosso, Marco Pedrana, Marco Rafalá, Marco Tavian, Marco Weisspfennig, Marcus Brissman, Marcus Burggraf, Marcus Fernberg, Marcus Flodin, Marcus Fransman, Marcus Gabriel Fors, Marcus Hast, Marcus Hellberg, Marcus Henriksson, Marcus Igarashi, Marcus Mccoy, Marcus Noble, Marcus Schönbeck, Marcus Smith, Marcus Stahl, Marcus Uhrvik, Marcus Vesterberg, Marcus Wirebrand, Mareike O'neil, Margaret Geiger, Maria And Henri Laine, Maria Högberg, Maria Markenroth Nordström, Mario Croner, Mario Milioti, Marius Crowne, Mariusz Kutek, Mark Amurao, Mark Bruce, Mark Burton, Mark Cox-Palmer, Mark Davis Jnr, Mark Delsing, Mark Drew, Mark E Thompson, Mark Eberhardt, Mark Ewing, Mark Falvo, Mark Fenlon, Mark Grehan, Mark Heggen, Mark Hopkins, Mark Johnson, Mark Laing, Mark Lane, Mark Lewis, Mark Mckibben, Mark Miller, Mark Nettle, Mark Nunn, Mark Phillippi, Mark Poff, Mark Purkaple, Mark Rathbun, Mark Sadowsky, Mark Shear, Mark Stafford, Mark Story, Mark Szarek, Mark Turner, Mark Wallce, Mark Van Elswijk, Markku Tuovinen, Marko Niskanen, Markus Hallström, Markus Johnson, Markus Kothe, Markus Linderum, Markus Lütkemeyer, Markus Minkkinen, Markus Nord, Markus Plötz, Markus Sanderfelt, Markus Schönell, Markus Svensson, Markus Tenghall, Markus Tuppurainen, Markus Wagner, Markus Widmer, Marley Diazdelvalle, Marshall Jacobson, Marshall Miller, Martha Van Drunen, Martin Ackerfors, Martin Bengtsson, Martin Bourque, Martin Brosser, Martin Coborn, Martin Cutbill, Martin Fors, Martin Foster, Martin Garland, Martin Grape, Martin Hall, Martin Insulander, Martin Jarl, Martin Johansson, Martin Jonsson, Martin Kaså, Martin Kölbl, Martin Larsson, Martin Monrad, Martin Månson, Martin Nichol, Martin Olsson, Martin Rennie, Martin Schwarz, Martin Stenmarck, Martin Svensson, Martin Söderberg, Martin Tulloch, Martin Weld, Martin Venaas, Martin Zackrisson, Marvin Langenberg, Mary Salmonsen, Mason Jackson, Mathew Fisher, Mathew Hargrove Farabee, Mathias Forsmark, Mathias Green, Mathias Palmberg, Mathieu Brunet, Mathieu Lapierre, Mats Rytther, Mats Sjögren, Mats Sjövall, Matt Birdsall, Matt Conn, Matt Conroy, Matt Keyser, Matt Laband, Matt Leitzen, Matt Macgregor, Matt Morris, Matt Paine, Matt Snodgrass, Matt Sturm, Matt Warren, Matt Winter, Matt Wiseman, Matteo Noti, Matthew Barker, Matthew Bauer, Matthew Bernard, Matthew Blaszczynski, Matthew Buist, Matthew Caron, Matthew Clarke, Matthew Coote, Matthew Deturck, Matthew Dickson, Matthew Dodds, Matthew Fairfax, Matthew Farmer, Matthew French, Matthew Gallo-Walsh, Matthew George, Matthew Guilliams, Matthew Henley, Matthew Hobbs, Matthew Jensen, Matthew Kay, Matthew Kirby, Matthew Krous, Matthew L Davis, Matthew Molloy, Matthew Orwig, Matthew Ruane, Matthew Sanders, Matthew Sears, Matthew Sochocki, Matthew Stevenson, Matthew Taylor, Matthew Townsend, Matthew W. Sutton, Matthew Wang, Matthew Wasiak, Matthew Watkin, Matthew Wetzel, Matthew Widener, Matthew Vieyra, Matthew Wood, Matthias Kleindienst, Matthias Pall Gissurarson, Matti Jäääro, Mattias Ahlberg, Mattias Andersson, Mattias Arvola, Mattias Berglund, Mattias Bergman, Mattias Erichsén, Mattias Falck, Mattias Henriksson, Mattias Johansson, Mattias Ludvigsson, Mattias Petter Johansson, Mattias Sundling, Mattias Swing, Matty, Mauno Joukamaa, Maurice Strubel, Mawson Tilley, Max Christiansson, Max Downton, Max Grüntgens, Max Hardenbrook, Max Haskvitz, Max Herngren, Max Herzl-Betz, Max Norin Barrhäll, Max Snider, Max Verloop, Max Werner, Max Zomborszki, Maxim Grunewald, Maxime Pépin, Maximilian Reichardt, Megan Matteson, Megan Willis, Mel White, Melanie Hall, Melissa Yenty, Micael Fryksäter, Micael Åkesson, Michael Auzinger, Michael Bedggood, Michael Ben Silva Iii, Michael Bernhard, Michael Berthiaume, Michael Bowman, Michael Brand, Michael Brandolino, Michael Brown, Michael Chandler, Michael Charge, Michael Clelland, Michael Cobb, Michael Collins, Michael Cosimano-White, Michael Curtis, Michael Dulock, Michael Eland, Michael Fox, Michael Georges, Michael Glennemo, Michael Goodrick, Michael Grasegger, Michael Heilemann, Michael Heinsohn, Michael Hemmingsson, Michael Hjerppe, Michael Hunt, Michael J Perry, Michael Jacob Burns, Michael Kwan, Michael Leader, Michael Lizardi, Michael Lord, Michael Losure, Michael Marshall, Michael Miley, Michael Miller, Michael Murray, Michael Nevarez, Michael Obrien, Michael Ordidge, Michael Ostermaier, Michael Owen Hill, Michael Parker, Michael Prescott, Michael R Knutson, Michael Ramsey, Michael Rodino, Michael Ruth, Michael S Seman, Michael Sands, Michael Scott, Michaël Servotte, Michael Seymour, Michael Simoniello, Michael Skelton, Michael Springer, Michael Stahre, Michael Surbrook, Michael Szczepaniak, Michael Trevino, Michael Williams, Michael Wuttke, Michaeljon Hayden, Michal Klosowski, Michał Skwarek, Michal Zeman, Michele Masini, Michelle Borden, Michiel Barten, Mick Moss, Miguel Courchesne-Perras, Mihai Vancea, Miika Turtiainen, Mika Robert Pehkonen, Mikael Almstedt, Mikael Andersson, Mikael Bergström, Mikael Brauer, Mikael Dahl, Mikael Degerfält, Mikael Eriksson, Mikael Falk, Mikael Haglund, Mikael Hansson Warhuus, Mikael Hedman, Mikael Hedström, Mikael Jakobsson, Mikael Jansson, Mikael Kilgren, Mikael Lundgren, Mikael Nordström, Mikael Theorin, Mikael Tysvær, Mikael Widenfalk, Mike Bowie, Mike Button, Mike Cupples, Mike Delaney, Mike Foster, Mike Gerth, Mike Hall, Mike Pereira, Mike Pierce, Mike Poon, Mike Schulenberg, Mike Weber, Mike Willis, Mikel Matthews, Mikelis Zalais, Mikey Hermann, Mikkel Rasmussen, Mikko Kuosa, Mikko Parviainen, Milan Garcia, Milan Janosik, Miles Mcmahan, Mille Björkman, Milosz Golebiewski, Milton Tegebjer, Mischa D Krilov, Miss Dora Bucknole, Mitch Haggman, Mitchel Bonnema, Mitchell Fensome, Moazzam Ullah, Moe Lane, Mohit Sadhu, Morgan Ellis, Morgan Hazel, Morgan Hughes, Morgan Ivarsson, Morgane Ferreira Coelho, Morgane Munns, Morten Boye Amundsen, Morten Greis Petersen Fakkelskov, Morten Strårup, Murl E Westheffer, Muura Parkkinen, Måns Broman, Mårten Björk, N Dixon, Nat Barmore, Nate Gulizia, Nathan Anderson, Nathan Bisker, Nathan Emery, Nathan Hill, Nathan Hillen, Nathan Mezel, Nathan Miller, Nathan Raj, Nathan Reed, Nathan Streeper, Nathan Trail, Nathan Wickham, Nathan Yeoman, Nathanial Hicks, Nathaniel Dozier, Nathaniel Roth, Nathaniel Schafer, Nathaniel Welchert, Neal Obermeyer, Neal Rasmussen, Neil Anderson, Neil Fasteen, Neil Googe, Neil Laird, Neil Martin, Neil Mason, Neil Mcgurk, Neil Munro, Neil Thompson, Newt Newport, Niall Gordon, Niall Ogrady, Nic Ager, Nic Durham, Nicholas Hayhoe, Nicholas Hopkins, Nicholas Kerr, Nicholas Middleton, Nicholas Patrick Bloom, Nicholas Poonamallee, Nicholas Rasmussen, Nicholas Roach, Nicholas Sceusa, Nicholas Schmidt, Nicholas Sukalac, Nicholas Zakhar, Nick Clements, Nick Demaagd, Nick Eden, Nick Herrmann, Nick Jones, Nick Kupiec, Nick Lange, Nick Murray, Nick Pitman, Nick Rowe, Nick Trettel, Nick Winley, Nicklas Andersson, Nicklas Ohlsen, Niclas Ryberg, Nico Grupp, Nico Tzieply, Nicola Mcblane, Nicolas Berkowitsch, Nicolas Christakis, Nicolas Jamain, Nicolas Phillips, Nicolas Roos, Nicolas Rouanet - Citymeo, Nicole Carlson, Nicolette Tanksley, Niels Højgaard Sørensen, Nigel J Kim, Nigel Phillips, Nigel Soederhuysen, Nigel Wright, Nik Mennega, Niki Corradetti, Nikkholai Miller, Nikki Lemon, Niklas Backer-Meurke, Niklas Brandt, Niklas Fällman, Niklas Herrström, Niklas Jalmerud, Niklas Lindblad, Niklas Martin Gustavsson, Niklas Meurling, Niklas Nilsson, Niklas Norén, Niklas Widell, Niko Silvennoinen, Nikolai Kotchetkov, Nikolai Voiloshnikov, Nikolaos Papanikolaou, Nikolaos Stamelos, Nils Löw, Nils Wellander, Nils Åström, Nils-Erik Johansson, Nina Moritz, Noah Brummer, Noah Jacobus, Noah Plunkett, Noah Soudrette, Norman Kummer, Norman Walsh, Ola Lantz, Ola Persson, Ole Morten Eriksen, Ole Sandbæk Jørgensen, Oleg Krapilskiy, Oleksandr Kotovskov, Olive Roberts, Oliver Brackenbury, Oliver Dabnor, Oliver Gross, Oliver Jönsson, Oliver Rankloo, Olivier Bos, Olivier Lefebvre, Olivier Murith, Olle Eklund, Olle Jonsson, Olle Sahlin, Olly Hill, Olof Hägglund, Olof Joensson, Olow Nyman, Oly Darke, Omari Brooks, Orlando Hill, Oscar Hafvenstein, Oscar Ima, Oscar Rios, Oscar Sahun Reguant, Oskar Christensson, Oskar Dahlbom, Oskar Drenske, Oskar Rognås, Ota Ulc, Owen Goss, Owen Harris, Owen Mcgauley, Owen Robinson, Paal Mann, Pablo Gallastegui, Pablo Hernández, Pablo López Aránguez, Pablo Sancho, Paige Winburne, Panificio Zanini - Emanuele Bonomo, Parker Abbott, Parker Kassewitz, Pascal Koos, Pascal Sutter, Pasi Heinonen, Pasquini Chiara, Patrice Esmieu, Patrice Mermoud, Patrick Barger, Patrick Barry, Patrick Birtles, Patrick Dunn, Patrick Dwyer, Patrick Gamblin, Patrick Gilmartin, Patrick Healey, Patrick Jarman, Patrick Kiefer, Patrick Kraft, Patrick Mcgeachie, Patrick Ogenstad, Patrick O'rielly, Patrick Redding, Patrick Schwieren, Patrick Simmons, Patrick Walsh, Patrick Wright, Patrick Zadnik, Patrik Byhmer, Patrik Gustafsson, Patrik Hermansson, Patrik Johansson, Patrik Lif, Patrik Nordebo, Patrik Olterman, Patrik Påfvelsson, Patrik Spånning Westerlund, Patrik Stroem, Patrik Svensson, Patryk Adamski, Paul Aubry, Paul Bendall, Paul Corbin, Paul Currie, Paul Davies, Paul Dipastina, Paul Dodson, Paul E Goodman, Paul Epstein, Paul Garrett, Paul Granich, Paul Hales, Paul Heid, Paul Hodgeson, Paul John Davis,

RIKSENERGI

Paul Johnson, Paul Künnap, Paul M Beakley, Paul Magee, Paul Martens, Paul Ouderkirk, Paul Pod, Paul Rivers, Paul Stöwer, Paul Tomes, Paul Wilde, Paul Vogt, Paul Yee Han Yuen, Pauline Högh, Paulo Picolomini, Paweł Kubiak, Pawel Seczkowski, Pavel Sokolov, Paweł Zdanowski, Pavol Rabatin, Pc Thornton-Smith , Pedro Gil, Pedro Pablo Calvo Morcillo, Pekka Viklund, Penné, Peppe Bergqvist, Per Blom, Per Håkansson, Per Larsson, Per Mevius, Per Olofsson, Per-Erik Andel, Per-Gunnar Valegård, Per-Ingemar Andersson, Per-Oskar Odermalm, Peter Askling, Peter Brichs, Peter Callander, Peter Carducci, Peter Coffey, Peter Cornelius, Peter Eriksson, Peter Griffith, Peter Hall, Peter Holland, Peter Hollinghurst, Peter J Troia, Peter Jilmstad, Peter Jonsson, Peter Kadletz, Peter Karlström, Peter Lindqvist, Peter Mazzeo, Peter Mikkelsen, Peter Miller, Peter Northcott, Peter Peretti, Peter Povey, Peter S. D'arpa, Peter Siefert, Peter Städe, Peter Svärd, Peter Van Den Berghen, Peters Bertrand, Petra Mayer, Petre Julien, Petri Leinonen, Petri Nordeman, Petter Bengtsson, Petter Cronsten, Petter Holmberg, Petter Segerås, Petter Wäss, Petter Öhman, Peyton Pearson, Phil Bales, Phil Dennis, Phil Ward, Philibert Benoit, Philip Bolger, Philip Eisner, Philip Emmens, Philip Gwynn, Philip J Macaoidh, Philip J Reed Jr, Philip Ledgerwood, Philip Poole, Philip Tynne, Philipp Dopichaj, Philipp Winkler, Philippe Marcil, Phill Massey, Phillip Bailey, Phillip Harte, Phillip Speer, Phong Tran, Phyllis Whittlesey, Pier Paolo Falsini, Pierre Andersson, Pierre Hall, Pierre Ohlsson, Pieter Spealman, Piette Fabien, Piia Puranen, Piotr Kraciuk, Piotr Michalczyk, P-O Bergstedt, Pol Le Tue, Pontus Folkesson, Pontus Kjellberg, Pontus Rosenlöf, Preston Woody, Pride C St.Clair, Pyke Van Zon, Pål Lövendahl, Quadrat Alban, Quentin Marsac, Quincy Millerjohn, Quinton Daigre, Rachel Bostwick, Rachelle Shelkey, Rade Flatter, Rafael Cerrato Castellote, Rafael Cordero, Rafal, Rahul Venugopal, Ralf Achenbach, Ralf Kienle, Ralph Mazza, Ralph Thumm, Randall Padilla, Randel Evans, Randy Mosiondz, Randy Pacetti, Randy Wolfmeyer, Raneff Winters, Raphael Chiu, Raphaël Lallement, Rasmus Alstrup Jensen, Rasmus Boldt Madsen, Rasmus Leo, Rasmus Nicolaj West, Rasmus Rasmussen, Raul Manjavacas Cañego, Ravi Karnik, Raymond Dominic Toghill, Raymond E Schneider, Raymond L Walters, Raymond L. Dibble, Reamonn O'connell, Reed Little, Rees Hinton, Reese Clawson, Reid Halabura, Remi Letourneau, Rene Arruda, René Hänsel, Rene Kerkdyk, René Schultze, René Toft, Reuben Beattie, Rex Balboa, Rey-Coyrehourcq Sébastien, Rhys Miller, Rhys Nelson-Harrop, Ricardo Barragan Jr, Ricardo Fuente Muñoz, Ricardo Garcia Hernanz, Ricardo I Rosales, Ricardo Lebres, Ricardo Marcelo Lozano Gil, Rich Palij, Rich Redman, Rich Wilcox, Richard Bartram, Richard Brown, Richard Cloes, Richard Fitzgerald, Richard Francis, Richard Geldard, Richard Hayes, Richard Hulme, Richard Martinez, Richard Mcbrain, Richard Neary, Richard Newby, Richard Norris, Richard Odegrip, Richard Sobey, Richard Sorden, Richard Thomson, Richard Wüster, Rick Knight, Rick Mansfield, Rick Sorgdrager, Rick Spears, Rickard Lindqvist, Rickard Nordström, Rickard Vesterberg, Ricky Anderson, Rik Nicol, Rikard Blomberg, Rikard Falk, Rikard Larsson, Rishi Kundi, Risto Vuorio, Rita Harris, Rob Boyd, Rob C Sansone, Rob Heinsoo, Rob Klug, Rob Macandrew, Rob Mccreary, Rob Wieland, Robbie Luppi, Robbie Munn, Robert & Jeanna Lundgren, Robert A Stull, Robert Arnholm, Robert Biddle, Robert Björn, Robert Bobick, Robert Bouwman, Robert Brown, Robert Casey, Robert Cook, Robert Corr, Robert De Luna, Robert Esch, Robert Guenther, Robert Haddon, Robert Hoehn, Robert J Kelsall, Robert Jones, Robert Kelsey, Robert Kenny, Robert Lupfer, Robert Lüddecke, Robert O'rourke, Robert Ott, Robert Parker, Robert Peacock, Robert Perkins, Robert Pfaff, Robert Rees, Robert Sagris, Robert Snow, Robert Strickland, Robert Teodoropol, Robin Droste, Robin Hoskins, Robin Jonsson, Robin Kocaurek, Robin Landén, Robin Pittman, Robin Thomas, Robineau Olivier, Rod Meek, Rodolfo Schmauk, Roger Frye, Roger Mainor, Roger Orth, Roger Sjögren, Roland Lidstrom, Romain Beaulieu, Romain Dussupt, Ron Beck, Ron L Davis, Ron Smay, Ron Szameitpreuss, Ronald Davis, Roney Lundell, Ronnie Levin, Ronny Hansson, Ronny Thörnvall, Rory Oliver, Rose Jinkins, Ross Adam, Ross Ireland, Ross 'Marquis' Lewis, Ross Payton, Ross Thompson, Rowan Gray, Rowland Gault, Roy Hancock, Ruben Filho, Ruben Schreuder, Ruben Tigelaar, Rudy Jahchan, Rueff Jérémie, Rufino Ayuso Fernández, Rune Astrup Lien, Rune Belsvik Reinås, Rune Printzlau, Rune Warhuus, Ruslan Avdonin, Russ Herrold, Russell Akred, Russell Biser, Russell Hartley, Ruud Van Der Loo, Ryan A Bonatesta, Ryan A Martinez Stevens, Ryan Anders, Ryan Brenders, Ryan Dallaire, Ryan Elliott, Ryan Fung, Ryan Hall, Ryan Harden, Ryan J Bevan, Ryan Jervis, Ryan Johnson, Ryan Kuhar, Ryan Mccartney, Ryan Michaud, Ryan Motz, Ryan Rogers, Ryan Say, Ryan Shellito, Ryan Yeager, Rüdiger Querfurth, S. Groot, Saajan Patel, Sabrina Klevenow, Sage Latorra, Sali Lutoli, Salvador Gimeno Zanón, Salvatore Ciano, Sam Beedon, Sam Courtney, Sam Drummond, Sam Heazlewood, Sam Moss, Sam Sampson, Samantha Lobello, Samantha Scott, Samantha Wallwork, Sami Merilä, Samir El-Sabini, Samson Hall, Samuel Axelsson, Samuel Clamons, Samuel De Goede, Samuel Franklin, Samuel Genoese, Samuel Haggren, Samuel Pearce, Samuel Till, Samuel Tung, Samuel Tymoczko, Samuel William Reinhardt, Samuel Young, Sander De Visser, Sander Lebau, Santhan Vutha, Sara Engström, Sara Gorecki, Sara Grocott, Sara Holm, Sarah Buchanan, Sarah Daniels, Sarah Kennington, Sarah Parsons, Sarah Robbins, Sascha König, Sascha Tanner, Saskia Hagemann, Sauli Samila, Schuiten Alban, Scot Jandly, Scot Schneebeli, Scott A. Reed, Scott Alex, Scott Beca, Scott D. Alden, Scott Dippel, Scott Jarvis, Scott Kenney, Scott Lauchlan-Ford, Scott Lee Ellis, Scott Macauley, Scott Mellors, Scott Philip Mcclellan, Scott Rampley, Scott Taylor, Sean Bentley, Sean D Hoffman, Sean Dowling, Sean Gordon, Sean Iwans, Sean Izaakse, Sean Laverty, Sean M Smith, Sean Omara, Sean Pelkey, Sean Riedinger, Sean Walsh, Sean Werner, Sean Wix, Sebastian Bessler, Sebastian Kehrle, Sebastian Kunnari Levin, Sebastian Macleod, Sebastian Nielsen, Sebastian Permevik, Sebastian Schuster, Sebastian Utbult, Serge Lejeune, Seth Blumberg, Seth Glenn, Seth Johnson, Seth Lindberg, Seth Picchi, Seth Rogers, Seth Spurlock, Severin Brettmeister, Severin Heiberg, Shad Scarboro, Shane, Shane Fitzgerald, Shane Flaherty, Shane Hickey, Shane Langnes, Shane Mclean, Shane Walden, Shannon Maclean, Shannon W Lentz, Shaun Clinton, Shawn Murphy, Shawn Orban, Shelby Eickholt, Sherri Marx, Sho Uehara, Sicily Fredericks, Sierra Dennehy, Sigrid M Rea, Sigurd Teigen, Sigvard Holmström, Siiri Hedlund, Simon Barber, Simon Blakemore, Simon Brake, Simon Burnett, Simon Durkin, Simon Ekhamra, Simon Engmalm, Simon Engqvist, Simon Grunditz, Simon Holmes, Simon Hornyánszky, Simon Larsson, Simon Nantel, Simon Nilsson, Simon Sams, Simon Sjöström Grönkvist, Simon Spicer, Simon Sundling, Simon Tye, Simon Vlahovic, Simone Gallerini, Simonin, Skjalg Kreutzer, Skye Alcorn, Skylar Simmons, Smith T Holloway, Sofia Fransson, Solene Van Hoeydonck, Sonja Fulbright, Spencer Cole, Spencer Sanders, Staffan Andersson, Staffan Björk, Staffan Lindsgård, Staffan Rosenberg, Stan Andrus, Stanislaw Mitko, Stecker Julien, Stefan Agartsson, Stefan Anundi, Stefan Breuker, Stefan Eld, Stefan Feltmann, Stefan Groenewoud, Stefan Hestermeyer, Stefan Johansson, Stefan Karlsson, Stefan Köhler, Stefan Norin, Stefan Rice, Stefan Sahlin, Stefan Stresow, Stefan Tidén, Stefan Tobiasson, Stefan Wertheimer, Stefano Baldantoni, Sten Peter Larsson, Stephan Schwarz, Stephan Voltz, Stephane Blais, Stephanie Grosch, Stephanie Mcalea, Stephanie Spears, Stephanie Wagner, Stephen, Stephen Crawford, Stephen Hindmarsh, Stephen Jallins, Stephen Jones, Stephen Kane, Stephen Keith, Stephen Lester, Stephen Lincoln, Stephen Livengood, Stephen Master, Stephen Mcglone, Stephen Miller, Stephen O'brien, Stephen Sanders, Stephen Sauer, Stephen Trumbach, Stephen White, Sterling Baldwin, Sterling Brucks, Stewart B Skeel, Stewart Burwood, Steve Burnett, Steve Collins, Steve Cooper, Steve Dempsey, Steve Dismukes, Steve Foote, Steve Gott, Steve Kohls, Steve Murray, Steve Nicol, Steve Ramirez, Steve Round, Steve Sick, Steven, Steven, Steven A Lee, Steven Danielson, Steven Gomez, Steven Harbron, Steven King, Steven Medeiros, Steven Moy, Steven Northup-Smith, Steven Owen, Steven Ungaro, Steven Wall, Stevie-Ray Kertland, Stig Lindqvist, Strahinja Acimovic, Stuart Alexander, Stuart Lee, Stuart Mcclelland, Stuart Miller, Stuart Niblock, Stuart Park, Stuart Peake, Stuart Platt, Stuart Watkins, Styrbjörn Åkesson, Summer Gammill, Susan King, Susan Marleau, Swaelens Jonathan, Swann Klein, Sven Alfonsson, Sven Barth, Sven Hartmeier, Sven Liepertz, Sven Martensson, Svend Andersen, Sverker Norlander, Sverre Torp Solberg, Sylvain Pronovost, Sören Kohlmeyer, Søren Thulesen, T Mosquera, Tad Leckman, Tage Borg, Talha Khan, Tamara York, Tamas Malindovszky, Tania Rodrigues, Tanya Beeson, Tanya Osborne, Tanzil Rahber, Taran Winnie, Taylor Hall, Taylor Labresh, Taylor Moore, Ted Spilsbury, Teemu Salminen, Teodor Knigge, Theo Riches, Theodore Delphia, Theodore Polwarth, Theresa Verity, Thijs Meuwese, Thijs Van Quickenborne, Thijs Vriezekolk, Thobias Bjerlo, Thobias Kroon, Thomas Baker, Thomas Beland, Thomas Blythe, Thomas Burke, Thomas C Abella, Thomas Caspersen, Thomas Christensen, Thomas Courbon, Thomas Craig, Thomas Deeny, Thomas Delplace, Thomas Drevon, Thomas Duelund, Thomas Fitch, Thomas Fägerhall, Thomas Gernon, Thomas Giaquinto, Thomas Gustafsson, Thomas Heinig, Thomas Krømke, Thomas Langford, Thomas Lilja, Thomas M Wilson, Thomas Mcdonald, Thomas Nilsson, Thomas Norris, Thomas Perry, Thomas Quanci, Thomas Rayner, Thomas Santilli, Thomas Schubert, Thomas Sedlmair, Thomas Sleeth, Thomas Turnbull, Thomas Vanhala, Thomas Vanstraelen, Thomas Wernberg, Thomas Verschueren, Thomas Widgren, Thomas Vignal, Thorsten Schramm, Tiago Panaro De Oliveira, Tieg Zaharia, Tiffany Maclean, Tijn Rams, Tim Arthur, Tim Cant, Tim Coxford, Tim Höpker, Tim Jenkins, Tim Jensen, Tim Mixell, Tim Notari, Tim Parkinson, Tim Persson, Tim Salisbury, Tim Schnars Ii, Tim Struck, Tim Trensmar Hellman, Timea Tabori, Timo Wirtz, Timothy Bannock, Timothy Darby, Timothy Davis Ii, Timothy Deschene, Timothy Lund, Timothy Mcgowan, Timothy Moeyaert, Timothy Mushel, Timothy Nguyen, Timothy Pskowski, Timothy Reynolds, Timothy Roller, Timothy Young, Tirelli Matteo, Tj Nieset, Tobias Anderberg, Tobias Brock Korsgaard, Tobias Edin, Tobias Linder, Tobias Niemitz, Tobias Nyblom, Tobias Radesäter, Tobias Ronnqvist, Tobias Sjöblom, Tobias Thryselius, Toby Fagence, Toby Hardwick, Todd Biggs, Todd Brunner, Todd Dayton, Todd Gibel, Todd Howard, Todd Jacobson, Todd Showalter, Todd Williams, Tom Adriaenssen, Tom Bowers, Tom Burdak, Tom Butkiewicz, Tom Coster, Tom Field, Tom Hackett, Tom Hoefle, Tom Huber, Tom Klimas, Tom Kronhöffer, Tom Lienert, Tom Lynch, Tom Lynch, Tom Rosin, Tomás Alarnes Piñeiro, Tomáš P ibyl, Tomas Sisohore, Tomas Tidén, Tomas Zeljko, Tomasz Sapir, Tommi Koivula, Tommi Putkonen, Tommy Day, Tommy Fredriksson, Tommy Sääf, Tondar Malmgren, Toni Fräki, Tonny Andreasen, Tony Dowler, Tony Sanson, Tony Söderqvist, Tor Klestrup, Torbjörn Blixt, Torbjörn Bomble, Torbjörn Eklund, Torbjörn Johansson, Torbjörn Johnson, Torbjörn Wihlen, Tore Halse, Torsten Hildebrandt, Torsten Maibohm, Torsten Rahm, Tory Davis, Toshihiko Kambayashi, Travis Bryant, Travis Glidewell, Travis Homan, Travis Howe, Travis Myers, Travis Stout, Travis Torgerson, Trent Boyd, Trent Peterson, Trevor Bramble, Trevor Brick, Trevor Fetherstonhaugh, Trevor Gere, Trevor Gicklhorn, Trevor R Placker, Trevor Sparks, Tristan Bridge, Trond Roaas, Troy Miller-Perry, Truls Magnus Aamodt Gulbrandsen, Tug Baker, Tulio Calsaverini, Nino Soave, Daniel Pegoraro, Tyann Duran, Tyler Chapman, Tyler Crumrine, Tyler Helsel, Tyler Hill, Tyler Panetta, Tyler Thompson, Ulf Henriksson, Ulf Johansson, Ulrich Drees, Ulrich Feindt, Wade Holmes, Wade Tripp, Wade Wallace, Waldemar Yuen, Waleed Mansour, Valentin Veschambre, Walter Beckwith, Valter Östberg, Vaniez Cedric, Varapol Mapunya, Warren Niffenegger, Warren Zahari, Vegar Farsund, Vendevogel Alain, Wenjie Ji, Vera Vartanian, Vermeylen Hans, Veronica Peshterianu, Veronica Sjöberg, Veronika Matkovi , Veronikis Spyros, Vesa-Matti Sarenius, Wesley Lutz, Wesley Teal, Victor Engelmartin, Victor Fiszer, Wictor Hoffman, Victor J. Wyatt, Victor Kuder, Victor Lussan, Victor Strömberg, Victor Torres, Victoria Langford, Victoria Törnkvist,

## TROUBLEMAKER

## GROWN-UP